MARKETING OF NEWSPAPERS: AN OVERVIEW

MARKETING OF NEWSPAPERS

An Overview

R. PADMAJA

KANISHKA PUBLISHERS, DISTRIBUTORS
NEW DELHI-110 002

KANISHKA PUBLISHERS, DISTRIBUTORS
4697/5-21 A, Ansari Road, Daryaganj
New Delhi-110 002
Phones : 2327 0497, 2328 8285
Fax : 011-2328 8285
e-mail: kanishka_publishing@yahoo.co.in

First Published 2008

ISBN 978-81-8457-035-9

PRINTED IN INDIA

Published by Madan Sachdeva for Kanishka Publishers, Distributors, 4697/5-21A, Ansari Road, Daryaganj, New Delhi-110 002, Typeset by Sunshine Graphics, Delhi, and Printed at Nice Printing Press, Delhi.

Preface

In modern age, communication has become an integral part of human life. Man has used communication, which includes symbols or sounds (oral) to link him with external world. In the process, he realised its potential of fulfilling his socio-economic needs, and established contacts with others belonging to varied cultural and ethnic backgrounds, cutting across geographical boundaries.

The invention of script, which facilitates easy communication among people, gave a new dimension. The advent of the printing press extended reach out capacity of communication. By the turn of twentieth century, the advancement of science and technology led to the development of other channels of communication such as Radio, Film and Television, which were put to greater use for dissemination of information, as well as for propaganda. Because information plays a vital role in disseminating various views, it is increasingly used to influence the opinion of people. Newspaper is one among them, influence people in every walk of their life.

The demographic and sociological studies relating to newspaper readers so far are very limited. One of the biggest problems for managers of newspaper business is the lack of research data, other than half-yearly NRS, IRS data. So there is lacuna in newspaper research data. Not only that today the newspaper industry is in recession. Though there is increase in readership, it is not increasing on par with population growth. The cost of production of newspaper has been increased enormously after introduction of colour printing. There is greater difference between the cost of production and the selling price, which leads newspaper industry in huge losses. However, the industry is sustaining only because of support from advertising revenue. The competition for this business is also high because of electronic media. Evidently, if proper strategies are developed and adapted, faster achievement of the goals is more likely.

There is a need for studying about reader preferences and adapting proper strategies to improve readership.

The present study concentrates on newspaper industry to know the efficiency of distribution system and reader preferences in Indian context. The survey analysis of newspaper agents, retailers, distribution boys and newspaper organisational heads, readers and other media habits of readers gives clear picture about readers opinions relating to various items in newspapers. The study was conducted in Visakhapatnam city of Andhra Pradesh in India, because it consists of cross section of readers who read different newspapers.

I chose this topic with the lofty intention of making an original contribution to an area that was hitherto not much researched. But many a time I felt if I was lost in the wilderness. I would not have been able to get to this stage without the help of many individuals. I can only extend a token of appreciation for the invaluable help rendered by them.

I wish to express my deep sense of reverential gratitude and indebtedness to my Research Director, Prof.U. Babaji for the confidence he reposed in me and for encouraging me to explore an area which was not much researched in India. Despite the many demands made on him as Head of the Department, he spared his time to guide me and to review my work and to make corrections. I wish to express my gratitude to my Joint Research Director Dr. V. Krishna Mohan, for his able guidance, encouragement, critical comments from time-to-time and help me in accessing the right information sources and generosity in allowing me to encroach upon his precious time.

I am highly indebted to Sri G.J.V. Jagannadha Raju, founder Chairman of Visakha Institute for Professional Studies, Visakhapatnam, who have not only provided me a place in the Teaching Faculty of Management Studies, but also encouraged me a lot in the matters of career development by elevating me as Head of the Department of Management Studies.

I am also thankful to Prof. B. Parvatewara Rao, Chairman, P.G. Board of Studies for extending all kinds of support during the course of study.

I thank all Heads of Newspaper Oraganisations in Visakhapatnam especially *Eenadu*, *The Hindu*, *Deccan Chronicle* and

Vaartha, for according me permission to visit the Newspaper organizations to collect data. I also thank Dr. D.V.R. Murthy, Professor in Journalism Department, Andhra University, Visakhapatnam, for exhorting me to combine idealism with practicality and for being empathetic when I was struggling to balance my work and research.

I am indebted to Dr. S. Haranath, Co-ordinator, Childline, Department of Social Work for guiding me in the field of conducting survey and for extending his full support to conduct survey of Readers. I also wish to acknowledge the help of Sri M. Gopala Rao, Tech. Asstt. of Dr. V. S. K. Library, Andhra University, Visakhapatnam, who has been very kind in helping me use their library facilities and also assisted me while entering data in to computer system.

I wish to thank my husband Mr. P.V.S.V. Prasad, for his expectations of me, for his constant encouragement in every academic pursuit of mine. I am lucky to have got married into a family which encourages intellectual pursuit, I thank my father-in-law Sri P. Subba Rao and mother-in-law Smt. Vijaya Maha Lakshmi for their support and who completely looked after my little daughter Kusuma Madhooha throughout the period of my work.

Words do not suffice to describe my feelings of gratitude towards my parents Sri R. Siva Rama Krishna Rao and Smt. R. Udaya Lakshmi for their moral support given to me and without their unstinted support, I could have neither started nor completed this work. Finally, I thank all my family members for their support given to me to finish this work.

Needless to say that all matters of analysis interpretation, judgment, opinion, errors or omissions are entirely my responsibility.

R. Padmaja

Contents

Contents

Abbreviations

1.	A&M	: Advertising & Marketing
2.	ABC	: Audit Bureau of Circulation
3.	AEJMC	: Association for Education in Journalism and Mass Communication
4.	AINEF	: All India Newspaper Employee Federation
5.	AIR	: All India Radio
6.	AITUC	: All India Trade Union Congress
7.	AMIC	: Asian Media Information and Communication Center
8.	BBC	: British Broadcasting Corporation
9.	CII	: Confederation of Indian Industry
10.	CMS	: Centre for Media Studies
11.	CPI (M)	: Communist Party of India (Marxist)
12.	DAVP	: Directorate of Advertising and Visual Publicity
13.	DTH	: Direct To Home
14.	FDI	: Foreign Direct Investment
15.	FII	: Foreign Institutional Investor
16.	FMCG	: Fast Moving Consumer Goods
17.	HRD	: Human Resource Development
18.	I&B	: Information and Broadcasting
19.	IGNOU	: Indira Gandhi National Open University
20.	IJU	: Indian Journalist Union
21.	IMRB	: Indian Market Research Bureau
22.	INS	: Indian Newspaper Society
23.	IRS	: Indian Readership Survey

24.	ISP	: Internet Service Provider
25.	KM	: Kilometre
26.	MRC	: Media Research Council
27.	MRTP	: Monopolistic Restrictive Trade Practice
28.	NAA	: Newspaper Association of America
29.	NNA	: National Newspaper Association
30.	NRI	: Non-Resident Indian
31.	NRS	: National Readership Survey
32.	NRSC	: National Readership Survey Council
33.	NUJI	: National Union of Journalist of India
34.	PC	: Press Council
35.	POTA	: Prevention of Terrorism Act
36.	PTI	: Press Trust of India
37.	PTSD	: Post Traumatic Stress Disorder
38.	RNI	: Registrar of Newspapers for India
39.	RTC	: Road Transport Corporation of India
40.	T.V.	: Television
41.	UGC	: University Grants Commission
42.	UNI	: United News of India (News Agency)
43.	USA	: United States of America
44.	USP	: Unique Selling Proposition
45.	WAN	: World Association of Newspapers
46.	WTC	: World Trade Centre

1

Introduction

The Newspaper is a publication issued periodically, usually daily or weekly, to present information about current events. 'One comes every day, but I don't know which it is' and this is often the view of readers who find nothing to distinguish one paper from another.[1] The Roman *Acta Diurna* (C.59), posted daily in public places, was the first recorded newspaper. The invention and spread of printing in the 15th century was the major factor in the early development of the newspaper. The advancement of technological changes over the past decade has been somewhat mind-boggling for veteran newspaper professionals who have been used to long established methods of production which have been abandoned for a whole new array of publishing facilities and concepts.[2] The high cost of responding to competition combined with the increased cost of newspaper production have resulted in a general consolidation in the Newspaper Industry. This consolidation has helped the industry implement new technology and delivery mechanism.[3] The first daily paper in England was the *Daily Courant* (1702). English newspapers began to reach the masses in the 19th century. Important newspapers of today are *The Times of London* (founded in 1785) and *The Manchester Guardian*. Some of the oldest continental newspapers are, *Avisa Relation Oder Zeitung* (Germany), *LeFigaro* (France), *Osservatore Romano* (Vatican). The first newspaper to appear in the American Colonies was a news sheet of public occurrances, which was issued in Boston in 1860. During the 19th century many famous U.S. newspapers appeared: *The New York Evening Post* (1801); *The New York Sun*, founded (1833) by B.H. Day; *The New York Herald* (1835) and the *New York Times* (1851). Other important American newspapers are *The Washington Post; Los Angeles Times; Christian Science Monitor* (Boston); Atlanta Constitution; *Chicago Tribune; USA Today*, a national newspaper; and *Wall Street Journal* (New York), which in 1980 became the best-selling daily newspaper in the U.S. In the 20th century great newspaper empires were built in England and in the U.S. by 1980 the Australian magnate Rupert Murdoch was publishing newspapers in Australia, Britain and the United States. Since the invention of the *Telegraph*, which facilitated the rapid gathering of news, the great news agencies have sold their services to many newspapers. Improvements in typesetting and printing (especially the web press) have made such technological developments as photographs have revolutionised the newspaper industry. The advent of computer technology has allowed many newspapers to offer information through commercial on-line computer services and they are able to spare more attention and space to each problem. The newspaper articles give much more information about events today. The advantage of newspapers is that they can cover stories than any other news media. Newspapers in any country aim at informing and satisfying the growing interest of people in news, views, events and happenings.[4] They also cover stories in great detail. 'The main findings were that, the major traffic in a newspaper are the headlines, the captions and the photos. Only a minority of readers reach the half way point of most stories, which means there is a big drop between headlines/captions and those who read the whole story.'[5] However, the newspapers present information later than Radio or Television. The great advantage of newspapers over Radio and Television is that they can report stories in depth. Readers can skip items that don't interest them. Newspapers also can print certain materials that appeal to only small percentage of readers. "The newspaper should not fall but keep up its desired level of quality. First, it must have the facilities to do good printing. It must be able to pay enough to get conscientious, well-educated staff members. It must be able to receive a variety of services from news agencies as well as to collect needed national and world news with its own correspondents. It must either have a rather sizable circulation, or it must develop a special elite readership which will offset a small circulation."[6] Newspaper readers encompass all income brackets, educational levels, age groups and ethenic backgrounds. They live in cities, suburbs, towns, resorts, and rural areas. By all demographic standards, the newspaper is a solid mass-market medium, representing about 68 per cent of adult population.[7] The demographic factors that effect the newspapers are literacy, income and leisure. Historically, newspaper reading tends to be lowest among people in their teens and early twenties. 'Then it always bumps back up as people reach 30 and settle into homes and need access to the kind of information that newspapers provide,' says Frederick Toccills, director of news media and products with *Newsday*.[8] The literacy and income have been increasing steadily. The future will see a greater population in the upper age groups. Hence, the market for the newspapers is ever growing. Newspapers only have to adopt to the changing times, taste and types of customers. As a whole, the newspaper industry has wrapped its arms around emerging technology, and this adoption has not been restricted to conventional Internet sites. Stories are now being distributed through Web-enabled phones, pagers, e-mail and palms.[9] A busy executive is now able to down load stories from the *Wall Street Journal* and the *New York Times*, anytime and anywhere. Companies such as Audible Inc. even provide digests of the papers. Files can be down loaded from its website Audible.com and played on carry–along CD players. Experts in the Newspaper Industry expect these new delivery systems to be profitable soon.[10]

In India now, almost all newspapers are completely accessible through the Internet and prcvide up-to-date news and information. Major changes that can be expected is in the field of technology used in the printing and the number of units per each organisation. The competition between the vernaculars and English newspapers may increase because of the present educational system. Newspapers are by no means obsolete. The traditional benefits to the reader are obvious, but today's customers expect more. Newspaper organizations now-a-days identify themselves as a commercial enterprise and the newspaper is a commodity, rather a public institution to serve the society. Although newspapers draw sustenance from profits, total dedication to profits cannot be the goal of this institution.[11]

In over two hundred years of its existence, the newspaper media has survived many challenges—from Radio, Television and now Online, as also from time to time setbacks due to the shortages of essential inputs like paper and import restrictions etc. It has done this essentially by staying in step with the whirl of technology—seeing it not as an impediment but an impetus to growth.[12] Whether the industry as a whole can deliver on these expectations remains to be seen, but there is potential for positive change.[13] Last but not least is the marketing strategies and the organisation policies which should be customer oriented and not industry oriented.

Newspapers in Global Scenario

A nations's socio-political system and philosophy generally determined its press system. Hence, the nation's leading newspapers form the important print media and are socially responsible. For example, the communist newspapers considers itself socially responsible, and carries out its responsibility to the social system of the country where it operates. The same thing might be said of the so-called "authoritarian" newspapers, as they exist in Spain.[14]

A newspaper in the United States, which by its pluralistic nature would tend to undermine national policy and disrupt national harmony, would be anathema in a nation like Spain. In U.S.A. special newspapers also exist for special interest groups, religious denominations, political affiliations, labour unions, and professional and fraternal organizations.[15] Spanish newspapers, the most serious like *ABC* and *YA of Madrid* and *La Vanguardia Espanola* of Barcelona, are exceptionally responsible to Spanish society, and it should be added that, they supply a surprising diversity of orientations and view points within the confines of the national policy. In other words, newspaper of a nation, even one under considerable government control, will still prove its eliteness through its subtle ties, skillful restraint and capacity to make the most of the situation in which it finds itself. In many ways, it takes more journalistic ability and courage to put out an important newspaper in a country such as Spain than in a country like Britain or Sweden. The British press is divided into two categories; broad sheets and tabloids. *The Guardian, Daily Telgraph* are in broad sheet category and *Daily Mail, Daily Mirror, Sun, News of the world* under tabloid category. Tabloids hold sway over the British Press.[16]

Another important pattern among the world's important newspapers is that of economic diversity. This pattern, of course, is related to the political context, but actually is quite different. For example, one important newspaper in a libertarian nation can run into dire difficulties while another in the same country prospers and grows. An important daily is not determined by how much property it owns or the profit it makes. Important newspapers throughout the world exemplify a wide range of economic development and prosperity, but their overriding concern is with serious news, which is quite apart from differences in economic health.[17]

The third pattern of the important newspapers is geographical. This pattern is closely related to national development. Most of the important newspapers are published in developed or developing countries, although there are a few that represent the developing of transitional nations. Europe and North America are the principal homes of the elite newspapers. This is not surprising since these two continents are the most industrialised, the most technologically advanced and most literate of all the continents. As the economic bases become stabilized, and literate and well-educated populations of other continents grow, the evenness of dispersion of the newspapers throughout the world should improve significantly. Presently, however, important daily newspapers are scattered about the earth in a very uneven fashion. This pattern of clusters and vast gaps greatly hinders the total impact of serious, concerned journalism in the world as a whole. If international information in newspapers in a balanced communication traffic, as originally useful for third world countries and they would be able to make the core countries of the industrialized and technological world better informed.[18]

Asia

Asia, with the exception of China, Japan and India, is virtually without an important newspaper. Of the three, Japan stands out for its great progress in quality journalism and popular journalism too. *Asahi* is without doubt the best quality daily in Japan and shows that an important daily paper can, with editorial flexibility and sagacity, develop a large circulation within a free-market press system.[19] Japanese Newspapers abandoned the holiday also, in order to deliver the news as soon as possible at a time when the situation at home and abroad is changing drastically.[20] In India, the problems of the newspapers are much more acute than in either the CIS (Commmon Independent States), China or Japan. There are many reasons for this, but the chief is the phenomenon of too many languages. At present the major newspapers of India are published in English, understood only by the educated, mainly found in a few of the large cities. And even within the English reading public, the circulation of the English elite newspapers are segmented since there are five elite newspapers in the country. These are *The Hindusthan Times* of Delhi, *The Telegraph* of Kolkata, *Deccan Chronicle* of Hyderabad, *The Hindu* of Chennai and *The Times of India* of Mumbai. But marketers are trying to improve the readership by technology upgradation and regionalisation. Not only improving Indian readership, but also trying to cater to the needs of ethnic Indians. The Newspaper published in Tamil, for Tamil speaking Singaporeans is an example, though they can read newspaper through Internet also.[21]

Africa

In Africa, outside Egypt in the extreme north east and the Republic of South Africa in the far south, there is no significant elite newspaper and even in these two republics considerable government sensitivity has hindered development of quality of newspapers. Egypt, with its nationalized newspapers, takes second place to South Africa as a nation with a pluralistic press. In South Africa, in spite of government sensitivity towards press, the newspapers, especially those in English, act as search lights of inquiry and criticism. They are able to shine, eventhough slightly filtered. They often concentrate on dark areas where the regime is most sensitive. South Africa claims to have the freest newspapers on the continent, and within the English language press are papers which are equal in quality and tone to the important newspapers of other nations of the world.

The Middle East

In the Middle East, newspapers are caught between severe problems. Governments throughout the region are generally suspicious of the newspaper and sensitive to its criticism.

Latin America

Latin America, in spite of awesome economic development and literacy problems, has somehow managed to develop a rather sizable group of important newspapers.[22] This region of the world has far more-advanced newspapers in all respects than is generally found in Asia and Africa. One obvious explanation for this is that Spanish is almost a common language of the newspapers of Latin America, whereas in both Asia and Africa the polyglot of languages and dialects makes the development of newspapers of substantial influence and circulation extremely difficult if not impossible.

Australia

In Oceana, Australia alone has a press which includes newspapers of the important daily type. Barriers to newspaper growth in island are mainly, *(i)* small population, *(ii)* technological under-development, *(iii)* scarcity of trained journalists, *(iv)* geographical isolation from the main stream of international concerns. In Australia several papers might be included among the important newspapers and others are aspirants. The *Age of Melbourne* is usually considered the most serious and influential newspaper.

North America

In North America the elite newspapers thrives. The *Globe* and *Mail of Toronto,* with a circulation of more than 2,30,000 is Canada's only truly national newspaper. It is also considered as the country's best newspaper. Although there are important newspapers in every major section of United States, most of them are concentrated along the East Coast and in the Middle West. In the East are such sophisticated newspapers as *The New Baltimore Sun* and the *Miami Herald.* In the Middle West a few of the leaders among the important newspapers are *The St.Louis Post-Dispatch, The Minneapolis Tribune* and the *Kanas City Star.* Quality papers of national and international prestige tend to fade out in the plains and Mountains area of the West, with *The Denver Post* ruling a vast empire from its strategic position. Along the West, there is *Los Angeles Times* which is the fastest growing U.S. daily. After September 11, 2001, a significant sales boost, topper newspapers in the U.S. Gannett Company's *U.S.A. Today* remainded the country's top selling newspaper.[23] But average daily circulation of USA for six months ended March 31 slips 3.4 per cent to 2.21 million compared with the earlier year period. *Wall Street Journal* remained (published by Dow Jones Capital and Company) in the second position. This business daily is at 0.05 per cent circulation gain to 1.82 million compared with the year earlier period. *Newyork Daily* newspaper faired better than industry's Newyork Times Company's *Newyork Times* registered 3.8 per cent in daily circulation to 1.19 million. News Corporation's *New York Post* saw circulation rise 15.4 per cent to 562,639. Circulation of *New York Daily News,* rose to 2.2 per cent to 733,099. The rest of the industry, which has been struggling for decades to reverse declining circulation couldn't take advantage.[24]

According to a Newspaper Association of American analysis of ABC figures (2003), average daily circulation for the 820 reporting newspapers fell 0.6 per cent. The steepest decline among the top 10 papers was at Tribune Company's *Los Angeles Times*, where average daily circulation (including Saturday) fell by 5.3 per cent to 985.798. This decline was expected and was due to price increase made throughout 2001.[25]

Table–1.1
TOP TEN NEWSPAPERS OF U.S.A. IN 2003

Name of the Newspaper	*Circulation/Day (Copies)*
U.S.A. Today	2,616,824
Wall Street Journal	2,091,062
New york Times	1,676,885
Los Angeles Times	1,379,258
Washington post	1,029,966
Chicago Tribune	1,002,166
New york daily news	805,350
Dallas morning news	785,876
Philadelphia Inquirer	749,793
Houston Chronicle	747,404

Source: Audit Bureau of Circulation (2003) of America.

Europe

If the press of North America is well-developed and the important newspapers are numerous, the newspapers of Europe might be said to be over developed and the important daily newspapers are numerous. A variety of quality newspapers are to be found in Europe. There are three important dailies among Western Europe led by the super serious *Neue Zurcher Zeitung* of Switzerland *Le Monde* of France, the *Times* and the *Guardian* of Britain. The European newspapers offer the reader a wide selection of packages and political orientation. There is a paper whose journalistic style and philosophy as well as layout appeal to any kind of serious newspaper reader.

The newspapers aimed at the enlarging masses of literate persons with low journalistic expectations. This is reflected in increased space given to 'features' and 'sensational pip' on one hand and growing fascination with 'sophisticated technology' on the other. The newspaper industry enjoyed a banner year in 1997 with 19.5 per cent for operating income. Revenues were also increased.[26] This was because of better staffing and more promotional efforts. For 1999-2004 period overall growth is expected slightly faster than 5.6 per cent rate posted in the 1994-99 period. But actually advertising slump hits earnings at newspapers, and the U.S.A. newspaper, *Chicago Tribune* also set Voluntary Retirement Programmes to cut its work force.[27] In order to increase growth in circulation, the newspaper businessmen have to follow 'adaptive' culture than 'defensive' culture.

It is a difficult time for newspapers wanting to rise their circulation and readership levels. The decline of independent, personalized and creative journalism aiming above the lowest common man lead to slow death of important newspapers during late 20th century. To flourish and not just to survive in this increasingly competitive market, the print media has shed its sleek, barefoot-messenger-of-news image. Rather, it has cultivated a plump Santa Claus image. All newspapers, English or regional language, give more space if not pages to business and finance. The number of independent business/finance newspapers has swelled. There is a special section for business in every news bulletin. Similarly, computer and telecom related publications have seen an upswing. Virtually every newspaper has a city/lifestyle supplement that goes beyond austere news. As the world rejuvenates itself with time, so must the media. With one publication trying to outsell the other, this increasing freedom is not always free from misuse.[28] A reaction could, of course, set in against, this trend toward sensational and superficial newspapers which are misusing freedom to increase circulation and readership. World is tuning to news items as real life gets deadly, because of so many natural calamities, crimes, accidents etc.[29] That is most of the people are interested in news items because of so many disasters, crimes, accidents etc.

Some newspaper organisations are going for mergers also.[30] Better integration of Newspaper Organisations for acquisitions improve performance of newspaper organizations and capture the benefits of greater coordination.[31]

National Scenario

The press is considered to be one of the most effective media of communication available and it will be helpful to a marketing man in reaching the most influential and educated section of society. The press includes daily newspapers, magazines and periodicals. Among them the newspaper which is published daily or atleast four days a week is the most important source of information about current affairs.

The printed word in India, carries an aura of sanctity and authenticity. The print medium, more so the newspapers, therefore, wield much clout. And so, it can be a powerful ally of the people, guiding them and educating them and leading to development. The newspapers played a glorious role in the independence struggle. Barring the few Anglo-Indian nerwspapers which had enoromous resources, both in terms of money and talent, the Indian owned papers were impecunious, often persecuted and harassed and yet they had the fortitude to stay and fight on.[32] Addressing a gathering of Indian journalists in London on 18th, August, 1947, shortly after the Indian independence Bill received the assent of the British Monarch, Lord Histowell, the last Secretary of State for India said "The Indian newspapers have every reason to be proud of the part they have played in the great constitutional change and of the good influence they have exercised on Indian opinion." Nepolian Bonparte said that "Four hostile newspapers are more to be feared than a thousand bayonets".

Newspaper reading is a habit. For a large number of literate persons it is as much a part of daily life as eating and sleeping. Their day starts with newspaper reading. It guides and supports children in acquiring greater knowledge.[33] Not withstanding the Radio and Television 'Explosion' because of their popularity due to reasonable prices and wide availability, the importance of the newspapers has not diminished. More and more people continue to read the newspaper everyday. After 1947, there was big growth in number of newspapers and there were 3,000 newspapers in India. In 1981, it grew to 19,144 newspapers[34] and by 1996, it rose to 39,149 newspapers.

The newspaper has been defined as "an unbound printed publications, issued at regular intervals, which presents information in words, often supplemented by pictures." Any printed or cyclostyled periodical carrying news of public interest, of comments on it is also a newspaper. According to the Indian Post Office Act, every publication consisting wholly or in great part of political or other news or of articles relating thereto or to other current topics, with or without advertisements, shall be deemed a newspaper subject to the following conditions, namely *(a)* that it is published in numbers at intervals of not more than 31 days and *(b)* that it has bonafide list of subscribers.

Indian journalism had its first when James Augustus Hicky started his *Bengal Gazette* on January 29th, 1780 at Serampore near Calcutta. Hicky's venture was followed by a number of others in quick succession. The most significant of these was "John Bull in East" in 1821, which was subsequently changed into the "Englishmen". Unlike American and some other constitutions in which freedom of the press is maintained as one of the fundamental freedoms, the Indian constitution does not specifically mention freedom of the press. The Fundamental Rights clause of the Indian constitution threatens freedom of the press as aspect of the larger "Freedom expression." Article 19(1) of the constitution guarantees, "The right to freedom of speech and expression to all citizen."[35] This freedom has been interpreted by the courts to include freedom of the press under the constitution (First Amendment Act of 1951). "Though in India there was no constitutional provision distinctly for press freedom, this freedom was inherent in the freedom of expression as a fundamental right."[36] Parliament can pass legislation reasonably restricting the right in the interest of the security of the state, incitement to an offence. The words "reasonable restriction" make such legislation justifiable. The Registrar of Newspapers for India[37] (RNI) has divided the newspapers as follows.

Chains: More than one newspaper under common ownership from more than one centre.

Groups: More than one newspaper under common ownership from the same centre *Multiple Units*: More than one newspaper of the same title, language and periodicity under common ownership. A newspaper issued at least four times a week is called a daily and one appearing at an interval of a week or more is known as periodical.

Classification of Newspapers

The newspapers have been classified into three categories based on their circulation. They are: *(i) Big Newspapers:* A newspaper with a circulation of more than 50,000 copies per publishing day, *(ii) Medium Newspapers:* A newspaper with a circulation between 15,001 and

50,000 copies per publishing day and *(iii) Small Newspapers:* A newspaper with a circulation upto 15,000 copies per publishing day. In the early days newspapers enhanced their scope of activity especially in Calcutta, Bombay and Madras. "The first newspaper in Madras, *The Madras Courier,* came into existence in 1785 as an officially recognized newspaper founded by Richard Johnson. *Bombay Herald* came into existence in 1789."[38]

The Sayyed-Ul-Akhbar is generally mentioned as the first Urdu newspaper started in Delhi in 1837. It was edited by Syed Mohammed Khan, though Ordoo Akhbar of Delhi probably started publication in 1836.[39]

'In Telugu, the first newspaper published in the sixties of the last century owned its inception to missionary effort. *The Hitavadi* which was published weekly ceased to exist after a few years. Rao Bahadur K.Veeresalingam Pantulu, scholar, educationalist and social reformer made a beginning in Telugu Journalism with his weekly the *Viveka Vardhani* devoted to social and language reform. In 1886, the first news weekly was started by A.P. Parthasarathi Naidu. It was published from Madras under the name of *Andhra Prakasika.* The first two papers to be published from outside Madras were the *Godavari* and *Andhra Kesari* from Rajahmundry. First daily newspaper was *Desabhimani* by Devagupta Seshachala Rao. It was started first as a fortnightly, then as weekly and bi-weekly and finally daily newspaper. Andhra's first successful daily paper was *Andhra Patrica* was started as weekly from Bombay in 1908 by Nageswararao. *Andhra Prabha* was started in 1939 and edited by Khasa Subbarao and later by Narla Venkateswarao. The *Prajasakhti* published from Vijayawada which has now been succeeded by *Visalandhra* the communist daily. *Krishna Patrika* was started in 1902 by Konda Venkatappayya and Dasu Narayana Rao. Other weeklies which were successful are *Prajamitra, Anandvani* edited by V. Kalidas, *Janavani* edited by Darmarao and *Prajabandhu* edited by D. Acharya and *Swatantra* published both in Telugu and English by Kasa Subba Rao.[40] In Andhra state social reformers like Kandukuri Veeresalingm, Kasinadh Nageswara Rao, Tanguturi Prakasam and Pattabhi Setaramayya have contributed for the growth and development of newspapers. They have inspired youth to take up the art of writing for the various newspapers.[41]

Malayala Manorama of Kottayam is one of the the leading dailies of Kerala today, was formed 79 years ago by Kandathi Varghese

Mappilai who brought an instinct for news.[42] After the attainment of Independence, Indian newspapers have grown in numbers, in circulation, technological sophistication, in specialization and its earnings. The present day newspapers are reaching even remote areas not connected with pucca roads and communication facilities.

The newspapers have enlightened their readers, enlarged their knowledge and influenced decision-making of individuals. The newspapers also play an important role in nation building. In urban areas 70 per cent of Indians report having a newspaper.[43] It is the responsibility of newspapers to open the eyes of the government when it goes in a wrong direction. Newspaper should be a people's forum and the views expressed by the readers are to be considered by the government in planning and implementing various socio-economic developmental programmes. Newspapers should appeal to the good slide of people and aim at achieving the emotional integrity of the country.[44]

Indian society is witnessing momentous changes in social and economic spheres. The newspapers too are changing along with the society. They are acquiring new technologies and modernizing to discharge their functions better. "The newspaper is really a super market. The Papers give you rows and rows of schemes with hundreds of different stories to sample for. So we can pick and choose."[45] We can read any section of newspaper which we are interested which is not possible in other media.

Some of the popular Indian Newspapers are *(i) The Times of India* (English), *(ii) Dainik Bhaskar* (Hindi), *(iii) The Hindusthan Times* (English), *(iv) Anand Bazar Patrica* (Bangla), *(v) Dharitiri* (Oriya, English), *(vi) The Telegraph* (English), *(vii) The Asian Age* (English), *(viii) The Indian Express* (English), *(ix) Dinathanthi* (Tamil), *(x) Malayala Manorama* (Malayalam), *(xi) Dainik Jagran* (Hindi), *(xii) Eenadu* (Telugu), and *(xiii) The Hindu* (English).

The circulation of Indian newspapers registered 24 per cent rise in daily circulation in 2002-03 compared with the previous year of 2001-02. In 2001-02 financial year, the circulation was 115 million copies and in 2002-03 year, the circulation recorded was 142,005,543 copies daily. Among multi-edition dailies, *Dainik Bhaskar*, with 18 editions in Hindi claimed the largest circulation at 1.717 million copies and next highest was *Times of India* in English with 1.384 million copies. Among the single edition dailies *The Hindusthan Times* in English claimed a circulation of 1.112 million copies while *The Hindu*, also in English came second with a figure of 0.922 million copies.[46] Out of 7,158 newspapers that sent their annual statements in 2002-03, 5371 were owned by individuals while 950 were owned by joint stock companies.[47]

Table–1.2

TOP ENGLISH NEWSPAPERS IN URBAN INDIA IN 2003

Newspapers	*Readership (All figures in '000s)*
The Times of India	6925
Hindusthan Times	2983
The Hindu	2733
The Telegraph	1312
Deccan Chronicle	1032
The Economic Times	966
The New Indian Express	888
Mid-day	846
Deccan Herald	832
Indian Express	668

Source: National Readership Survey 2003 – Round 1, by National Readership Studies Council, an autonomous division of Audit Bureau of Circulations, Mumbai.

Table–1.3

COMPARISON OF PRINT MEDIA REACH WITH OTHER MEDIA

Media Reach	*Per cent Penetration*
Print	52
Terrestrial TV	90
Cable and Satellite	60
Radio	45
Cinema (Movies)	6
Internet	8

Source: National Readership Survey 2003 (Round 1) by National Readership Studies Council, an autonomous division of Audit Bureau of Circulations, Mumbai.

The Times of India's readership increased to 33 per cent compared with previous year according to NRS survey results. Among *Times of India* readers, more than 75 per cent of them belong to the highest socio-economic class 'A' amd more than half the readers belongs to households with a monthly income of over Rs. 10,000.[48]

Need for the Study

The newspaper has been one of the oldest media for mass communication. Due to the technological development, there has been tremendous raise in the number of newspapers being published, to serve the needs of the growing population. Competition has increased not only among newspapers, but also from other media like Television, Radio and Internet. To meet this competition newspaper organisations have to adapt many changes and introduce many policies. Still the Newspaper Industry is facing many problems. One of the biggest problems of the newspaper industry is lack of adequate research data.

Many strategies relating to market development and production were introduced. Pricing strategies, Advertising strategies, Product and Promotional strategies were introduced in many newspaper organisations. Though newspaper organisations change their policies and adapt new technology, some of them are not in a position to survive in the present day circumstances. Only few of them which are highly sophisticated, which have modern technology, which constantly innovate can with stand and survive in the present day competitive situation. Most of the newspapers in India are facing a severe threat from other media as well as other sophisticated newspaper organisations.

The spread of literacy and increase in purchasing power across the country has a direct relationship with the readership. Literacy rate from 1997-99 increased to nine per cent. From the Table 1.4, it is evident that the readership increased only by four per cent.

Table–1.4

READERSHIP FIGURES OF PRINT MEDIA IN 1997 AND 1999

Year	*Per cent of Adults in India Who Read Newspaper and Magazine*	*Per cent Increase from 1997-99*
1997	45	–
1999	49	4

Source: National Readership Survey 1999 by National Readership Studies Council, an autonomous division of Audit Bureau of Circulations, Mumbai.

Newspaper circulation is generally directly proportional to literacy levels and standard of living. But the numbers released by the A.B.C. reveals a different view.

REGIONAL PRINT MEDIA FROM 1998-2000

Language	*1998*	*1999*	*2000*
Marathi	28,58,631	28,20,662	28,82,122
Hindi	54,71,103	5,718	69,09,447
Malayalam	20,15,556	20,92,018	20,79,277
Tamil	10,86,817	11,10,335	11,76,960
Telugu	10,21,064	9,53,796	10,47,391
Bengali	15,00,144	16,06,066	16,96,539

From the table it is clear that the worst hit has been the Marathi press with a sharp fall that is five per cent in circulation. Another big loser has been the Telugu press with a four per cent drop. The reason for the decrease of readership is the spread of television. The people are preferring to switch the channels rather than flip pages. The regional press is bearing the burnt of this change in media consumption habits. IRS 2002 points to a dip in print media readership. Among dailies, *Dainik Jargan* topped the list, followed by *Dainik Bhaskar* and *Malayala Manorama.*[49]

Literacy growth from 1999-2002 is 13 per cent increase (NRS survey). But the readership is not proportional to the increase in literacy levels. There was only 10 per cent increase in readership from 1999-2002.[50] Notwithstanding inconsistencies in readership surveys, a time series analysis at macro level for 1972-2002 period reflects broad trends. Whatever spurt there was in readership of dailies in particular has come more along with the television boom. Since the year 2000, the reader base in India has grown from 163 million to 180 million, a growth of 10 per cent. In fact, in the case of daily newspapers the growth during the period was 20 per cent. Today nearly 160 million people read a daily. Also more housewives read a daily today than ever before. But taking a long-term view one could also say that television has slowed down the growth of print media. And, as could be seen, the growth rate in readership was higher in rural than in urban areas. The trend calls for a breakthrough to come out of a slow phase since the growth potential is many times more. In the last couple of years the overall readership of newspapers has increased only by about four per cent both in rural and urban areas. In 1999, the readership of newspapers decreased by 2.4 per cent when compared with previous figure of 127 million readers.

At this juncture, it is pertinent for researchers to investigate the causes for slow rise in Readership and Circulation which have not gone up on par with the population increase and literacy growth. It is also important for the researcher to know strategies evolved by some of the newspapers to overcome the threat, to face competition prevailing in market, to know changes made to product according to the requirements and satisfaction of the readers. Many suggestions are made available in this study and make them available to newspaper organisations for their successful functioning and about the importance of newspaper distribution in proper marketing.

Review of Literature

The review of literature is divided mainly into three categories. International, National (Indian) and State (Andhra) literature.

International literature for convenience is again divided into three classes.

- *(i)* Content analysis.
- *(ii)* Ownership.
- *(iii)* Marketing of Newspapers (Including Circulation and Readership).

International Studies on Content Analysis

Franklin.Bob and David Murphy[51] in their research discussed the format and content of local alternative papers, investigative journalism by the alternative papers, the market's influence on content radical papers, and the problem of financial viability of local press in Great Britain. They examined the traditional local press, discussed the traditional view of news gathering, diversity within the traditional local press and the definition of local news and the local weekly press and local and regional daily press. They also commented on the future of local press in their research.

The survey conducted by M.Mank Muller, Julie[52] revealed the following results. The candidates images were distinct in press releases and news stories and candidates positions were represented differently in both. Here candidate means the person who contested in the elections. He also said, candidates were differently successful in getting news media to reflect their positions and he concluded news media covered substantive concerns that were not included in candidates press releases. This study was based on content analysis.

The study conducted by K. Demers (1998)[53] revealed the following results. He mainly concentrated on editorial content. This study tested the editorial vigour hypothesis using an alternative methodology, the data provided partial support for the corporate structure theory, the more structurally complex the newspapers, the more news sources perceived that paper as being critical of them and their institutions. The author argued corporate newspapers are more critical because they are more likely to be located in pluralistic communities, which contain more social conflict and criticism of dominent groups and value systems, because they are more insulated from local political pressure.

Elli, P.Lester-Roushanzamir and Usha Raman studies[54] (published in 1996) revealed that newspaper reporting aimed at children has proliferated yet children news has seldom been the subject of study. This conclusion is based on the study conducted by author on Olympic news coverage for children in the Atlanta-journal constitution.

In the study conducted by Claire E.Taylor and her associates[55], she concentrated on the local press coverage on environmental conflict in Louisian (2000). This study was based on environmental content analysis. The study examined 600 items in the local press coverage of environmental conflict during 10 years period showed that a community daily in a small, but heterogenous system did indeed favour government/industry sources rather than activists, citizens. It supported local industry in editorials and staff opinion columns.

In the study conducted by C. Anthony Giffard and Nancy K. Rivenburg[56] (2000) the hosting of global media events in order to enhance the images is examined. The study examines *Associated Press, Reuters* and *Interpress* coverage of six major United Nations Summit meetings for their presentation of host nations. This study was based on content analysis.

Stephen Lacy conducted research (2001)[57] to determine the sample size for newspaper content analysis in multi-year studies. Basing on this study she suggested selecting nine constituted weeks (nine issues from Monday, nine from Tuesday etc.) from five years is more efficient than 10 constituted weeks.

Joseph C. Harry[58] study was a comparitive analysis of small and near by big city newspaper covering the same environmental conflict. Results showed that some community newspapers might perform more like their big-city counterparts for sustained periods of time.

Kis Kodich[59] examined the Nicarguan newspapers in 1990s which turned to Non-Nicarguan sources for ideas on how to appeal better to readers. Using a combination of content analysis, survey, participant observation and interviews this study finds that many Nicarguan newspaper journalists clearly admire the journalism of other countries and seek the training of outsider owners and managers of Nicarguan newspapers also encourage and facilitate this foreign influence. This study finds Nicarguan newspapers may be changing as a result of this mixing of cultures, yet there are also signs of resistance to these changes at newspaper establishments. This study was based on content analysis.

Kaarin Wahl-Jorgensen[60] examined how editors in the San Francisco Bay area speak about how the letters to the editor successfully balance the two visions of the community. The letter section is seen as customer service feature that boosts the newspaper's financial success (published in 2001). This study was based on content analysis that is 'letters to the editor.'

Mark Deeuze,[61] in his paper (published in 2002) compared the main findings of surveys among Dutch journalists with results from recent projects in Germany, Great Britain, Australia and United States. He dicussed about cross-national research. The cross-national comparison is used as a means to describe and interpret a national news culture of journalists using the Netherlands as a case study.

John J. Pauly and Melissa Eckert[62] discussed about the Myth of 'local' (2002) in American journalism. He said that term local has received less scrutiny than other keywords of the profession, such as objectivity, public and independence. Yet references to local news figure prominently in many contemporary discussions of newspapers readership, coverage, management and mission. Study explained the importance of local news.

Dietram A. Scheufele, James Shanaham and Sei-Hill Kim[63] explained how media influences local political involvement, issue awareness and attitude strength. According to their study demographic variables and idealogical differences are not influencing people's involvement in politics but local newspaper views are having an impact on people's political involvement, issue awareness and attitude strength. Their opinion survey on a local newspaper revealed that, by covering certain aspects of an issue more prominently the media increase the salience of these aspects among audience members. This study concluded that the media by emphasizing certain attributes of an issue, tell us, 'how to think about' this issue as well as 'what to think about.'

Dharma Adhikari, Tracy Everbach and Shahira Fahmy[64] in their ethnomethodological study (2002) is based on news decision-making at a small Mid-western city. It involved six weeks long persistant behavioural observation of news, budget sessions, core of the gatekeeing process, news routines level. Through the qualitative paradigm they identified four typologies of determinants-time-space-dimensions, content based on considerations, nature of news, inter-subjectivity and external pressure—as crucial to the sociology of news decided for the front page of the newspaper.

Fredrick Fico and Olivia Balog of Michigan State University conducted (2002)[65] research to examine the dominance by partisan and non-partisan sources. In this comparitive analysis Partisans dominated the space and attention in conflict stories. Few stories gave partisan opponents a balanced treatment. Reporters who had a higher priority for conflict stories were more likely than others to produce balanced stories. Stories displayed more prominently were likely to be balanced.

A content analysis by Guy Florida and Wayne Wanta[66] compared staffwritten stories on the *New York Times'* op-ed pages to those written by guest columnists. Results show that guest column topics and focuses were vastly different from staff writers, supporting a "diversity Hypothesis." Staffwriters, however, were more opinionated. Results also show that few voices outside U.S. politicians and experts were heard after the september 11th , 2001, terrorist attacks showing mixed support for a "convergence hypothesis."

Elza Ibroscheva[67] study examined the news coverage of the three Mile Island and the Chernobyl nuclear accident, the role of political ideology in deciding the content of news in two elite U.S. newspapers, the *New York Times* and the *Washington Post,* and two elite soviet newspapers, *Pravda* and *Izvestiya.* Study concludes that both the

U.S. and the Soviet news media were heavily influenced by the war climate and the dominant ideology of each society.

The paper presented by Chango Lee, Texas-Austin (2002)[68] compares how The *New York Times, Arab News* covered the U.S. attack on Afghanisthan, which was response to the September 11th terrorist attack on the U.S. The study consists of a content analysis complemented by textual anlysis. On the whole, the results showed, *The New York Times* displaying a more Pro-war position and *Arab News,* a more anti-war one. Articles in the former focused on military operations and war supporting nations.

The study of Autumn Miller and Dente Ross (2002)[69] analysing news, feature and editorial content in *Boston Globe* found historical negative frames of Native Americans continue. The virtual absence of American Indians and unattributed negative content marginalize American Indians.

The 'use of sources in local news' is a study (2002) conducted by Kristy H.Nich.[70] The purpose of this study was to examine the types of sources used in written, front page stories of local newspapers and to examine whether circulation size is related to the sources these newspapers use. This study's results indicated that smaller local newspapers rely on fewer government sources and more non-government sources than larger local newspaper; and newspapers rely less on government officials as sources than national newspapers.

The study conducted by Yonghoi Song (2002)[71] titled "Sourcing Patterns of National and Local Newspapers" compared the sourcing patterns of national and local newspapers in order to see the degree of official and elite source dominance in political news as non political news. The findings show that local newspapers rely more heavily on offical sources than national newspapers do. The trend is more obvious in the coverage of non-political news. The results of this study suggest that the newspaper sourcing patterns reflect the the structure, the community they serve.

International Newspaper Ownership Studies

Neiva-Elizabeth[72] used the example of postwar consolidation of the American newspaper industry,1953-1980 He said that the process of newspaper industry evolution is because of arbitary market forces and also because of individuals innovative schemes. This conclusion was arrived at by examining the technological labour-related and regulatory forces behind the industry's dramatic change in ownership structure. The study was related to evolution of newspaper industry.

Bronars and Stephen.G.[73] presented a paper that consists of simple non-parametric tests that can be used to distinguish between competing models of union employment determination and applies this test to the market for typographers in the newspaper industry.

Picard, Robert. G.[74] conducted survey and it focussed on editors and their roles, interlocking directorships and economic power and monopoly and socialization.

Noon Mike[75] conducted research to assess the success of National Union of Journalist (NUJ) in negotiating the introduction of computerized editorial systems in provincial newspapers. It employs quantitative as well as qualitative survey to suggest that the NUJ has been exemplary in using the new technology agreement as a bargaining tool in order to limit the negetive effects of technological change and to secure notable benefits particularly pay increases.

Jan Bekken[76] in his study discussed about the exploitation of news boys by the newspaper industry.

Picard, Robert G, Brody, Jeffrey H.[77] conducted research on newspaper industry which provided an overview of newspaper industry and its current situation. They presented some historic milestones in the development of the U.S. newspaper industry. It described about the typical production cycle of a daily, morning newspaper. It outlined the activities that takes place on different days in the production cycle of a weekly newspaper. They addressed issues that affect the newspaper industry's future, including technology and labour issues, contemporary editorial issues and problems and some legal and regulatory issues and concerns.

Kathleen A. Hansen, Mark Neuzil and Jean Ward[78] (1998) examined the effects of newsroom topic teams on news routines and newspaper quality. It is based on census survey of journalist at the Star Tribune and The St. Paul Pioneer press. The study finds that the effects of the team systems on the news process and news quality have been mixed, but predominantly negative, in the assessment of these journalists.

Doobrev and Stainisslav, D.[79] examined the alignment strategies of state owned Bulgarian newspapers in the light of the theoretical insights provided by adaptation and selection of perspectives of organizational evolution. He argued that impact of internal restructuring is closely tied to the location of change in the organizational structure.

Abby Dress,[80] in his study analysed the shutting down of *NewYork Newsday* by *Times Mirror* which is its parents organization. The launch of *Newyork Newsday* in 1983 was doomed to failure, regardless of the newspaper's promise and its national expansion from *Newsday*'s Long Island base in *Newyork City*. The plan for profitability advocated by senior management was approved by it parent, *Times Mirror* which welcomed a presence in the highly visible New York market, which is already dominated by three other daily newspapers. However, the effects of media conglomeration on *Times Mirror* for bottom line results would pull the plug on the Newyork venture that was nearing its provisional term and beginning to show positive results.

George L. Daniels and C. Ann Holifield[81] in their study presented the longitudinal analysis of the effects of organizational changes and change of management efforts at CNN Headline news on newsroom employees, attitudes, morale and likelihood of quitting jobs. The study found that for newsroom mangers, organizational change was a losing proposition resulting in staff member's perception of greater unhappiness with their jobs. Newsroom employees were most negative changes they thought hindered their ability to produce high-quality journalism and change management efforts had only limited impact on job satisfaction and commitment.

The study conducted by Randal A. Beam[82] showed, that senior editors from market-oriented newsrooms express less uncertainty about their newspaper's environment than editors from the other newspapers. They also feel more confident that they can adapt their paper to changes in its environment.

Joe Strupp[83] examined various policies like policies on publishing, ethics, etc. He reviewed various articles relating to newspaper policies of American newspapers.

Randy Dotinga[84] in his study explained the advantages when one media converges with another media. Newspapers with Television media or Internet gains readership. In his study he quoted

American media like newspapers,Television media and some magazines.

The impact of public ownership, profits and competition on a number of newsroom employees and starting salaries in mid-sized daily newspapers were the issues involved in a study conducted by Alan Blanchard and Stephen Lacy.[85] This study comprises 77 dailies between 25,000 and 1,00,000 circulation. It was found that publicly held daily newspapers produced higher profit margins than did privately held dailies. Ownership and higher profits were associated with smaller newsroom staffs. Public ownership positively related with starting salaries. Also the presence of competition was positively correlated with newsroom size and starting salary. The impact of profitability on newsroom size was progressively greater for newspapers with higher than average profit margins.

Glen, L. Bleske[86] explained the problems of news employees. It was pointed out that text books on editing talk about copy editing in an idealized newsroom, where poor work can be upgraded. The books tell students of the romance of the editing, but they are light on the reality of burnout, deadline pressures, and the overburdened copy editors. This case study spent two nights with copy editors who pushed their copy through their computers. They are more like technicians than wordsmiths and the textbooks don`t talk about disappointments that the editors face.

Lijing Arthur Chang[87] in his study explores factors behind newspaper reporters turnover, intentions and the link between their intent to leave their newspaper and their intent to leave journalism. A total of 361 Texas newspaper reporters were surveyed. Findings showed that overall job satisfaction, pay, staff size, age, gender and marital status of newspapers reporters effects turnover intentions. The reporters intent to leave their newspapers is also to be a significant predictor of their intent to leave journalism.

Alyssa Eckman and Thomas R. Lindlof[88] conducted ethnographic case study of how one newspaper organization undertook the redesign of its advertising products. Examining the design and production of advertorials enables us to see and understand moments when the values of the interpretive communities of advertorialists (advertising) and journalists are invoked. This case study examines the potential for internal conflict within a new organization as distinctly oppositional interests – advertising and news-seek to control a newspapers' symbolic goods.

Frank, E.B.[89] study was based on newsroom at two different periods provides a time of changes in journalistic belief systems and the influence of convergence of work groups. Analysis supports finding that the local work culture is strong and quick to socialize new members. The findings suggest that friction between work Groups in newly converged newsrooms may relate more to turf battles and power issues than fundamental beliefs about journalism role and function in today's society.

Bruce Garrison[90] discussed reporters and editors, use of electronic mail in US daily newspaper newsrooms. The study was based on national mail survey of reporters and editors of randomly selected daily newspapers during fall of 2001. Respondents described the levels and types of use of electronic mail job and their concern about electronic mail. The study found a growing role for electronic matters concerned about how and under what circumstances it may be used successfully in gathering information for news stories.

Johnston and Dolores Flamiano[91] conducted interviews at four newspapers, the authors found that the critical issues facing the journalists and newspapers included overcoming the negative images of the newspapers in the community, reconnecting with ignored communities, and using minority gatekeepers to provide an additional perspective on stories. It was found that the newspapers were generally still operating under different paradigms that measured success in diversity in terms of numbers and targeting of minority communities.

Philip Meyer and Minheong Kim[92] examined 400 newspapers and found that those with above-average staff size (adjusted for circulation size) in 1995 were more successful at retaining circulation in the next five years. They explained that variance was small but significant.

Bill Silcock and Susan Keith[93] study focused on newswork language, routines and culture conflicts that can occur in the convergence process. This paper reports on a pilot study that sought to identify areas where news operations and journalism schools that adopt convergence in the future may encounter language and culture challenges.

International on Marketing of Newspapers

Jay Fogarty and Fredrik Gren and Levis Ubinas of Mckinsey[94] and company in a speech delivered at the World Association of Newspapers Annual Conference in Kobe, Japan in 1998 explained about the reasons for losing of advertising revenues. They suggested some methods to improve revenues. Some of them are go and talk to the customers, conduct market research, so on.

Staurt H. Schwartz[95] in his study advised the newspaper staff to pay heed to market survey and caliberate both selection and presentation of news more carefully to the audience preferences.

Thomson R. Stephen[96] research investigates the circulation and readership profile relation using a simple simultaneous equation framework. The model is then estimated across a sample of British and Irish daily and Sunday newspapers. In his study he found that the proportion of readers belonging to the more affluent social categories exert a strong positive influence on advertising.

Gall and Gregor S.[97] research demonstrates both intuitively and empirically, that advertisers actually benefit from the geographic concentration of newspaper industry. A regression, using thirty-five cities, showed advertising prices were positively related to competition, although the coefficients were statistically insignificant.

Pierce Brooks, Winter Harold[98] research provides a theoretical distiction between two pricing schemes. The distinction relies on the degree of consumer heterogeneity in reservation prices. Specifically, they use data from the newspaper industry in which some two edition newspaper firms are mixed bundles and others are pure bundles.

Cable, John, R.[99] research results on the U.K. newspaper industry offer some evidence of stable, overall mobility relationships, but the absence of long run equilibrium relationships at the market share level suggest these may be misleading.

Van-Kranenburg, H.L., Palum, Franz, C.P. Fann, Geerard.A[100] in their research investigate the life cycle characteristics of the market for daily newspapers in The Netherlands since 1848. Life expectancy depends on the cyclical evolution of the number of daily newspapers through time. The life cycle of the competitive newspaper industry in the Netherlands is characterised by turning period of turmoil during Second World War. Models that aim at estimating the expected life time of newspapers should acknowledge the cyclical characteristics of the industry.

Bently, C.[101] study revisits a land mark investigation of newspaper readership published 50 years ago. Like the work of Bernard Berlson, it attempts to discover why newspaper readers miss their paper when they can't receive it. The study reviews research on readership and uses individual stoppages caused by normal delivery problems at a daily newspaper net work.

Slade and E. Margaret[102] collection of data from the Canadian newspaper advertising industry is used to assess the private profitability of tying in the market where the Standard efficiency motives (e.g. price discrimination, cost saving and quality control) are unlikely to apply. The empirical assessment is based on a model leveraging in which suppliers of the tied good are paid a commission rather than a fee for service. This model demonstrates that tying is profitable under a wide range of circumstances. Furthermore, it is found that, with newspapers, tying and monopoly power go hand in hand.

Vivek and Chaudari[103] in their research address some of the issues associated with a monopoly in newspaper industry. In particular they analyse the pricing policies for a newspaper proprieter under different market structures. This theory is supported by empirical investigation of the Australian newspaper industry.

Hugh J. Martin[104] in his study uses economic theory to develop a long run standard for comparison of newspaper profits. Profits earned by fifteen publicly owned newspaper companies during an eleven year period are compared to publishing company profits and to yields from government and corporate bonds. The comparison shows that average newspaper company profits could be considered excessive.

Hendricks and Patrick[105] explores how newspaper industries in the Netherlands and the United States have evolved from the beginning of the 1980s until the mid-1990s, focussing on the strategic behaviour of individual newspaper companies in response to changes in their business environment, based on a series of seventy-three interviews with newspaper executives in the United States and the Netherlands. Reports on the economic fundamentals of newspaper publishing; the industrial context of newspaper firms: vertical integration and horizontal mergers and acquisitions; and strategies of expansion through diversification and innovation, consider implications for the near future of newspaper, newspaper organizations, and the newspaper industry.

Fee, C. Edward, Hadlock, Charles, J.[106] examined the relationship between management turnover and market structure for newspapers in 50 large cities from 1950-1993. They found that competitive markets display greater turnover rates than monopolistic markets and that turnover rates are increasing in the degree to which a newspaper trails its competition in market share. They discussed the implications of these findings for theories concerning competition and managerial employment contracting. The results appear most consistent with the hypothesis that the greater likelihood of liquidation in competitive markets leads to elevated turnover rates.

Leonard, N. read and Karen[107] in their study utilized survey and interviewing method to examine top level advertising managers. Opinions of the substitutability of server media options within the context of National advertising planning are taken into consideration. Newspapers were seen as reasonable substitutes for magazines and Radio.

Mary Alice Shaver and Stephen Lacy[108] in their exploratory study of forty dailies found a negative relationship between the number of radio and television stations and daily newspapers ROP (Run of Paper) advertising which means the paper can place the advertisement on any page or in any position it desires. A weaker relationship was found between number of radio and television stations and total advertising linage in daily newspapers. The markets used here varied greatly in competition's impact on linage. It appears that intermedia advertising is monopolistically competitive with some media being better at some types of advertising than others. These results hold implications for antitrust actions because on the assumption that intermedia competition is extensive in newspaper markets.

E. Adams[109] in his study cites examples of price fixing and collusion practices used among newspapers in several cities across the United States during the late 1890s and early 1900s. An examination of E.W. Scripps papers reveals secret agreements or combinations that were utilized among competitors to gain market advantages or to limit competition. The practices included, but were not limited to profit pooling, price fixing, collusion and contract, exclusively. The extent to which these agreements were established in differing markets and the candid discussion among the parties involved suggest these agreements were widespread in their use by Scripps newspapers.

Steve J. Collins[110], Texas at Arlington, conducted a student survey at a public university in southwest, examined the variables that predict campus newspaper readership. Although satisfaction with the student paper was quite high, the majority of students reported reading no more than one in every four issues. Consistent with the Community Integration Hypothesis, time spent on campus, participation in campus activities, student group membership, living on campus all predicted high levels of exposure to the student paper. Readership was negative correlated with year in school.

Frank E. Fee Jr. Carolina[111] study examined the nature of purported disconnect between readers and journalists. Direct comparison of these groups shows significant differences in the belief systems held by the journalists and non-journalists about the role of journalism. Findings also challenge at least some of the claims of the public journalism movement about reader wants and needs, and suggest that practices to help readers may be unwelcome.

The research conducted by Jean Kelly, Jan Knight, Jason Nedly, Lee Peck and Guy Reel[112] showed that straight news and narrative stories often did not differ in their ability to engage readers, and in some cases the narrative stories have actually been more effective. Secondary analysis revealed that story subject-matter did not influence readers' assessments of story traits.

The study conducted by Wilson Lowrey[113], tests the assumption that non-linear web news stories benefit readers. The study also explores impact on non-linearity of narrative structure on reader feedback. Findings suggest readers of non-linear stories perceived and had more control over the reading process than did readers of linear stories, but there were no significant difference in perceived credibility, perceived involvement by the readers, or in knowledge acquisition. Readers of linear stories were significantly more likely to focus on story content in feedback about the story.

Research Studies on Indian Newspapers

Indian Institute of Mass Communication[114] conducted a research project during the 1967 Indian general election, and two specific points were selected for assessment, namely what role did the press play in *(a)* educating the electorate about the election process and *(b)* enlightening the people on the policies and programmes of the different political parties and found that readers were more interested in political news.

The Indian and Eastern Newspaper Society[115] in their research assesses the changes in press advertising pattern both from the point of view of products and nature of advertising, covering four English dailies published in Bombay, Calcutta, Madras and Delhi. Data collected and presented compares the year 1973 and 1975. It was found that advertising pattern was improved and was made attractive in 1975 compared to 1973.

Mazharul Haque[116] investigated the news content of a sample of seven Indian metropolitan dailies through a systematic content analysis. The findings of the study not only demonstrates the types of news Indian newspapers contain but also provides a basis for studying news content from a cross-cultural standpoint in the future, comparing Indian news content to that of the west.

D. V. R. Murthy[117] conducted research on four Indian Dailies *The Hindu*, *Eenadu*, *The New Indian Express* and *Andhra Jyothi*. This study consists of analysis of development news that is analysis of editorials and letters to the editor. He explained the proportion of different news items like development politics and government acts, war, defence and protests, economic activity, travel transport, crimes, moral problems, conflicts, accidents and disasters, science and invention, public welfare and popular amusements, general human interests, scheduled caste/scheduled tribe, women, etc. He also explained the proportion of different news items like local news, state news, national news, foreign news, etc., in newspapers.

Robin Jeffrey[118] worked on Indian Regional language newspapers. He examined how these language papers *Eenadu* and *Punjab Kesari* have become an important part of life for a vast constituency of India, importantly, it is about the forces that are at play behind the making of news. He found that people read newspapers because of local news coverage. Some readers look for different key pieces. People get attracted towards puzzles and some readers read recipies, the comics, the feature stories, legal ads, etc.

Elizabeth Burch[119] study investigates framing of the environmental sustainability and development debate within two of India's leading English-language newspapers reputed to follow opposing political ideologies:the pro-government, *The Times of India* and the anti-government *The New Indian Express.* It was found that the paper's political ideologies did not necessarily affect coverage. Themes of advocacy versus objectivity, freedom of the press, market journalism and cultural values strongly motivated environmental reporting. Intra-organizational cultural factors were most influential in framing coverage of the environment.

Bela Trivedi, Kosha Takera's[120] study is based on media convergence in India. His research showed that media convergence in India is likely to be accelerated and in the near future Indian society will no longer be influenced by one media alone. This convergence will have significant and far reaching implications and impact on Indian society, according to these two researchers.

D.V.R. Murthy's[121] study concentrated on the history, growth and conflict in international communication on a positive note. He traces the emergence of developmental communication and how the Indian press has been covering developmental news. It gives an introduction to selected folk forms of Andhra Pradesh and how these folk forms are used for effective developmental communication. It carries a fine explanation of how news tactics should be reoriented to adapt to the changing expectations of the civic society.

Kiron Bansal's[121] content analysis study concentrated on news coverage of four Indian newspapers. The results of the study are as follows. "Modern society is flooded with a vast range of media. Newspapers provide a variety of information to readers and help them in making informed choices. Different types and categories of news events occurring at local, regional, national and international levels, selected on the basis of news values and newsworthiness form the core of a newspaper. International news bringing events from beyond national boundaries is a good indicator of the emphasis a newspaper places on global issues. The selection, placement and treatment accorded to international news, in addition to information dissemination, indicate the priorities and approach of a newspaper. In view of globalization, it becomes even more important that international news be given adequate space and projection in newspaper columns so that it contributes towards international goodwill and peace and helps in the understanding of cross-cultural relations. An overview of the Indian press will help to appreciate the projection of international news in the Indian press and situate it in a larger context."

Review of Literature Relating to State (Andhra Pradesh)

Murthy[123] conducted research on four Indian Dailies *The Hindu, Eenadu, The New Indian Express, Andhra Jyothi.* This study consists of analysis of development news that is analysis of editorials and letters to the editor. It explained the proportion of different news items like development politics and government acts, war, defence and protests, economic activity, travel transport, crimes, moral problems, conflicts etc. Accidents and disasters, science and invention, public welfare and popular amusements, general human interests, scheduled caste and sheduled tribe and women etc. It also explained the proportion of different news items like local news, state news, national news, foreign news etc in newspapers.

Another study by Murthy[124] concentrated on the history, growth and conflict in international communication on a positive note. He traces the emergence of developmental communication and how Indian press have been covering developmental news. It gives an introduction to selected folk forms of Andhra Pradesh and how these folk forms are used for effective developmental communication. It carries a fine explanation of how news tactics should be reoriented to adapt to the changing expectations of the civic society.

Bobby Vardhan's[125] study is on Indian press and national movement aims at making a useful contribution to journalism. It attempted to provide an extensive examination of the role of the press in all its length and breadth. This study concentrated on the nationalist period from 1857 to 1947. The press, for the purpose of the study, refers to the daily newspaper, the periodicals, and some journals. It exercises views of the leaders who volunteered their patriotic services. It profiles some individuals involved in the freedom struggle. It looks at the various revolutions and movements during the freedom struggle.

Eventhough a considerable amount of research has been done in the field of newspaper marketing, most of the research works were based on foreign newspapers and only a few research works were available on Indian newspapers. Again no research work is available basing on market analysis and distribution of newspapers and readers satisfaction except NRS and IRS studies. Not only that no research work is available till now on the marketing of newspapers in Visakhapatnam City. As physical distribution is given utmost importance in newspaper marketing, it is pertinent for researcher to choose the topic of Marketing of Newspapers : A Study of Selected Newspaper Organisations, Intermediaries and Readers in Visakhapatnam City. That is why this particular topic was chosen for the present study.

Aim of the Study

The Present Study aims at analyzing different newspaper markets and readers' behaviour in Visakhapatnam City. It tries to ascertain the selected newspaper distribution network, readership preferences and the coverage of different news items and compare the news content of the sample newspapers.

Objectives of the Study

The following are the specific objectives of the study.

(a) To know market potential of selected newspapers in Visakhapatnam City.

(b) To understand media habits like watching television, listening to the radio and reading magazines, internet usage etc., and compare the media habits of Visakhapatnam readers.

(c) To ascertain readership and analyse competition among various newspaper organizations in Visakhapatnam City.

(d) To examine the newspaper reading habits of readers in Visakhapatnam City.

(e) To analyse the opinions of readers about coverage of different news items and their areas of interests relating to different newspaper attributes.

(f) To study the distribution network of Visakhapatnam newspaper organizations and analyse distribution problems.

Methodology

(a) ***Area of Study:*** The area chosen for the study is Visakhapatnam city. Since, the population of Visakhapatnam city consists of readers who read a variety of newspapers. The diversity of readers in reading different newspapers enables effective comparison of a cross-section of the society and for the study of preferences of readers who read different newspapers. Hence, the study was conducted in Visakhapatnam City.

(b) ***Geographic Segmentation:*** For convenience the entire Visakhapatnam City is divided in to four zones.

First zone consists of : *(i)* One town; *(ii)* Main road; *(iii)* Official colony; *(iv)* Ramnagar and *(v)* Dabagardens.

Second Zone consists of: *(i)* M.V.P. colony; *(ii)* Potinamallaya-palem; *(iii)* Sagarnagar; *(iv)* Doctors colony; *(v)* Pandu Ranga Puram; *(vi)* Kirlampudi; *(v)* Akkaya Palem; *(vi)* Dwarakanagar and *(vii)* CBM compound.

Third Zone consists of : *(i)* Gopalapatnam; *(ii)* Buchirajupalem; *(iii)* Santhi Nagar; *(iv)* Journalist colony; *(v)* Madhavadhara VUDA colony; *(vi)* Marripalem; *(vii)*Muralinagar; *(viii)* 104 area; *(ix)* Vepagunta and *(x)* Simhachalam.

Fourth zone consists of: *(i)* Hindusthan Zinc quarters; *(ii)* BHPV town ship; *(iii)* Sheela nagar; *(iv)* Steel plant; *(v)* Rajiv Nagar; *(vi)* Pedagantyada; *(vii)* Sriharipuram; *(viii)* Scindia and *(ix)* Gajuvaka.

(c) ***Sources of Data:*** The data was collected both in Primary and Secondary ways. Primary data was collected through questionnaires. Five different questionnaires were prepared and administered. One to readers, to know about their preferences, media habits and reading habits. The second one is for selected newspaper organisational heads, to know the present scenario and future of newspaper Industry. The third-one is to Retailers (panshop owners) to know about newspapers which are fast moving and so on. The fourth one is to Newspaper Agents to know about the distribution system of newspapers. Fifth-one is to the Distribution boys to examine the distribution and also the distribution problems in newspaper organisations.

Secondary data is from company manuals, journals, periodicals, newspapers, National Readership Surveys, Indian Readership Surveys, Registrar for Newspapers in India (RNI), magazines like A&M, Business world, Business India etc.

(d) ***Universe of the Study***

Selection of newspapers: Eight newspapers were selected for the present study keeping in view of their Circulation, Geographical location, Readership and Language. They are *(i) The Hindu, (ii) Deccan Chronicle, (iii) The New Indian Express, (iv) The Times of India, (v) Eenadu, (vi) Vartha, (vii) Andhra Bhoomi, (viii) Andhra Prabha.* (Profiles of the selected newspapers appear in Chapter III).

Universe for Readers Survey

Basing on the circulation of selected newspapers in Visakhaptanam City, the sample was selected. The circulation of some newspapers in Visakhapatnam city are as follows:

Table 1.5
CIRCULATION FIGURES OF THE EIGHT SAMPLE DAILIES

Daily	*Total (India)*	*Visakhapatnam*
Eenadu	8,41,890	40,000*
The Hindu	9,04,654	25,000*
Vaartha	2,00,000	11,700*
Deccan Chronicle	2,33,139	22,061
The New Indian Express	2,51,895	5,000*
Andhra Bhoomi	65,869	7,700*
The Times of India	12,61,799**	500*
Andhra Prabha	20,000	800*

Source: Audit Bureau of Circulation (Mumbai) report, December, 2002.
* Approximate figures.
** New Delhi and Chandigarh circulation figure was not included because the figure is not received by the time of audit period.

The Hindu, Deccan Chronicle, The New Indian Express, The Times of India are considered elite English dailies. The other four are premier Telugu newspapers in Andhra Pradesh. *The Hindu* has the highest circulation among the English dailies of the region, and *Eenadu* has the highest circulation among Telugu dailies.

Two considerations went into the selection of the two different Language dailies.

1. English being the associate official language and the main medium of intellectual exchange among the elite in the country, the English dailies are read by the majority of policy-makers, decision-makers and administrators.
2. The language newspapers are read by the masses and reach the majority of the population in the region.

The universe for this study comprises all the readers who read eight newspapers in Visakhapatnam City during the calender year September 2002-February 2003. Illiterates and Children below 15 age group are excluded from this study. Universe for Agents Survey comprises all 200 agents (Approximately) in Visakhapatnam City. The universe for distribution boys survey comprises of total number of 1200 distribution boys (Approximately) in Visakhapatnam City. The universe for retailers' study comprises of total number of 400 retailers.(Approximately) in Visakhapatnam City. The universe newspaper organisational study comprises of the total number of newspaper organisations and their heads.

(e) ***Selection of the Sample***

Readers. While selecting the sample, keeping in view of the time and financial resources available for the researcher, it was thought that a sample of 500 readers represent a sample of 0.5 per cent of all readers. So more than 0.5 per cent of the total population was chosen for this study. The actual sample chosen was 600, as readers population is one lakh. (Approximately). (Out of 600, 576 Questionnaires were good in all respects. So sample size became 576). In the sample of 600 readers in order to get accurate results, entire sample is divided basing on age, educational level, income, occupation and gender. Readers are classified into males and females basing on gender. Age groups are started from 15 years and classes constitute 15-20 years old, 21-25 years old, 25-30 years old so on. Income levels include *(i)* Less than Rs. 5,000, *(ii)* Rs. 5,001 to Rs. 10,000, *(iii)* Rs. 10,001 to Rs. 15,000 *(iv)* Rs. 15,001 to Rs. 20,000, *(v)* Above Rs. 20,000. Education levels consists of five groups. They are *(i)* Up to 10th class; *(ii)* Inter, *(iii)* Degree, *(iv)* PG (General), and *(v)* PG (Professional). Basing on employment status readers are divided into Businessmen, Employees, Students and Housewives.

*Agents:*While selecting the sample, it was thought that 15 agents represent a sample of 7.5 per cent of total agents in Visakhapatnam City. So 15 number of agents were examined.

Retailers: While selecting the sample, it was thought that 50 retailers represent a sample of 12.5 per cent of total retailers in Visakhaptnam City. So a number of 50 retailers were examined.

Distribution Boys: While selecting this sample, it was thought that 50 distribution boys representing a sample of 4.2 per cent of total distribution boys in Visakhaptanm City. So a sample of 50 distribution boys were examined.

Organisational Heads. In universe of seven organisational heads, questionnaires were administered to *Eenadu, The Hindu, Deccan Chronicle and Andhra Bhoomi, Vaartha* organisational heads because, these are the newspapers, have large circulation in Visakhapatnam City. So these four organisational heads were interviewed.

(f) ***Instruments used in Data Collection:*** Five different questionnaires were administered to elicit information from the Readers, Agents, Retailers, Distribution boys and Organisational heads.

Questionnaire for readers: It is constructed in English and some of the questionnaires were administered by the researchers herself because some readers though literates, they cannot read and understand the English language. The information pertaining to demographic factors like Gender, Age, Income, Educational qualifications were studied. The readers' preferences relating to various news items like Local news, Regional news, National news and International news were examined. The impact of price reduction, quality and quanity, coverage of news items of various newspapers over the readers were also examined.

The questionnaire consists of four parts. In Part I, demographic factors like gender, age, income, educational qualifications were examined. In Part II, newspaper reading habits and preferences of readers for selected newspapers like *The Hindu, The New Indian Express, Deccan Chronicle, The Times of India, Eenadu, Vaartha, Andhra Bhoomi, Andhra Prabha* of Visakhapatnam were examined. It consists of newspaper reading habits and preferences like name of newspaper reading, readership preference of reading newspaper, time spent on reading newspaper, time of reading newspaper, nature of buying newspaper that is either by subscription or from newspaper stands, time of receiving copy of newspaper, areas of interest of readers relating to various news items like local news, regional news, national news and International news. It also consists of impact of newspaper attributes like price, quality etc., on newspaper reading habit of readers and reading of newspaper through internet. The content was examined basing on the extent of coverage given to different news items like local news, national news and so on.

In Part III, various media habits of readers were examined. Media habits include Watching Television, Listening to the Radio, Reading Magazines and Surfing Internet.

In Part IV, various reading habits other than reading newspapers were examined. Other reading habits include Magazine reading, Journal reading and Periodical reading. In magazine reading Telugu Language and English Language magazines were examined.

Questionnaire for Distribution boys: It consists of questions relating to demographic profile of distribution boys, information relating to name of Publications distributing, arrival time to paper points, number of papers distributed, areas of distribution, time taken for distribution, participation in cash collection, days required to finish cash collection work, remuneration for work done, incentives and finally problems faced by the Distribution boys were examined.

Questionnaire for Retailers: By using this questionnaire, demographic factors were studied. In this the name of Publications selling, arrival time of newspapers, newspapers which are fast moving, reasons for fast moving, incentives and problems faced by retailers were examined.

Questionnaire for Agents: By using this questionnaire in addition to demographic factors of agents, it also examined Publications dealing with, area of operation, volume, duration of carrying newspaper business, investment made, time of receiving paper bundles, returns on investment made, number of distribution boys under his control, salary structure, reasons for choosing newspaper business, ranking of newspapers, opinion on reading newspaper through internet, opinion on future of newspapers and finally problems faced by newspaper agents.

(g) ***Data Collection:*** The data was collected both in primary and secondary ways. The primary data was collected during the calender year September 2002-February 2003. Primary data is collected through questionnaires. Five different questionnaires were prepared and administered for Readers, Selected Newspaper Organisational heads, Panshop Owners (middlemen), Agents, Distribution boys. A pilot study has been conducted to identify the operational and

semantic problems inherent in the questionnaire for readers. Modifications were made on the basis of advice given by various experts. The researcher strived to make the questionnaires comprehensive even while ensuring that the questions are neither too difficult nor too simple. Efforts were made to prevent respondents from conferring with each other while answering the questionnaires.

The researcher administered 600 questionnaires for readers who read eight selected newspapers in Visakhapatnam City during the calender year September 2002-February 2003. Fifteen questionnaires were administered to newspaper Agents during normal hours (9 a.m. to 5 p.m.) in Visakhapatnam City. Fifty questionnaires were administered to Retailers (pan shop owners) during normal hours (9 a.m. to 5 p.m) in Visakhapatnam City. Fifty questionnaires were administered for Distribution boys. These questionnaires were administered to Distribution boys, everyday, early in the morning before 4.30 a.m. when boys were waiting for paper bundles at paper points in Visakhapatnam.

The secondary data collected was for a four year period starting from March 1999 -March 2004. Secondary data was collected from company manuals, journals, periodicals, newspapers, NRS & IRS surveys, Reports of RNI, PTI[126], PIB[127] etc., and magazines like *A&M, Business World, Business India, Industrial Economist,* etc.

(h) ***Data Analysis:*** The main objective of the study is to analyse readers' preferences about different newspapers in Visakhapatnam City and to know about areas of interest relating to various news items in newspapers. For this purpose, the inter relationships between demographic and socio-economic background of various readers were analysed. The analysis was made to find out the relationship between demographic factors and preferences of readers relating to various newspaper attributes like price, coverage of items, areas of interest and so on. Secondary data was used to analyse primary data. Age-wise classification of readers, income-wise classification of readers, educational qualification-wise classification of readers was based on classification in NRS surveys.

(i) Units of Analysis: The units of analysis for this study were: *(i)* News item, *(ii)* Reader:The readers are segmented basing on geographical location, age, education, income, occupation and also gender, *(iii)* Agents or middlemen, *(iv)* Panshop owners or retailers and *(v)* Distribution boys.

(j) ***Operational Definitions***

(i) *News item:* a News item is any item on a timely event with a current dateline, on account of that event reported by the newspaper's own correspondents' or reporters or items from wire services. These include human interest stories.

(ii) Readers are the people who read a newspaper.

(iii) Agents or Middlemen are the people who act as mediators between newspaper subscribers and newspaper organizations.

(iv) Panshop owners are the traders who are selling newspapers in retail.

(v) Distribution boys are the people who supply or distribute newspapers to the readers. These people are appointed by the agents.

The following items were excluded from being considered as units of analysis for this study. *(a)* Children and young people below 15 years of age, *(b)* Illiterates who cannot read newspaper.

(k) ***Subject Categories***

Income: Income means personal income. It means the amount which is actually received by the individuals or households in a country during the year.[128]

Competition: It refers to that market situation in which rival firms try to increase their profits at one another's expense.[129]

Price of newspaper: The value of newspaper expressed in monetary terms.

(l) ***Geographical Categories***

Local news: It gives information on happenings in the city, advertisements in relation to the city regarding educational institutions, shopping etc., weather forecasts of the city, list of various engagements in city, a special column by *name around the city* is present containing various welfare activities, medical camps, awards etc., in relation to the City.

Regional news: It gives district-wise presentation of happenings, a column containing a brief coverage of various aspects and *Regional appointments.*

State news: State news means it covers news mainly from the state. It occupies about one- two pages depending on the news.

National news: It gives information regarding political happenings, social events, Government policies and decisions of the entire nation (India).

International news: It covers in-depth news from around the world, pictoral coverage of latest happenings etc. Two pages are generally allotted to cover this news.

Business news: It gives Corporate news, Stocks, Finance, Shares, Commodities, Bombay Stock Exchange, exchange rates and Bullion Markets.

Sports news: It means coverage of sports news, in-depth analysis about national, regional and international sports. It covers news about Cricket, Tennis, Bridge, Snooker, Golf, Billiards, Football, Racing, Athletics, Hockey, Chess, Squash, Basketball, Weightlifting and so on. Three pages are allotted daily to the sports news in most of the newspapers. Generally Photographs from all sports are also published in newspapers.

Editorial news: It means an opinion piece that projects the view point of the newspaper on a particular policy, programme, or event. It gives a digest of facts, evaluates them and arrives at a logical conclusion step by step.

Limitations of the Study

1. The study covered the geographical location of Visakhapatnam City only.
2. Newspaper organisations lack sufficient past records, journals etc., to supply required data.
3. Due to rigorous door-to-door sales promotional activities some of the customers did not like to respond to queries of the researcher with enthusiasm as they lost patience with the sales promotion people. However, the researcher explained the purpose of visit and tried her best in sustaining their interest level to the extent required.

4. What the respondents have said is believed to be their true response and hence, no statistical test has been performed to study non-response bias and consistency of individual response.

The Scheme of the Presentation

The study is presented in seven chapters. The Scheme of Presentation in each chapter is as follows:

Chapter I: Design of the Study. This Chapter consists of introduction about newspapers, newspapers in global and national scenario. It explains the research methodology adopted in the study. The research methodolgy contains need or significance of the study, review of literature, aim of the study, objectives of the study, methodology of collecting data and limitations of the study.

Chapter II: Development of Newspaper Industry : An overview. It gives detailed description about origin and development of newspaper *industry* in India. It explains about origin of press, origin of newspapers, about vernacular newspapers, growth of newspapers in India, Reasons for growth of newspapers in India, role of newspapers in integrating society, ownership of newspapers, competition in newspaper industry, Foreign Direct Investment in newspaper industry, price wars among newspaper organisations, newspapers of Andhra Pradesh and finally about problems and prospects in newspaper industry.

Chapter III: Newspaper Organisational Profiles of Visakhapatnam and Newspaper Organisations. It contains a clear description about organisational profiles of selected newspaper organisations of Visakhapatnam City and summary report of interviews conducted with newspaper organisational heads in Visakhapatnam City.

Chapter IV: Marketing of Newspapers : An Analysis of System. It gives a brief description of marketing concepts, marketing scope in newspaper industry, existing marketing system of newspapers, and also explains about the strengths, weaknesses, opportunities and threats of current newspaper industry and performance of newspaper organisations in the present scenario.

Chapter V: Distribution of Newspapers: Role of Interme-diaries. It explains about the distribution of newspapers and the role of intermediaries in distribution of newspapers refering to selected newspaper organisations in Visakhapatnam City. It also contains views and perceptions of agents, retailers and distribution boys.

Chapter VI: Analysis of Customers Views, Perception and Satisfaction. It consists of a detailed analysis of customers' (readers') views about different newspapers in Visakhapatnam City, their perception about different newspapers and different media and their satisfaction towards different types of newspapers.

Chapter VII: Summary, Findings and Suggestions. It contains summary of the entire study and some suggestions to newspaper organisations to improve their readership by improving different attributes of newspapers like quality, coverage etc., and also to improve the distribution system of newspapers.

Scope for Further Research

The newspaper industry now-a-days facing so many problems because of stiff competition from different media. To overcome this problem and to increase readership, study about reader's preferences is not enough. Comparison of different media habits of people with newspapers and finding out reasons for decline in readership of newspapers is also important. This can be taken up for further study. Not only that, the newspaper industry is getting revenues not only through readership. It is getting revenue through advertisements also. So the methods to increase advertisement revenue by newspapers organisations can also be taken up for further study.

REFERENCES

1. Suhas Chakravarthy (1997), *Press and Media: The Global Dimensions*, Kanishka Publishers, p. 1.
2. Herbert Lee Williams (1982), *Newspaper Organisation and Management*, Surjeet Publications, p. 46.
3. Wells Burnet Moraiarty (2003), *Advertising Principles and Practice*, (Sixth Edition), Pearson Education, p. 239.
4. Shaikh Abdus Salam (1998), *Bangladesh Media and India: An attitudinal Approach*, Reprinted by J.S.Yadava, Pradeep Mathur, *Issues in Mass Communication – The Basic Concepts*, Kanishka Publishers in Association with Indian Institute of Mass Communication, p. 152.
5. Garcia (2003), (President and CEO of Garcia Media, Who has redesigned more than 450 Publications from all over the world including *Wall Street Journal* and *The Miami Herald* (U.S.A.), *Die Zeit* (Germany), *EL Tiempo* (Colombia) and *Liberation* (France).
6. B.N. Ahuja (1993), *History of Press, Press Laws and Communications*, Surjeet Publications, p. 1.

7. Kim Long (1993), *The American Forecaster Almanac,* 1993 Business edition.
8. Rebecca Pirto Heath (March 1997), *In so Many Words* American Demographics, pp. 39-45.
9. Jane Hodges (April 29,1996), "Newspapers Plug Along in Quest for Web Answers." *Advertising Age*:S6; Dana.
10. Lori Lefeure (October 22, 2001), "Waiting for the Web," *Brand Week*: SR 22.
11. D.V.R. Murthy (2002), *Mass Communication Concepts and Issues,* Olive Green Publications, p. 122.
12. N. Bhaskara Rao (2003), "Opportunities and Challenges", *Vidura,* Vol. 40 (Jan-Mar 2003), p. 35.
13. Christy Fisher (1992), "Newspapers of the Future Look to Go High Tech as Experiments Abound." *Advertising Age* (Octobr 5, 1992): S3;
14. B.N. Ahuja (1993), "History of Press, Press Laws and Communications", Surjeet Publications, p. 1.
15. Christine Larson(1991), "Ethnic Issues," *Adweek* (May 6,1991):N3
16. D.V.R. Murthy (2002), "Study of Contemporary Trends in British Press", *The Hindu*, Friday, December 6, 2002, p. 5.
17. B.N. Ahuja (1993), *History of Press, Press Laws and Communications,* Surjeet Publications, p. 1.
18. Rene Jean Ravault, *International Information Bullet or Boomering,* Reprinted by Doris A.Graber,' (1994), *Media Power in Politics,* p. 403.
19. B.N. Ahuja (1993), *History of Press, Press Laws and Communications,* Surjeet Publications, p. 2.
20. Peter Landers (2002), "Japan's Newspapers Take Holiday from Traditional Vacation Days", *The Financial Express,* Saturday, March 16, 2002, p. 11.
21. Neel Chowdary (2002), Singapore, "Indian Media Generates Revenue by Beaming International Signal", *The Financial Express,* Friday, June 21, 2002, p. 4.
22. B.N. Ahuja (1993), *History of Press, Press Laws and Communications,* Surjeet Publications, p. 3.
23. IraTeinowitz (2002), "USA Today: No Longer a Newspaper", *Advertising Age,* Sept. 2, p. 18.
24. Reuters, Newyork (2001), "US Ruling on Freelancers to Hit Newspapers", *The Hindu Businessline,* Wednesday, June 27, 2001.
25. Mattew Rose (2002), "Circulation at U.S. Newspapers Slips, Trends Mixed at Largest Papers", *The Financial Express,* Wednesday, May 8, 2002, p. 7.
26. Vernonis Suhler Communication Industry Forecast (1999-2004).
27. Reuters, New York (2001), "Ad Slump Hits Earnings at Papers, Agencies", *The Hindu Businessline,* Saturday, June 16, 2001, p. 6.

28. Balbir K. Punj (2002), "Media: Fact & Fiction", *The New Indian Express*, Wednesday, May 15, 2002.
29. Shyam G. Menon, Lathavenkataraman (2002). "World Tunes to News Channels as Real Life Gets Deadly", *The Hindu Businessline*, Friday, April 19, 2002, p. 1.
30. Bruce Orval and Martin Peace (2002), "Media Megamergers aren't big Hits as Futuristic Synergies Prove Elusive", *The Financial Express*. Saturday, May 12, 2002.
31. The 55th *World Newspaper Congress* in Belgium from 26-29, May 2002, "New Strategies for Profit Growth."
32. Bobby Varthan (2000), *Indian Press and National Movement*, (Thesis), pp. 1-7.
33. Shilpa Sebastian Romeles (2002), "Learning with the Newspaper", *The Hindu*, Saturday, December 14, 2002, Young World Supplement, p. 4.
34. B.N. Ahuja (1993), *History of Press, Press Laws and Communication*, Surjeet Publications, p. 124.
35. B.N.Ahuja (1993), *History of Press, Press Laws and Communications*, Surjeet Publications, p. 143.
36. S. Mohan (2002), "Positive Critism is Media's Right, Say Former Supreme Court Judge", *The Hindu Businessline*, Thursday, December 12, 2002, p. 7.
37. Registrar of Newspapers for India is Commonly Known as Press Registrar Came in to being on 1st July, 1956.
38. J. Natarajan (1995), *History of Indian Journalism*, Publication Division, Ministry of Information and Broadcasting, Government of India, p. 7.
39. J. Natarajan (1995), *History of Indian Journalism*, Publication Division, Ministry of Information and Broadcasting, Government of India, p. 57.
40. J. Natarajan (1995), *History of Indian Journalism*, Publication Division, Ministry of Information and Broadcasting, Government of India, pp. 244-46.
41. Poturi Venkateswara Rao (2000), *History of Telugu Newspaper*.
42. J. Natarajan (1995), *History of Indian Journalism*, Publication Division, Ministry of Information and Broadcasting, Government of India, p. 7.
43. Gallup India Private Limited, Banglore Survey, 2002.
44. Jayachandra Reddy (2002), "Criticism by Media should be Welcomed.", *The Hindu*, Thursday December 12, 2002, p. 7.
45. David Nyhan, *Newspapers in Campaigns* Reprinted by Doris A Graber (1994), *Media Power in Politics*, p. 171.
46. Times News Network, "Radio Biggest Gainer in Delhi" *The Times of India*, December 23, 2003, p. 13.
47. Registrar of Newspapers for India 2002-03 Reports.
48. Times News Network, "Radio Biggest Gainer in Delhi" *The Times of India*, December 23, 2003, p. 13.

49. *The Hindu* (June 23, 2002), Sunday Magazine, p. 3 (National Readership Survey).
50. *The Hindu Businessline(2003),* Wednesday, April 30, 2003, p. 6.
51. Bob Franklin and David Murphy (1991), "*Making the Local News: Local Journalism in Context,* London: Routledge.
52. Mark Miller, Julie (1998), "Framing the candidates in presential primaries", *Journalism and Mass Communication Quarterly,75/2,* pp. 312-325.
53. David K. Demers (1998), "Structural Pluralism, Corporate Newspaper Structure and News Source Perceptions. Another Test of the Editorial vigor hypothesis", *Journallism and Mass Communication Quarterly,75/3,* pp. 572-593.
54. Elli P. Lester-Roushanzamir,Usha Raman (1999), "The Global Village in Atlanta: A Textual Analysis of Olympic News Coverage for Children in the Atlanta Journal Constitution.", *Journalism and Mass Communication Quarterly, 76/4,* pp. 699-712.
55. Claire E. Taylor and Her Associates (2000), "Local Press Coverage of Environmental Conflict", *Journalism and Mass Communication Quarterly,77/1,* pp. 175-192.
56. C. Anthony Giffard and Nancy K. Rivenburg (2000), "News Agencies, National Images and Golbal Media Events", *Journalism and Mass Communication Quarterly,* 77/1, pp. 8-21.
57. Stephen Lacy (2001), "Sample Size for Newspaper Content Analysis in Multiyear Studies", *Journalism and Mass Communication Quarterly,* 78/4, pp. 836-846.
58. Joseph C. Harry (2001), "Covering Conflict: Astructural-Pluralist Analysis of How a Small-town and Big City Newspaper Reported an Environmental Controversy", *Journalism and mass communication quarterly,78/3.*
59. Kis Kodrich (2002), "Finding New Way : Nicarguan Newspapers in Globalised World", *Journalism and mass communication quarterly.* 79/1, pp. 101-121.
60. Karin Wahl-Jorgensen(2002), "The Normative-economic Justification for Public Discourse: Letters to the Editor." *Journalism and Mass Communication Quarterly,* 79/1, pp. 121-134.
61. Mark Deuze (2002), "National News Culture: A Comparison of Dutch, German, British, Australian and Journalists", *Journalism and Mass Communication Quarterly,* 79/1, pp. 134-150.
62. John J. Pauly (2002), Melissa Eckert, "The Myth of 'The Local' in American Journalism", *Journalism and Mass Communication Quarterly,* 79/2, 2002. pp. 310-27.
63. Dietram A. Schenfele, James Shanaham and Sei-Hill Kim (2002), "Who Cares about Local Politics? Media Influences on Local Political involvement,issue awareness and attitude strength." *Journalism and Mass Communication Quarterly* 79/2, pp. 7-26.

64. Dharma Adhikari, Tracy Everbach and Shahira Fahmy(2002), "Watching the Watch Dogs: An Etheno Methodological Study of News decision making at a midwestern newspaper," *AEJMC Publications idivision, 2002.*
65. Fredrick Fico and Olivia Balog (2002), "Partisans and Non-Partisans in News Coverage of Local Conflict", *AEJMC Publications Division,* 2002.
66. Guy Forida and Wayne Wanta,U.S.(2002), "Gate-keeping on the Newyork Times op-ed pages: How Diverse is the Content?", *AEJMC Publications Division,* 2002.
67. Elza Ibroscheva, Carbondale (2002).
68. Chango Lee, Texas-Austin (2002), 'News Coverage of the U.S. Attack on Afghnisthan: A Comparison of the New York Times, Arab News,' *AEJMC Publications Division,* 2002.
69. Autumn Miller and Dente Ross (2002), "They are not us: Framing of American Indian by the Boston Globe", *AEJMC Publications Division,* 2002.
70. Kristy H. Nich Lousiania at Lafayette (2002), "Source Diversity and Newspaper Size: Use of Sources in Local News", *AEJMC Publications Division,* 2002.
71. Yonghoi Song, Missouri Columbia (2002), "Sourcing Patterns of National and Local Newspapers: A Community Tructure Perspective", *AEJMC Publications Division,* 2002.
72. Neiva-Elizabeth (1996), "The Chain Building: The consolidation of the American Newspaper Industry, 1953-80", *American Journal of Business Histroy Review* in 1996, pp. 1-42.
73. Bronars and Stephen. G. (1998), "Non Parametric Tests of the Efficiency of Union Employment Contracts", Cambridge University Press, p. 41.
74. Picard, Robert. G (1998), "*Press Concentration and Monopoly: New Perspectives of Newspaper Ownership and Operation*", pp. 231
75. Noon.Mike (1991), "Strategy and circumstance: The success of the NUJ's new technology policy" *British Journal of Industrial Relations,* 29(2), (June 1991), U.K. pp. 259-76.
76. Jan Bekken (1995), "News Worker:Toward a History of the Rank and File", University of Minnesota Press in U.S.
77. Picard, Robert. G., Broady, Jeffrey. H (1997), "*Newspaper Publishing Industry*", Boston, pp. 224.
78. Kathleen A.Hansen, Mark Nevzil and Jean (1998),' Newsromm Topic Teams: Journalist's Asssessments of Effects on News Routines and Newspaper Quality.' *Journalism and Mass Communication Quarterly,* 75/4, pp. 803-822.
79. Doobrev and Stainisslav.D.(1999), "The Dynamics of Bulgarian Newspaper Industry in a Period of Transition:Organisational

Adptation, Structural Intertia and Political Change", *Industrial and Corporate Change (Journal of Bulgaria)*, September, 1999, pp. 573-605.

80. Abby Dress (1999), "Running out of Time: An Analysis of Shutting Down New York *Newsday* by *Times Mirror*", *Journalism and Mass Communication Quarterly*, 76/4, pp. 745-756.
81. George L.Daniels and C.Ann Holifield (2001), "Times of turmoil short and Long Term Effects of Organisational Change of News Room Employees." *Journalism and Mass Communication Quarterly*, 78/3.
82. Randal A. Beam (2001), "Does it Pay a Market Oriented Newspaper?" *Journalism and Mass Communication Quarterly*, 78/3, pp. 466-484.
83. Joe Strupp, "Newsroom Consider Policies, Port Blair Newyork Times Scandal Forces Changes", *Editor and Publisher Online*.
84. Randy Dotinga, 'Convergence Gains Critical Mass: Making the Dream Reality.' *Editor and Publisher Online*.
85. Alan Blanchard and Stephen Lacy (2002), "The Impact of Public Ownership, Profits and Competition on Number of Newsroom Employees and Starting Salaries in mid-sized Daily Newspaper." *AEJMC Newspaper Division 2002*.
86. Glen, L. Bleske (2002), 'The Romance and Reality of Copy Editing: A Newsroom Case Study.' *AEJMC Newspaper Division*.
87. Lijing Arthur Chang (2002), "Exploring the Turnover Issue: Why Newspaper Reporters Intend to Quit their Jobs", *AEJMC Newspaper division*.
88. Alyssa Eckman and Thomas R. Lindlof (2002), "Negotiating the grey Lines: An Ethnographic Case Study of Organisational Conflict, better Advertorials and News", *AEJMC Newspaper Division, 2002*.
89. Frank, E.B. (2002), "Whose Values are News Values? What Journalists and Citizens Want", *AEJMC Newspaper Division*.
90. Bruce Garrison (2002), "The use of Electronic Mail as a News Gathering Resource", *AEJMC Newspaper Division*.
91. Johnston and Dolores Flamiano (2002), "Practicing Diversity: An Exploratory Study of Implementing Diversity in the Newsroom",' *AEJMC Newspaper Division, 2002*.
92. Philip Meyer and Minheong Kim (2002), "How Many Newspeople does a Newspaper Need?", *AEJMC Newspaper Division, 2002*.
93. Bill Sillock and Susan Keith (2002), "Translating the Tower of Babel: Issues of Language and Culture in Covered Newsroom: Pilot Study", *AEJMC Newspaper Division, 2002*.
94. Jay Fogarthy and Fredrick Gren and Levis Ubinas (1998), "Rapidly Increasing Newspaper Revenue through Redesigning Advertising Sales", *Mckinsey and Company*, June 1998.
95. Staurt H Schwartz(2002), *Wall Street Journal*.
96. Thomson R. Stephen, (March 1989), "Circulation Versus Advertiser Appeal in Newspaper Industry", *Journal of Industrial Economics* in U.K., pp. 259-271.

97. Gall and Gregor, S. (December 1993), "The Employer's Offensive in the Provincial Newspaper Industry", *British Journal of Industrial Relations* in U.K., pp. 615-24.

98. Ierce.Brooks, Winter, Harold (Dec 1996), "Pure Versus Mixed Commodity Building", *Review of Industrial Organisation,* U.S, pp. 811-21.

99. Cable, John. R. (February, 1997), "Market Share Behaviour and Mobility: An Analysis and Time Series Application", *Review of Economics and Statistics of* U.K. pp. 136-141.

100. Van-Kranenburg H.L.Palem, Franz C.P. Fann, Geerard, A. (October 1998), "The Life Cycle of Daily Newspapers in Netherlands (1848-1997)", *De-economist Journal,* pp. 475-94.

101. Bently, C. (2000) , "50 Years Later, What it Means to Miss the Paper."

102. Slade and E. Margaret (October 1998), "The Leverage Theory of Trying Revisited: Evidence from Newspaper Advertising", *Southern Economic Journal,* pp. 204-222.

103. Vivek Chaudari (March 1998), "Pricing Efficiency of Ciruclation Industry: The Case of Newspapers", *Information Economics and Policy Journal of Australia* in March 1998, pp. 59-76.

104. Hugh, J. Martin (1998), "Measuring Newspaper Profits: Developing a Standard of Comparison.", *Journalism and Mass Communication Quarterly,* 75/3,1998.

105. Hendricks and Patrick(1999), "*A Lost Cause? Strategic Mangement of Newspaper firms in the United States and in Netherlands*", p. 251.

106. Fee, C.Edward, Hanlock, Charles.J. (April, 2000), "Management Turnover and Product Market Competition: Empirical evidence from the U.S. Newspaper Industry", *Journal of Business (American magazine),* pp. 205-243.

107. Leonard, N. Read and Karen (2000), "A Demand Side View of Media Substitutability in National Advertising. A Study of Advertiser Opinions about Traditional Media Options", *Journalism and Mass Communication Quarterly,* 77/2.

108. Mary Alice Shaver and Stephen Lacy (2002), "The Impact of Intermedia and Newspaper Competition on Advertising Linage in Daily Newspapers", *Journalism and Mass Communication Quarterly.*

109. Edward E. Adams (2002), "Collusion and Price Fixing in the American Newspaper Industry: Market Preservation Trends", *Journalism and Mass Communication Quarterly,* 79/2,2002, pp. 1890-1910.

110. Steve.J.Collins, (2002), "The Community Integration Hypothesis' and other Predictors of Campus Newspaper Readership", *AEJMC Compilation 2002.*

111. Frank E.Fee Jr Carolina (2002), 'Whose Values are News Values? What Journalists and Citizens Want.' *AEJMC Compilation, 2002.*

112. Jean Kelly, Jan Knight, Jason Nedly, Lee peck and Guy Reel, (2002)," On the straight and narrative:The effect of writing style on readers' perceptions of narrative story quality.", *AEJMC compilation, 2002.*

113. Wilson Lowrey (2002), 'The non-linear Web Story:An Assessment of Readers Perceptions, Knowledge Acquisition, Readers Feed back', *AEJMC Compilation 2002.*

114. Indian Institue of Mass Communication (1968), "Role of Daily Newspapers During Elections: Report of a Content Analysis of the Indian Dailies Coverage of Election News and Items", *Indian Institute of Mass Communication,* New Delhi, 1968, p. 12.

115. Indian and Eastern Newspaper Society (1976), "Analysis of press Advertising:1973-75", *The Indian and Eastern Newspaper Society,* New Delhi (1976). p. 7.

116. S.M. Mazharul Haque (1988), *What is News in India? A Content Analysis of the Elite Press"*, University Press of America, Lanham, MD (1988), p. 190.

117. D.V.R. Murthy (2000), *Developmental Journalism and Indian Press: A Content Analysis of Selected Newspapers"*, Thesis.

118. Robin Jeffrey (2000), *The Great Indian Newspaper Revolution: Capitalism, Politics and Indian Language Press,* Oxford University Press, New Delhi (2000), p. 234.

119. Elizaberth Burch (2001), "Framing an Environmental Controversy in India's English Language Press: A Study of Text in Context", *The International Journal of Environmental Studies,* Vol. 4, 2001.

120. Bela Trivedi, Kosha Takera (2001), "Social Dimensions of Media Convergence in India", *Media Asia,* AMIC, 28/3, 2001.

121. D.V.R. Murthy (2002), *Mass Communication-concepts and Issues,* Olive Green Publishers, p. 150.

122. Kiron Bansal (2002), "International News Coverage in Four Indian Newspapers: A Content Study", *Meida Asia,*AMIC, 29/4,2002, p. 31.

123. D.V.R Murthy (2000), *Developmental Journalism and Indian Press: A Content Analysis of Selected Newspapers,* Theis.

124. D.V.R. Murthy (2002), *Mass Communication-concepts and Issues,* Olive Green Publishers, p. 150.

125. Bobby Varthan (2000), *Indian Press and National Movement,* Thesis.

126. Press Trust of India is India's Largest News Agency Which is Non-profit Sharing Cooperative Owned by the Country's Newspapers.

127. Press Information Bureau is a Nodal Agency of the Government to Disseminate Information to the Print and Electronic Media on Government Policies, Programmes, Initiatives and Achievements.

128. M.L. Seth (1981), *Macro Economics,* p. 494.

129. *Ibid.*

2

Development of Newspaper Industry: An Overview

Origin of Press

The press in modern times has become a powerful social institution known as the 'Fourth Estate'. It facilitates the exchange of thoughts and helps to solve many complex processes on a large scale in the shortest time. The press became an indispensible weapon to stir the conscience of the people, to enlighten them with new ideas. The press is also an instrument to develop modern culture ushered in the science and arts.

The press emerged in India in the wake of the British rule and its consolidation.[1] It was started for the first time by westerners and in the English language. It exhibited before Indians a novel method of communication which was unknown so far in India. This new method of communication was adapted in this country at different places by different groups as and when factors facilitating such an adaption materialized. Presently it will be seen how initially the English language press came into existence in India. Printing was not known in India before the year 1556. It was introduced here for the first time by the Portuguese for publishing biblical literature. In the British Indian territories, efforts to set up the first printing press were made by Bhimji Parekh, a native of western India. The Gujarati press emerged at an early date.

The press is considered to be one of the effective media of communication available and it will be helpful to a marketing man in reaching the most influential and educated section of society. It was an effective medium in the hands of nationalists as well as social reform groups. They exposed social evils like casteism, child marriages, ban on remarriage of widows, social, legal and other inequalities for which women were subjected. It also helped them in carrying out a massive campaign to educate the people on the eradication of untouchability.[2] The press includes daily newspapers, magazines and periodicals. They are the important carriers of news and comments. Among them the newspapers which are published daily or at least four days a week is the most important source of information about current affairs and the present study aims at studying this Newspaper Industry.

Origin of Newspaper

There are many who claim that newspapers originated in Rome during the reign of Julius Caesar in first century B.C. Chinese claim that it originated in China in 8th century A.D. Historical evidences are there to presume that in the medieval period Indian newswriters enjoyed the patronage of Akbar in mid-16th century in his recording office where they were supposed to record various information. Hence presence of newspapers or some kind of written documents of news and information was present in those days. The newspaper has been defined as "an unbound, printed Publications issued at regular intervals, which presents information in words, often supplemented by pictures. Any printed or cyclostyled periodical carrying news of public interest or comments on it is also a newspaper."

The first English newspaper was published in 1622. It was a weekly. The first French newspaper came out in 1631. The first English daily was brought out in 1702 and the first American daily in 1733. The first English newspaper published in India was the *Bengal Gezette* or *Hicky's Gezette* in 1780.[3] In 1766, Mr.William Bolts the author of *Consideration of Indian Affairs* proposed to set up a printing press in Calcutta. But before the proposal could materialise the select committee of council at Fort William directed him to quit Bengal and his attempt was not successful. However, a European, James Augustus Hickey, published the first newspaper *Bengal Gazette* on January 29th, 1780. But within ten months of its first appearance it incurred the wrath of the government and the following order was promulgated by the Governor-General, Fort William, in 14th November, 1780, "public notice is hereby given that as the weekly newspaper called the *Bengal Gazette* or *Calcutta General Advertiser* printed by J.A. Hicky, has lately been found to contain several improper paragraphs tending to vilify private characters and disturb the peace of the settlement, it is no longer permitted to be circulated through the channel of General Post Office." In 1843, all the English papers of Calcutta with an aggregate circulation of 4,000 had only 125 Indian subscribers.[4] But this order though it hampered the circulation of the paper, could not crush it. It was circulated in Calcutta and Hicky had it delivered through peons in the neighbouring places. Soon after W.Hastings attempted to crush the paper as well as its editor. In June, 1781, the editor was arrested under an order from the chief justice in connection with a suit instituted by the Governor and kept in jail. The paper however, used to appear regularly. Hicky was fined. Yet he conducted the paper. Hasting instituted suit after suit against Hicky and at last succeeded in strangling the paper.[5] In 1791, William Duane was arrested by the Bengal Government and ordered to be sent to Europe for publishing some paragraphs in the Bengal journal. By about 18th century, printing and distribution of newspaper started taking place at a relatively large scale. In 19th century mass circulated newspapers came to stay as a part of the worldwide expansion and growth of newspaper industry. Newspapers not only became an important tool for mass communication, but also came to be accepted as big business.

Today newspapers have become a part of life. Morning begins for millions in India and billions all over the world with the newspapers and a cup of tea or coffee. Newspapers have something to offer to everyone, national and the world news, the economic scene, education and business trade, art and culture. Different kinds of classified advertisements, matrimonial, tolets, properties lost and found, and several newspapers display advertisements of various products and services.

Print Media Milestones

1780 India's first newspaper (weekly) *India Bengal Gazette* is published.
1818 *Digdarshan* first Indian language paper.
1822 The Gujarathi Daily, *Bombay Samachar* started.
1947 Press Trust of India comes into existence.
1998 The total circulation of print reaches 12.6 crore copies.
2000 The total number of periodicals and newspapers in India reaches 43, 828.

History of Vernacular Newspapers

In India the vernacular press originated in 1780 by James Augustus Hicky. He started the weekly *Bengal Gazette* or *Calcutta General Advertiser.*[6] In 1782, the Governor-General sued Hicky for libel. Six months papers began publishing in Calcutta between 1780 and 1783.

In 1789, the weekly *Bombay Herald* became the first paper published in Bombay. *Bombay Courier* (1780) and *Bombay Gazette* (1791) followed into existence. P.M. Motivala, a parsee, started the Gujarati daily *Jam-e-Jamshed* in 1831. In 1851, two more papers *Rast Goftar* and *Akbar-e-Saudagar* also started in Bombay. The founder leader of the Indian National Congress, Dadabai Naoroji edited the *Rast Gafter.*

The vernacular newspapers stirred deep concern among British authorities. *The Minute*, edited by Thomas Muro on April 12th ,1822 reflected the general attitude of the British authorities toward the native press. He wrote, "A free press and the dominion of strangers are things which are quite incompatible and which cannot long exist together for what is the first duty of a free press? It is to deliver the country from foreign yoke and to sacrifice to this one great object every measure and consideration."

In 1836, J.C.Marshman reported that the apathy of the natives had brought down the number of vernacular newspapers from almost ten to five with circulation not exceeding 300 among a population of 70 million.

By 1839, Calcutta had 26 European owned newspapers, and nine Indian newspapers. Bombay had ten European owned and four Indian newspapers. The journals of the 19th century were pioneers in the field and they laid a solid foundation for the future growth of journalism. The journalism they practised was not motivated by profit.

History of Telugu Newspapers

The history of newspapers and journals in Telugu as in other languages is a saga of sacrifices and devotion to nationalistic ideals. Profit or other commercial aspects never were dominent considerations. Even the rare example of a financially successful venture like the *Andhra Patrica* can be said to have done so more due to the affection of the Andhra people to the newspaper than any other consideration.[7] There were some journals earlier but *Andhra*

Patrica started as a periodical in Bombay in 1908 soon became popular particularly, because the founder P.K. Nageswararao, himself an eminent scholar, sent copies free to libraries and reading rooms all over Andhra Pradesh. The content of the periodical reflect the history of Telugu during 20th century. The *Andhra Patrica* was shifted to Madras in 1914 and became a daily. On Nageswararao's death in 1938 his son-in-law, Sambu Prasad took over. In 1965, it was again shifted to Vijayawada. The paper was prominent in spreading Gandhiji's ideals to the nooks and corners of Andhra. The memory of *Andhra Patrica* remains a matter of pride to Telugus.

Apart from nationalist ideals, one other subject that occupied the attention of the founders of Telugu newspapers was the style[8] of the language. There was simple style as in *Vemana's* verses or *Sumathi Satakam*. Even Pothana's *Bhagavatham* can be said to be in a simple style of Telugu compared to poets like Nannaya or Srinatha. But grammarians especially during the 19th century locked up the language in an understandable literary straight jacket that caused a large scale revolt in the early 20th century. The most notable of the scholars who led this movement were Gurajada Apparao and Gidugu Ramamurthi. Their main rival was the *Parishat Patrica* in which such eminent scholars as Jayanthi Ramayya Pantulu, Veeresalingam, Vedam Venkatraya Sastri and others stoutly opposed what they felt was debasing the language in the name of simplication. Their fears to some extent have been justified by the success of the votaries of sort of poetic justice can be seen in the writings of these people which, submerged in an ocean of colloquialism, make little sense to Telugu readers themselves and can be understood only if translated into better Telugu or even into English. There have been many other newspapers and periodicals that came to prominence in the first-half of the 20th century. Some of these are *Krishna Patrica, Golkonda Patrica, Andhra Prabha, Andhra Sahityaparishat Patrica* and *Bharathi* (monthly). Nearly a hundred names are to be found in the list of the newspapers and periodicals of the 20th century.[9]

Growth of Newspapers in India

The press has matured into a full grown entity from 1947. In 1947 there has been a remarkable growth in the circulation of dailies as well as periodicals and this is apparent from the statistical data of the first press commission which reported on the state of the press in India. Soon after independence in 1954, it noted that there has been a rapid growth in the number and circulation of daily newspapers in the country both in English and in the Indian languages.

Table–2.1

GROWTH IN CIRCULATION FROM 1956-1993 (MILLION COPIES)

Year	*Dailies*	*Weeklies*	*Fortnights*	*Monthlies*	*Others*
1956	2.908	3.020	0.785	3.479	0.769
1966	6.320	5.883	1.268	7.060	1.156
1976	9.461	9.154	2.745	10.836	1.156
1986	21.849	18.201	5.901	15.836	2.264
1993	29.488	21.380	5.807	9.860	1.076

Source: Registrar of Newspapers for India Reports 1956-1993.

This decadal study except in 1993 confirms that the Indian press has advanced at a fast pace, considerably faster than the population which, of course, is growing. It also shows that after 1976 the growth has been all the more remarkable and the importance of monthlies in Indian life has somewhat diminished as the dailies and the weeklies have been gaining ground and even fortnightlies, which had a hesitant start, have maintained a fairly good growth rate.

The circulation figures provide a clear picture about 10 million in 1947 and 51 million in 1982 published in 84 languages. The circulation of newspapers in 1989 was 5,82,84,000. In the year 1992 it was 6,36,67,000. In the year 1996 the total circulation of the Indian press was 8,94,34,000 copies and had a distribution at the global level. The circulation of newspapers in 2000 was 12,69,63,763. In 1996, the press comprises of more than 39,149 newspapers and periodicals of which 4,453 are dailies in contrast to 3,000 newspapers and periodicals including 300 dailies in the beginning.

The 1990s have seen a remarkable growth in terms of reach and quality of newspapers. Circulation increase were led by language newspapers, especially *Anand Bazar Patrica, Malayalam Manorama* and *Punjab Kesari*. The total number of newspapers in circulation was 33,162 in 1993. Of them, 3,740 were dailies, 275 tri/bi weeklies, 11,136 weeklies and 18,461 other periodicals. The state-wise distribution showed that Utter Pradesh had the largest number of newspapers.

The circulation of newspapers or periodicals showed a substantial increase. Big newspapers are 153 with a circulation of more than 75,000 copies. Medium size newspapers are 421 with a circulation of 25,000 to 75,000 copies. Small category are 3,380 with a circulation up to 25,000 copies.[10]

Table–2.2
STATE-WISE CLASSIFICATION OF NEWSPAPERS IN 1990

State	*No. of Newspapers*
Uttar Pradesh	579
Bihar	380
Madhya Pradesh	346
Tamilnadu	306
Rajasthan	343
Maharashtra	325

Source: Registrar of Newspapers for India, 1990 Report.

The activities and functions of the Press Information Bureau have increased significantly over the years. Besides appraising the newspapers and News Agencies of Government policies, programmes and decisions, the Bureau is attached to different Ministries and departments providing public relations services, explanations and backgrounders to official pronouncements. It also organises press conferences and press briefings for newspaper representatives from time-to-time and provides pictoral services to dailies and periodicals.

The Bureau provides accreditation facility to the journalists. There are 1,322 accredited journalists, including correspondents of news agencies, newspapers, editors-cum-correspondents, correspondents-cum-cameramen, cameramen, cartoonists and cartographers from India as well as abroad. The bureau operates as an agency for the exchange of delegation of journalists between India and foreign countries under cultural exchange programmes. It has set up a National Press Centre in New Delhi to provide facilities of international standards like telecommunication centre and a hall for press conferences.

Total circulation of newspapers as on December 31st, 1983 was 5,53,91,000 copies as compared to 5,00,94,000 copies in 1982 indicating an increase of 10.6 per cent. There were 7,975 newspapers which supplied their circulation data for 1983. Out of them only 192 come in the category of big newspapers, 427 in medium category and 75,356 in small category.

Table–2.3
NEWSPAPERS IN INDIA IN 1983

Language	*Dailies*	*Tri/bi weeklies*	*Weeklies*	*Others*	*Total*
Assamese	3	3	26	52	84
Bengali	44	8	417	1113	1582
Bilingual	33	15	373	1220	1641
English	123	13	428	3276	3840
Gujarati	40	5	174	510	729
Hindi	470	27	2709	2730	5936
Kannada	85	3	161	406	655
Kashmiri	Nil	Nil	1	Nil	1
Malayalam	112	Nil	121	607	840
Marathi	127	17	370	617	1131
Multilingual	9	1	65	279	355
Oriya	14	Nil	40	245	299
Punjabi	24	Nil	184	243	452
Sanskrit	2	Nil	4	25	31
Tamil	106	4	129	618	857
Telugu	37	2	162	382	583
Urdu	148	6	672	552	1378
Others	40	3	65	191	299
Total	1423	108	6122	13105	20758

Source: Registrar of Newspapers for India Report, 1983.

Table–2.4
LANGUAGE, NUMBER AND CIRCULATION OF DAILIES AND OTHER NEWSPAPERS TAKEN TOGETHER IN 1992

Language	*Dailies*	*Tri Weeklies*	*Weeklies*	*Fort Nightlies*	*Monthlies*	*Quarterlies*	*Others*	*Annual*
Hindi	1541	106	5504	1840	2150	364	113	20
English	241	18	611	474	2090	1006	574	125
Assamese	10	2	48	29	41	10	8	1
Bengali	74	11	497	370	572	347	115	8
Gujarati	73	7	276	116	384	47	33	9

(contd.)

Language	*Dailies*	*Tri Weeklies*	*Weeklies*	*Fort Nightlies*	*Monthlies*	*Quarterlies*	*Others*	*Annual*
Kannada	184	5	273	161	371	34	15	2
Kashmiri	0	0	1	0	0	0	0	0
Konkani	0	0	2	1	1	0	0	0
Malayalam	178	1	147	133	575	41	16	8
Manipuri	10	0	3	5	3	3	2	0
Marathi	215	17	551	133	394	85	34	81
Nepali	1	2	9	4	7	16	5	0
Oriya	41	2	77	53	212	72	17	4
Punjabi	76	15	285	62	201	25	17	1
Sanskrit	3	0	6	2	13	13	3	0
Sindhi	8	0	30	9	31	6	2	0
Tamil	289	34	307	187	563	20	9	2
Telugu	77	2	201	143	322	20	6	1
Urdu	373	17	962	277	433	42	13	3
Bilingual	47	17	433	252	902	272	101	27
Multilingual	13	4	77	41	189	59	25	7
Others	48	11	75	23	101	43	7	0
Total	3,502	271	10,375	4,315	9,555	2,525	1,115	299

Source: Registrar of Newspapers for India Report (1992).

Table–2.5

NEWSPAPERS IN INDIA IN 1992

Language	*Dailies Number of Copies*	*Circulation of Dailies (in Millions)*	*All Papers Number of Copies*	*Circulation of all Papers (in Millions)*
English	99	3.849	386	9.010
Hindi	441	11.966	1,978	27.938
Assamese	7	0.201	34	0.555
Bengali	29	1.422	288	3.488
Gujarati	41	1.640	116	2.533
Kannada	21	0.696	71	1.952
Malayalam	38	1.732	97	5.637

(Contd.)

Language	*Dailies Number of Copies*	*Circulation of Dailies (in Millions)*	*All Papers Number of Copies*	*Circulation of all Papers (in Millions)*
Marathi	67	2.348	168	3.357
Oriya	28	0.897	76	0.577
Punjabi	37	0.809	113	0.926
Sanskrit	2	0.034	13	0.074
Tamil	52	1.301	112	3.844
Telugu	30	0.916	83	2.065
Urdu	86	1.394	297	3.013
Others	973	29.258	3,954	67.611
Total (Including others)	1951	58.463	7786	132.025

Source: Registrar of Newspapers for India, 1992 Reports.

Table–2.6
NUMBER OF NEWSPAPERS IN THE YEAR 1996 AND 1998 (LANGUAGE-WISE)

Language	*1996*	*1998*
English	5,912	6,517
Hindi	15,647	17,836
Assamese	195	208
Bengali	2,254	2,425
Gujarati	1,113	1,408
Kannada	1,340	1,455
Kashmiri	1	1
Konkani	5	6
Malayalam	1,214	1,329
Manipuri	34	41
Marathi	1,736	2,046
Nepali	52	54
Oriya	586	655
Punjabi	765	817
Sanskrit	48	5

(Contd.)

Language	*1996*	*1998*
Sindhi	94	101
Tamil	1,630	1,769
Telugu	898	1,035
Urdu	2,567	2,745
Bilingual	2,291	2,504
Multilingual	440	474
Others	327	352
Total	39,149	61,664

Source: Registrar of Newspapers for India Reports (1996-98).

Table–2.7

REGIONAL PRINT MEDIA (1998–2000)

Language	*1998*	*1999*	*2000*
Marathi	28,58,631	28,20,662	28,82,122
Hindi	54,71,103	5,718	69,09,447
Malayalam	20,15,556	20,92,018	20,79,277
Tamil	10,86,817	11,10,335	11,76,960
Telugu	10,21,064	9,53,796	10,47,391
Bengali	15,00,144	16,06,066	16,96,539

Source: Audit Bureau of Circulation (Mumbai) Reports, 1998-2000.

Table–2.8

STATE-WISE CLASSIFICATION OF NEWSPAPERS, 2000

State	*No. of Newspapers*
Uttar Pradesh	8,750
Delhi	6,543
Maharashtra	5,610
Madhya Pradesh	3,748
West Bengal	3,623
Rajasthan	3,220
Tamilnadu	2,616
Karnataka	2,354
Andhra Pradesh	2,258

(Contd.)

State	*No. of Newspapers*
Gujarat	1,987
Kerala	1,757
Bihar	1,656
Punjab	1,159

Source: Registrar of Newspapers for India (2000) Report.

Table–2.9

STATE-WISE CLASSIFICATION OF DAILY NEWSPAPERS IN 2000

State	*No. of Newspapers*
Uttar Pradesh	873
Maharashtra	536
Madhya Pradesh	493
Karnataka	442
Rajasthan	422
Bihar	407
Tamilnadu	376
Andhra Pradesh	331
Delhi	300
Kerala	216
West Bengal	161
Gujarat	158
Punjab	129
Haryana	109
Orissa	103

Source: Registrar of Newspapers for India Report (2000).

Table–2.10

AN OVERVIEW OF GROWTH OF NUMBER OF NEWSPAPERS:1964-2000

Selected Years	*Dailies*	*All*
1964	514	8,161
1968	636	10,019

(Contd.)

Selected Years	*Dailies*	*All*
1969	650	10,281
1974	822	12,653
1975	835	12,423
1976	875	13,320
1991	3,229	30,214
1999	5,157	46,655
2000	5,364	49,145

Source: Press Trust of India Reports, 1964-2000.

Between 1964 and 2002, newspapers have increased by more than six times. About 90 per cent of the total are periodicals. Dailies increased to 11 from six per cent until a few years ago. During the last 40 years, the number of daily newspapers increased 12 times, from about 500 to about 6000. The overall growth in circulation had kept up during the period. Circulation of dailies increased from nearly 80 lakhs in 1964 to 600 lakhs. The annual growth in terms of numbers in the last decade (1990-2001), when the television boom was allover, was steady at five to six per cent.[11] However, in terms of circulation, the growth has not been steady and nowhere matching the potential. That is why the structure and scope need to be speeded up.

Table–2.11
UNEVEN GROWTH IN CIRCULATION: DURING 35 YEARS (1964-1999)

Years	*Circulation (in Millions)*		*Per cent Increase in Circulation Over Previous Year*	
	Dailies	*All*	*Dailies*	*All*
1964	7.3	26.5	3.2	1.9
1968	7.6	27.0	5.7	5.5
1969	9.2	33.0		-1.0
1974	9.4	33.8	2.2	-3.5
1975	9.4	34.0	1.1	5.6
1991	58.8	130.0		
1999	59.1	127.0	0.55	-2.40

Source: Vidura, Vol. 40; January-March, 2003, p. 35.

Table 2.12

NEWSPAPER READERSHIP VIS-À-VIS TV VIEWING:30 YEARS FROM 1972–2002 (PER CENT OF ADULTS-URBAN)

Urban		
1972-NRS	37	No TV
1978-NRS	53	9
1983-NRS	47	18
1986-NRS	56	–
1990-NRS	44	71
1995-NRS	46	76
1997-NRS	45	78
2000-NRS	45	78
2002-NRS	54	–

Source: National Readership Surveys 1972-2002.

Newspapers had gained steadily until 1989-1990 when the T.V. explosion started. Rajasthan in the Hindi belt is a case in this regard. Notwithstanding inconsistencies in readership surveys, a time series analysis at macro level for 1972-2002 period reflects broad trends. Whatever spurt there was in readership of dailies in particular has come more along with the Television boom. Since 2000, the reader base in India has grown from 163 million to 180 million, a growth of 10 per cent.[12] In fact, in the case of daily newspapers the growth during the period was 20 per cent. Today nearly 160 millions read a daily. Also more housewives read a daily, today than ever before. But taking a long-term view one could also say that the television has slowed down the growth of print media. And, as could be seen, the growth rate in readership was higher in rural than in urban areas. The trend calls for a breakthrough to come out of a slow phase since in the year 2000, growth potential is many times more. In the last couple of years the overall readership of newspapers has increased by about four per cent both in rural and urban areas.[13] In the year 1995, *The Financial Express* launched its Ahmedabad edition. *Dainik Bhaskar* barging into Rajasthan and *Vaartha* starting an edition from almost every district of Andhra Pradesh.[14]

From 1990-96

(*i*) The number of newspapers increased upto five per cent.

(*ii*) The circulation increased by 12.8 per cent. There was continuous increase in circulation from 1990-96.

(*iii*) Circulation of big newspapers come down.(-1.6 per cent).

(*iv*) Circulation of small and medium scale newspapers increased (32 per cent).

(*v*) Number of newspapers under common ownership rose from 450-710.

(*vi*) Circulation of news interest dailies under common ownership rose from 13.8 million to 21.2 million.[15]

Table–2.13

NEWSPAPER READERSHIP VIS-À-VIS TV VIEWING:30 YEARS FROM 1972-2002 (PER CENT OF ADULTS-RURAL)

Rural		
1972-NRS	7	No TV
1986-NRS	8	5
1989-NRS	9	27
1995-NRS	10	30
2000-IRS	15	35
2002-IRS	24	–

Source: Vidura, Vol.40; January-March, 2003, p. 36.

Daily newspapers increased 4.01 per cent in number from 1999-2000.[16] Number of newspapers and periodicals in India in 2000 are 49,145. Their circulation is 12,69,63,763.[17] Total English newspaper readership is 20 million. English dailies lost about 28,000 odd gross readers.[18] From 1999-2002, literacy growth increased to 13 per cent and there is a 20 per cent increase in newspaper readership.[19] In March 2002 readership survey readership growth is 1.4 per cent where population growth is one per cent. In June 2002 readership survey 10 per cent increase in readership is formed in rural areas. The total newspaper readership is 180 million.

Reasons for Growth of Newspapers in India

The press in India has matured in to a full grown entity from 1947. In the beginning there were 3,000 newspapers and periodicals including 300 dailies. The number of newspapers are 20,758 in India in 1983. In 1996, the press comprises more than 39,149 newspapers and periodicals, of which 4,453 are dailies. In 2000, the number increased to 49,145. From 2000-02 there is a 10 per cent increase in number of newspapers. Total circulation of newspapers as on 31st December, 1983 was 5,53,91,000 copies as compared to 5,00,94,000 copies in 1982 indicating an increase of 10.6 per cent. The increase in circulation since 1992 is very significant. In 1992, the total circulation of all publications was 67 millions whereas by the end of 1996, the total circulation went up to 89 millions, an increase of 23 per cent. In 2002, the circulation stood at 180 millions, almost doubling the percentage during the six year period. Readership from 1999-2002 increased from 131 millions to 156 millions that is 20 per cent increase in readership. The study shows that the number of newspapers, circulation and readership of Indian press has advanced at a fast pace, considerably faster than the population of which of course is growing. The increase was the result of various strategies adopted by the newspapers and magazines for this growth (Table 2.14). Some of the reasons for this growth are reduction of cover price, offer of free gifts, mass advertising, hawker promotion, free sampling, promotion of Publications in schools, city supplements, and loyalty programmes. These apart, the contents of newspapers are also aimed at mass readership. Nearly 90 per cent of newspapers published from 25 cities. This is despite availability of basic infrastructure elsewhere. The number of locations however, has more than doubled over the last 25 years. "District editions" is a new approach with impressive results. We should have half of the districts originating a daily newspaper by 2005 by when 75 per cent of people are expected to be literate against 65 per cent in 2001.[20]

Table–2.14
CIRCULATION OF LEADING DAILIES BY THE END OF 2002

Name of Newspaper	*Circulation (copies)*
Times of India	21,18,985
Malayala Manorama	12,14,134
Dainik Bhaskar	11,45,217
Dainik Jagran	11,42,013
Gujarath Samachar	9,52,000
Aaj	9,10,130
Hindustan Times	8,38,005

(Contd.)

Name of Newspaper	*Circulation (copies)*
The Hindu	8,85,096
Eenadu	8,38,643
Rajasthan Patrika	5,72,026

Source: Audit Bureau of Circulation Report, Jan-June, 2002.

Reasons for Growth of Newspapers

1. *Literacy Growth*: Literacy levels increased from 1947-2002. This is one of the reasons for the growth of newspapers, since an increase in literacy rate would lead to an increase in the number of people who can read newspapers. From 1999-2002, the literacy growth increased by 13 per cent and newspaper readership increased to 20 per cent.
2. *Reduction of cover price:* The reduction of cover price, which started with *The Times of India* in 1996 spread to other newspapers. The concept was introduced by Samir Jain in his paper, *Times* who insisted on profits for the paper. Jain, a young man became the chairman of the Bennet and Coleman group, the publisher of The *Times* group of newspaper, the leading English daily in the country . He reduced the price of the paper to Re. one for his Bangalore edition. Eventually, other papers were forced to follow the paper in order to sustain the circulation. His single point agenda for the paper is only profits for the group. In 1996, the paper earned a huge profit of over Rs. 80 crore.

Describing Him, Coleridge (1993) Says

"Of all the newspaper owners in the world, I met no one so single-mindedly wedded to marketing as Samir Jain. It is a science of such fascination to him that he is scarcely capable of any statement without reference to it (profits). He reminded me of those Maharajas of an earlier period in India's history who visited the industrialised West and returned fired with innovations to impose on their sleepy subjects. Of all marketing converts, nothing delights him so much as describing his newspapers in dispassionate, marketing language: the product or offerings (*The Times of India*). An unsold offering is like an unsold airline seat or an hotel bed. Neither can be sold the next day. The opportunity is missed forever."

That set the pace for price war and papers like *The Hindu,* reduced the cover price in Andhra Pradesh. The papers are being offered for Re. one or Re. 1.50 P. Some newspapers even offer gifts to the subscribers. The offer of free gifts and the reduction of the cover price have contributed to the circulation hike. For example, elite magazines like *India Today, Outlook* offer free gifts while newspapers like *The Hindu, The Times of India* and *The New Indian Express* have reduced the cover price. The situation resembles the twentieth century England where some newspapers like *Daily Mail, Daily Express* and *Daily Herald* offered insurance cover, fountain pens, works of Shakespeare and Charles Dickens etc., to the subscribers to increase circulation.[21]

3. *Special supplements*: Supplements have contributed to the success of the newspaper. As a new strategy, the regional as well as English newspapers started wooing different segments of population by providing fare that is demanded by the readers. For instance, *Eenadu* in Andhra Pradesh introduced a daily supplement for women, 'Vasundhara' in colour, apart from bringing out the daily paper in colour. The five popular Telugu papers in Andhra Pradesh introduced a district edition known as mini editions for the particular district focusing on that district. In 1994, *Eenadu* went ahead of other newspapers. It divided the city of Hyderabad into nine zones and published news exclusively for that zone. The readers of a zone are not aware of the news events of other zones unless it is very significant. Along with the 12-page main edition, a 16-page tabloid in colour of that particular zone is supplied to the subscribers without enhancing the cover price. Consequently, the publisher and the reader are benefited. The publisher gets the local advertisements while the reader gets more news of his neighbourhood. In this process in, significant news has found place in the newspaper columns. Further, the paper also employed educated unemployed youth as stringers and called them as contributors to cover news belonging to all walks of life. The paper has also linked all state capitals and district headquarters with computer network for faster transmission of news and photographs, which enable the paper to take an early lead in the news coverage.

4. *Local advertising*: This is also one of the reasons for the growth and increase of readership of newspapers. Most of the newspapers advertising targeted at a locality of people. It is aimed at the people living in a city, a town, or a village or in specific areas of city or town. *Eenadu, Deccan Chronicle* recently *The Hindu* are more regional in nature. *The Times of India* and *The New Indian Express* also have local editions. This localization is because people are demanding more local news. Newspaper growth is also because of content and credibility. Some newspapers are having extensive local news coverage for crime, water shortages, school functions, political visits, drought exploitation, atrocities on women etc. Eg:*Eenadu.*
5. *Other strategies*. The papers also launched mass advertising to appeal to the readers. Two papers, for example, *The Hindustan Times* and *The Times of India* went on an advertising campaign to promote the paper in New Delhi. Similarly other papers too launched campaigns in different parts of the country. Mostly, newspapers depend on outdoor advertising and television for promotion.
   (a) *Hawker promotion*. In 1990s, the newspaper industry promoted the paper through hawkers in metropolitan cities like Mumbai, Delhi, Calcutta and others. Normally, the agents who get a huge commission are offering a large share out of their commission to the hawkers. For example, if a newspaper is priced at rupees two, an agent gets 60 paisa as commission, and out of which 50 paisa is given to the hawker. In this process, newspapers have increased their sales. The papers by offering huge commission are inducing the hawkers to sell the papers by motivating new segments of readers. One such strategy adopted by the papers is free sampling of the paper for one month.
   (b) *Sponsorship*. Sometimes, the newspaper organisation sponsors an event in the city to distribute the paper at the venue to popularise it. This is one of the strategies gaining momentum in the newspaper industry.
   (c) *Promotion in schools*. Two newspapers in India viz., *The Hindu* and *The Times of India*, promote a concept known as newspaper in education. The aim is two-fold: children

get educated on some topic in schools and the event is being sponsored by the paper and the paper obtains some subscription. The second aspect is the students get addicted to the paper and they in turn will become the future readers of the paper. The paper is offered to the pupils at a subsidised price. *The Hindu*'s Saturday supplement, *Young World* has succeeded in this regard.

(d) *Campaigning.* Door-to-door campaigning highlighting the contents of newspapers is a massive success for the newspapers. *Deccan Chronicle* of Hyderabad launched a massive campaign and succeeded in this regard.

(e) *Newsprint:* Of late newspapers reduced the size of the paper to offset losses on cover price reduction. The standard of the English paper has been reduced to 35 centimetres (Table 2.15).

Table 2.15

SIZES OF NEWSPAPERS AFTER REDUCTION IN 2002

Name of the Paper	*Width in Centimetres*	*Height in Centimetres*
The Economic Times	35	54.5
Times of India	35	54.5
The New Indian Express	35	56.5
Financial Express	35	56.5
The Hindu	38	56.0

Source: Industrial Economist, May 30-June 14, 2002, p. 18.

The newspapers claim that the trimming has benefited the reader in three ways: *(i)* Trimming helps the reader in handling the paper comfortably while travelling, *(ii)* the paper looks sleek and more contemporary, and *(iii)* the reader can easily navigate the paper to save time. Though the reasons outwardly offer an explanation for the reader for reducing the size of the paper, managements are also benefited. Management can save cost by trimming the paper, by reducing the number of pages, while retaining the same advertisement tariff. Despite reducing the size of the paper, the managements have increased the advertising tariff. For example, *The Hindu* trimmed the width of the paper from 16 inches to 15 inches. The saving is 6.25 per cent and newsprint saving is around nine tonnes per day. If this is multiplied at Rs. 25,000 per tonne, the paper can save around Rs. 2.25 lakh a day and Rs. eight crores per annum.[22] *The Hindu* also cut the number of pages to 24, from 32-40 pages. Obviously, the international newsprint prices have been increased from $ 425 to $ 710 per tonne. In 1991, the State Trading Corporation which imports newsprint and supplies it to newspapers increased the cost of newsprint on the ground that the newsprint was being bought on extended credit. The outstanding credit amounted to Rs. 60 crores.[23] The newsprint hike was above Rs. 4,000 in that year. As a result, *the Illustrated Weekly of India* scrapped its colour magazine, which was printed on glazed newsprint and instead brought out its broadsheet format, which was printed on standard newsprint. *The Hindustan Times* cut back on its 24-page edition by anything between four- eight pages daily. *The New Indian Express* pulled out its Saturday colour supplement. Subsequently, the government in 1996 again made an attempt to raise the newsprint cost which was stoutly opposed by the print media. The governments in power always play a hide and seek game with newspapers by increasing the newsprint price when they are facing the hostile press. This is one of the ways to control the belligerent press. The press argues that it is a threat to freedom of speech and expression. *The Hindu*, in its editorial, 'Press freedom and Indian situation dated January 13th, 1990 asked the National Front Government headed by V.P. Singh to lift certain restrictions on the import of newsprint while suggesting other things to the government. The paper pointed out that the press freedom can be guaranteed partially if the Government fosters it, and the other half, "equally important and crucial is the physical and monetary wherewithal that Publishers and editors need to discharge their responsibilities effectively. Particularly the paper suggested two measures for this purpose: *(i)* Newsprint imported as well as domestic, should be available in the quality and quantities required – the commitment being with respect to the comprehensiveness of readership reach and quality of production. Glazed newsprint should be supplied to newspapers, besides magazines, to attain international excellence in printing, *(ii)* Import duty on newsprint should be abolished. Customs and excise duties on printing machinery, components, raw materials (other than newsprint) should be reduced gradually, if it is thought unrealistic to eliminate them. It should be useful to remember that, in pre-Independent India, the rate of duty was less than 10 per cent. In addition to the above mentioned reasons, greater use of colour and higher quality editorial products are also some of the reasons for growth of newspapers.

Table–2.16
CLASSIFICATION OF NEWSPAPERS BASING ON OWNERSHIP IN THE YEAR 1983

Form of Ownership	*Number*	*Circulation (In Thousands)*	*Per cent Share in Total Circulation*
Individuals	4,834	20,300	36.7
Joint stock companies	541	81,200	36.3
Firms/partnerships	427	5,429	9.6
Societies/Associations	1,333	4,419	8.0
Trusts	263	2,966	5.4
Governments	231	1,413	2.6
Others	235	783	1.4

Source: Registrar of Newspapers for India, 1983 Report.

Ownership

After Independence, newspapers and periodicals grew considerably. A peculiar trend in the growth of newspapers is that they are owned and managed by top businessmen in the country. In 1952, there were only 3,000 publications including 330 newspapers in the country and their circulation was only 2.5 millions.[24] But, by the end of 2000, the number of publications went up to 49,145 with a combined circulation of over 180 million. (Table 2.17).

Table–2.17
NUMBER OF PUBLICATIONS BY THE END OF 2000

Type of Publication	*Total Number*
Dailies	5,704
Weeklies	17,748
Monthlies	13,616
Quarterlies	3,425
Annuals	431
Other periodicals	1,668
Total	49,145

Source: Registrar of Newspapers for India Report, 2001.

The ownership pattern also shows that individuals, followed by Societies and Associations, own the majority of newspapers (Table 2.18). However, the leading newspapers like *The Times of India, The*

Table-2.18
OWNERSHIP PATTERN OF NEWSPAPERS IN INDIA (2001)

Type of Ownership	*Total Number*
Individuals	37,945
Societies and Associations	4,894
Joint Stock companies	2,189
Firms and partnerships	1,695
Governments (State/Centre)	774
Trusts/Cooperative societies/Educational societies	1,648
Total	49,145

Source: Registrar of Newspapers for India Report 2001.

Hindu, Indian Express including *The New Indian Express, The Hindustan Times, Aaj Tak, Dainik Bhaskar, Dainik Jagran, Malayala Manorama* and *Eenadu* hold the largest market share in terms of circulation and readership. Since India is a diverse country with many languages and dialects, publications appear in nearly 100 languages and dialects. Principally, ten languages occupy prime place in newspaper publication with Hindi getting the top slot while Punjabi is in the lowest place (Table 2.19). In 2002-03; 5,371 newspapers were owned by individuals while 950 were owned by joint stock companies. This figure includes 3,410 Hindi newspapers with a combined circulation of 61,768,735 (almost 62 million) and 750 English newspapers with a combined circulation of 26,213,142 (26 million) copies.[25] The Indian Press had a missionary role during the nineteenth and twentieth centuries till the country attained Independence.[26] The press also played a key-role in national development during that period. However, the role of the press underwent a sea change during the post-Independence period.[27] The chief reason for this growth of the press and its role at present is the entry of businessmen into the profession of journalism. Now, big business houses own newspapers. The same newspapers which existed before Independence and played a crucial role in the freedom struggle, have become business enterprises. Sham Lal (1994),[28] the former editor of *The Times of India* recalled his days 60 years ago. He said: "When I worked in *The Hindustan Times* in the 30s, the newspaper industry was really only a cottage industry. We had about ten people on the staff–one reporter, one special correspondent, a couple of leader writers, four or five sub-editors and that was it. Today, it is like any other industry, with investments running into crores. And this has transformed the profile of newspapers in fundamental ways." The press became more and more commercialised.[29] The old concept of a newspaper representing ideas and the nation's ethos had worn out and the profession became an industry. The character of a newspaper and also the reading public changed radically. Because of this reason, glamorous magazines started appearing on the scene. The Indian glamorous press originated in India's glamour capital Bombay, and continues to thrive out of the showbiz city. Around mid-seventies, a bunch of publications hit the news stands, more or less competing for the attention of the same segment of readers and advertisers.[30] For instance, *Femina, Eve's Weekly, Gentleman, Society* or *Bombay* are a few examples. These magazines started dominating the media scene because of their colour printing. The colour race was perceived as a direct counter to television advertising, which was posing a threat to print medium. The only way to attract big corporate houses for their advertisements with huge budgets was to invest in modern technology, better paper and superior quality of printing. Apart from this, these magazines are meant for the affluent sections of the population and hence the readership.

Expansion of newspapers. After 1980, many structural changes have occurred in Indian journalism. Several newspapers started expanding to other areas. The advent of new technology facilitated this expansion. Earlier, there was a single newspaper in a particular language belonging to one owner. However, the present trend is to have chain editions or multiple editions. For example, *The Hindu* and *The Times of India* are published from eleven and nine places respectively. *Eenadu*, the largest circulated daily in Andhra Pradesh, is published from 23 centres in Andhra Pradesh.

Earlier, the papers published from the metropolitan centres were the latest to adopt new technology. Today, the papers published from even remote places have switched on to new technology of photo-type setting and pagination.[31] The introduction of facsimile editions helped the newspapers in publishing from a larger number of places. Thus, the newspapers began catering to the readers in all regions. The availability of transport also helped the papers to increase their sales. For example, the readership survey in 2002 found that there is an increase of ten per cent in readership in the rural areas. Significantly, six language papers in India viz., Marathi,

Hindi, Malayalam, Tamil, Telugu and Bengali[32] registered an increase in readership. Although the newspapers registered an increase in readership, the reach of newspapers is only 33.3 per cent of the population of the country. According to National Readership Survey 2002 shows print media is adding 17 million to its reader base. It means the growth is 10 per cent from 163 millions to 180 million. It is also significant that the newspaper circulation has gone up by 20 per cent i.e 131 million to 156 million during the last ten years. However, there are 248 millions adult literate in the country, who do not read any publication.[33]

Table–2.19

NUMBER OF NEWSPAPERS IN TOP TEN LANGUAGES (2001)

Language of Newspaper	*Total Number*	*Percentage*
Hindi	2,393	48.0
Urdu	525	10.5
English	390	7.8
Marathi	371	7.4
Tamil	356	7.1
Kannada	332	6.7
Malayalam	216	4.3
Telugu	164	3.3
Gujarathi	141	2.8
Punjabi	107	2.1
Total	4,995	100.0

Source: Registrar of Newspapers for India report, 2001.

Foreign Direct Investment in Newspaper Industry

Jawaharlal Nehru cabinet set a rule in September 18th ,1955 regarding the print media. The 1955 resolution has two operative sentences. "No foreign owned newspaper or periodical should in future be permitted to be published in India. And foreign newspapers and periodicals which deal mainly with news and current affairs should not be allowed to bring out Indian editions." The government on 25th June, 2002, decided to allow 26 per cent foreign direct investment in news and current affairs print media. The cabinet rewrote the 47 years old resolution that barred foreign direct investment in print media. At this moment it requires a clear understanding about the entry of Foreign Direct Investment (FDI) in Indian newspaper Industry.

Foreign ownership norms in print media down the years: September 13,1955; The Jawaharlal Nehru cabinet states no foreign owned newspaper and periodicals, which deal mainly with news and current affairs should be allowed to bring out Indian editions. On the issue of FDI, media groups are divided in to two groups. Media groups opposing FDI are *The Times of India, Hindusthan Times, The Hindu, Malayala Manorama* supported by some politicians, have used this as an argument to say that the opening up of print media would threaten India's security and allow foreign countries to influence public opinion. However, there is a large group of media houses that support FDI including *Business Standard, The New Indian Express, The Asian Age, The Pioneer, Deccan Chronicle, Business India, Mid-day, Dainik Jagran, Gujarat Samachar, India Today, Ananda Bazar Patrica, Raashtriya Sahara.*

Advantages to Print Media if FDI is Allowed

Infusion of fresh funds, they would enable aggressive marketing of their publications leading to healthy competition and there by producing qualitative news.[34] By tying vernacular newspapers with International brands to enter English market increases readership. FDI would bring sound mechanism to evaluate readership, thereby having a major impact on advertising. So advertising revenues increase. The no two and no three in the market would have a better chance to compete with the top player. More investment could be had to upgrade technology. It enables newspapers to improve quality. A focus on human resources, almost missing in Indian print media would come into play if FDI is allowed. Human resource practices would include appraisal system, training and development programmes. Because of more funds journalists would learn from the best practices and get better remuneration. It leads to knowledge creation. Returns may be more.[35] Newspapers become more efficient by better technology and quality.[36] FDI will increase productivity by bringing better technology, management culture, incentives for employees. Continuous flow of talent.[37] If FDI is allowed it increases more opportunities for people who work in the media. Possibility for better working conditions. Better terms of service. Monopoly which is bad, is eliminated as in the field of information, it should be prevented at any costs. It eliminates pricing practice that is predatory pricing, which means a practice of pricing product way below its cost price which stifles competition and reduces the freedom of choice. As a result it prevents the closing down of many good newspapers.[38] It increases competition and international linkages and generally positive influences and it leads to more coverage, better understanding and caliberated views and less steriotyping. FDI in print leads to thought provoking and balanced type of newspapers.[39] It improves international relations. Banks are averse now-a-days to lend money to newspaper industry, supposedly a high risk business and entry cost is further raised because of FDI bar. So if FDI is allowed, the publishing house can enter into the capital market. Skewed distribution of advertisement expenditure by dominant newspapers like *The Hindu, The Times of India* create price wars thus leaving the rivals in double blind of poor advertising revenues and static levels.[40] FDI in print some time leads to healthy growth in the media sector which will take care of information needs of society.[41] FDI in print sometimes leads to innovation and enhance quality of coverage. If FDI is not allowed reader who can afford the high imported price of publications get to read them and the publication is not affordable by common man. If FDI is allowed, a common man also can afford the high priced publication which is imported.

Disadvantages

Newspapers help to shape public opinion, provide political education. Foreign lobbyists will now be in a position to promote their vested interest by exerting their influence in sensitive areas in political and security related matters. How modest was the beginning of East India Company and how it spreads it tentacles first in realm of trade and then to areas connected with the country governance.[42] It destroys rich culture and heritage of India. Diversity in plurality was the strength of Indian media and if FDI is allowed, it would result in exploitation of the situation. It leads to unethical trends in areas of advertisement and circulation.[43] FDI is allowed foreign media interests to dabble in the internal politics of country. Cultural invasion will take place if FDI is allowed.[44] The newspapers play a pivotal role in a democracy and in forming public opinion. The foreigners negatively influence public opinion and upstage the democratic set up. If a multinational starts a newspaper in India it will think only about the profit it can make during a crisis and not about the country's interests. The Indian newspaper industry enjoys two basic rights. Freedom of speech and expression under Article 19(1) A of the constitution and the Freedom to practice profession, business or article under (1) G. But these constitutional rights are given only to Indian citizens and their publications. The consequences of extending the same facility to foreigners who have no commitment to the country or its people could be disastrous.[45] It is prejudicial to the security of state, public order and communal harmony. The FDI in print media would have the potential of 'polluting' the cultural life and changing the 'basic orientation' of the Indian mind in the long run.[46] Even though sources of funding, are limited there is 'phenomenal growth' in the number of newspapers and circulation over the past five decades. India ranks fourth in the world-after Japan, The U.S. and China in terms of number of newspapers published and total circulation according to a report in *Hindu Businessline*, even though there is no FDI.[47] Socio-political life will get affected.[48] It has power to influence minds.[49] If FDI is allowed in print media there is a threat for small and medium newspapers and they will close their firms as they are more profit oriented and there is a threat for social security and soverignity.[50] Our political system will be subverted by foreign migrates instead of just being subverted by Indian ones. They will influence the government policy. People who cannot afford to buy televisions have to buy three to four rupees newspaper and read them, if FDI in print is allowed, which become some what costlier. It endangers National security.[51] Newspapers abroad are, however quick to pick up tragedies. The Gujarat earth quake, Plague, communal clashes and the like which have a negative impact on people. If FDI is allowed, the coverage of Indian scene is negligible compared to the space devoted by Indian newspapers to the developments of west. They pick odd bits of information and weave stories with an air of profundity. With the opening of print media to foreign investors there could be danger of the aided newspapers required to make use of the stuff of foreign experts who in turn influence our mind set. It will be a pity as the flow of foreign capital would lead to an invasion of the tabloid culture.[52] FDI in print is against national interests and press freedom.[53]

Future Dynamics to FDI

The new market dynamics are set to shape up latest within one year. According to Sastry, at least one global player would come to India latest by March 2003, without naming any Publications, Sastry said talks for tie-ups between global and Indian media houses would begin soon. Meanwhile, a pink daily has already announced its intention of a tie-up with a leading UK based newspaper. But a cautious official in the world has had a major input on the advertising pie. "All news organisations have been squeezed to such an extent that there is not much elbow room now," he said. Keeping in mind this scenario, huge movements are not expected immediately he added.[54]

Guidelines for FDI in News Category of Print Media

First, at least three-fourths of the directors on the board of the new entity and all key executives and editorial staff should be resident Indians. Second, the applicant and the new entity should disclose, at the time of application, the shareholders agreements and loan agreements that are finalized or proposed to be entered into. The Information and Broadcasting Ministry would have to be intimated of any subsequent change within 15 days. Third, the new entity should frame its articles/memorandum of Association to ensure compliance with the above. And finally, it would have to take prior permission from the Information and Broadcasting ministry before effecting any alteration in the foreign shareholding pattern and the shareholding of the largest Indian shareholder. The applicant would have to intimate the names and details of all NRIs who are proposed to be inducted in the board of the new entity. The company would also have to intimate the names and details of foreigners/ NRIs to be employed/engaged in the new entity either as consultants (or in any other capacity) for more than 60 days in a year, or as regular employees.[55] Soon after independence in 1954, it is noted that "there has been a rapid growth in the number and circulation of daily newspapers in the country both in English and in the Indian languages."

Circulation and Readership of Newspapers in India

The circulation of newspapers in 1989 was 5,82,84,000. In the year 1992, it was 6,36,67,000. In the year 1996, the total circulation of Indian press was 8,94,34,000 copies. The circulation of newspapers in 2000 was 12,69,63,763. In 1947, the number of copies of newspapers are 10 million, in 1982, the number of newspapers are 51 million, in 1989 the number of newspapers are 58 million, in 1992, the number of newspapers are 63 million, in 1996 the number of newspapers are 89 million, in 2000 the number of newspapers are 126 million, and in 2001, the number of newspapers are 115 million in number and in 2002-03 Newspaper Circulation in India is 142 million.

Table–2.20
CLASSIFICATION AND CIRCULATION OF NEWSPAPERS IN THE YEAR 1983

Form of Ownership	*Number*	*Circulation (In Thousands)*	*Per cent Share in Total Circulation*
Individuals	4,834	20,300	36.7
Joint stock companies	541	81,200	36.3
Firms/partnerships	427	5,429	9.6
Societies/Associations	1,333	4,419	8.0
Trusts	263	2,966	5.4
Governments	231	1,413	2.6
Others	235	783	1.4

Source: Audit Bureau of Circulation (1983).

Table–2.21
LANGUAGE AND CIRCULATION OF DAILIES IN 1993

Language	*Circulation (in Millions)*
English	3.849
Hindi	11.966
Assamese	0.201
Bengali	1.422
Gujarati	1.640
Kannada	0.696
Malayalam	1.732
Marathi	2.348
Oriya	0.897
Punjabi	0.809
Sindhi	0.034
Tamil	1.301
Telugu	0.916
Urdu	1.394
Total	29.258

Source: Audit Bureau of Circulation (1993) Reports.

Table–2.22
LARGEST CIRCULATED DAILIES IN 1994

Name of Newspapers	*Language*	*Circulation*
Times of India	English	813,166
Malayala Manorama	Malayalam	779,170
Gujarat Samachar	Gujarati	657,930
Eenadu	Telugu	558,463
Indian Express	English	544,112
Dainik Bhaskar	Hindi	542,148
Matrubhoomi	Malayalam	513,643
The Hindu	English	497,650
Anand Bazar Patrika	Bengali	484,886
Aaj	Hindi	473,173
Hindusthan Times	English	409,446
Daily Thanthi	Tamil	386,288
Navabharat Times	Hindi	378,283
Rajasthan Patrika	Hindi	365,420
Nowka	Marathi	350,450

Source: Audit Bureau of Circulation (1994) Reports.

Of the total of 89.434 million circulation of daily press in 1996, English constitutes 11.735 million, Hindi constitutes 37.231 million, Bengali, Malayalam, Gujarathi, Tamil, Urdu, Telugu etc., and other language groups constitutes 3 million.[56] In 2002-03 financial year, 3,410 Hindi newspapers with a combined circulation of 61,768,735 (almost 62 million) and 750 English newspapers with a combined circulation of 26,213,142 (26 million) copies. Multi-edition dailies, *Dainik Bhaskar,* with 18 editions in Hindi claimed the largest circulation at 1.717 million copies and the next highest was *The Times of India* in English with 1.394 million copies. Among "single edition" dailies, *The Hindustan Times* in English claimed a circulation of 1.112 million copies while *The Hindu,* also in English came second with a figure of .922 million copies.[57]

The spread of literacy and increase in purchasing power across the country should have a direct relationship with the readership. But the latest numbers released by the Audit Bureau of Circulation explain a different story. From the figures it is clear that the worst hit

REGIONAL PRINT MEDIA 1998-2000

Language	*1998*	*1999*	*2000*
Marathi	28,58,631	28,20,662	28,82,122
Hindi	54,71,103	57,18,001	69,09,447
Malayalam	20,15,556	20,92,018	20,79,277
Tamil	10,86,817	11,10,335	11,76,960
Telugu	10,21,064	9,53,796	10,47,391
Bengali	15,00,144	16,06,066	16,96,539

Source: Audit Bureau of Circulation Reports 1998-2000.

has been the Marathi press with a sharp fall that is five per cent in circulation. Another big loser has been the Telugu press with four per cent drop. The Tamil press however saw its circulation climb by a modest 1.8 per cent in the same period. There are only two solutions for this problem. First try to reaching out through the Internet. Second, expand the regional markets. Regional language publishing companies will try to capture as much as they can of a shrinking market. There could be a war breaking soon. The reason for the decrease of readership is the spread of television. People are preferring to switch the channels rather than flip pages, the regional press is bearing the brunt of this change in media consumption habits. Eenadu television, Gemini (Telugu) and Alpha (Marathi), in these two languages get a lion's share of the Rs. 677 crore in regional television advertisement pie after Tamil. Print media whose contribution is Rs. 4,000 crore in a total Rs. 7,000 crore of advertising revenue. But it has been shrinking. The solution is Internet. Through the internet overseas Indians people from other states also view their own regional papers and this increases ad revenue. Ramoji Rao of Eenadu group (Rs. 700 crore) has managed by venturing into television broadcasting five years ago. Srinivasan Vikathan group in 1977 put all the content of his four magazines into internet for free from the year 2000 onwards. We can read the newspaper and magazine without downloading the font. So many overseas Tamilians and Tamilians outside Tamilnadu can read the paper. Then he got more advertising revenue. The second solution is expanding geographically within India, has come from *Eenadu* (Telugu), *Dainik Bhaskar* (Hindi) and a few others. *Eenadu* has 29 editions across the state of Andhra Pradesh. These are packed with satellite edition for the district which gives local news and taps local advertising. In our country press penetration is 25 per cent except in Mumbai where it is 50-60 per cent. In Rajasthan *Dainik Bhaskar* was launched and press reach got doubled from 24 per cent to 50 per cent. *Dainik Bhaskar* has infact gone a step further and is talking about expanding into territories dominated by the English Publications. *Dainik Bhaskar* (Hindi) has successfully launched in Chandigarh where English dailies *Tribune* and *The New Indian Express* followed by *Punjab Kesari* and *Amar Ujala.*[58] NRS and *Org-Marg* survey shows 1,150 more readers after the launch of *Dainik Bhaskar* and reach is 42 per cent against 28 per cent. *Malayala Manorama* daily has circulation of 11 lakh. 70 per cent of three million Indians in the Gulf edition. It already sells 70,000 copies. It is planning to launch vending machines to down load the 44 pages paper of the net. As the advertising pie gets split among larger number of media, from television to internet to F.M and many more it makes sense for regional print to expand their basket. The more media vehicles they own or the large the geographics they cover the better their chances of survival. People are more comfortable in their own language. It really doesn't matter what vehicle regional languages use to reach them. The idea is survival.[59] Circulation increase was led by language newspapers, especially *Aanand Bazar Patrica, Malayala Manorama* and *Punjab Kesari.* The total number of newspapers in circulation was 33,162 in 1993. The circulation of newspapers or periodicals showed a substantial increase, Big newspapers numbering 153—with a circulation of more than 75,000 copies, medium size newspapers numbering 421 with a circulation of 25,000 to 75,000 copies, Small category numbering 3,380 with a circulation up to 25,000 copies. From 1990-96 the circulation of newspapers increased by 12.8 per cent. There was continuous increase in circulation from 1990-96. Circulation of big newspaper came down (1.6 %). Circulation of small and medium sized newspapers increased (32 % growth). Circulation of news interest dailies under common ownership rose from 13.8 million to 21.2 million.

Indian language press reach: The top three Indian language newspapers reach in 2002 is as follows.[60] *Dainik Bhaskar,* with 1,31,63,000 copies, *Dainik Jagran* with 1,26,70,000 copies, and *Malayala Manorama* with 1,00,32,000 copies of circulation. The five english newspapers ranked since 1999 are ranked as follows, basing on readership. *The Times of India* occupied top position. *The Hindu* is in second position. *The Hindusthan Times* occupies third position, *The New Indian Express* occupies fourth position and *The Telegraph* occupies fifth position.[61] Since 2000, the reader base in India has grown from 163 million to 180 million, a growth of 10 per cent. In fact, in the case of daily newspapers the growth during the period was 20 per cent. Today nearly 160 millions read a daily. Also more housewives read a daily today than ever before. But taking a long term view one could also say that TV has slowed down the growth of print media. And, as could be seen, the growth rate in readership was higher in rural than in urban areas.

UNEVEN GROWTH IN CIRCULATION: DURING 35 YEARS (1964-1999)

Years	*Circulation (in Millions)*		*Per cent Increase in Circulation Over Previous Year*	
	Dailies	All	Dailies	All
1964	7.3	26.5	3.2	1.9
1968	7.6	27.0	5.7	5.5
1969	9.2	33.0	—	-1.0
1974	9.4	33.8	2.2	-3.5
1975	9.4	34.0	1.1	5.6
1991	58.8	130.0	—	—
1999	59.1	127.0	0.55	-2.40

Source: Vidura, Vol. 40, Jan-March 2003, p. 35 (Press Trust of India Report)

NEWSPAPER READERSHIP VIS-À-VIS TV VIEWING: 30 YEARS (1972-2002) (Percent of Adults)

URBAN	*Readership*	*Viewership*
1972-NRS	37	No TV
1978-NRS	53	9
1983-NRS	47	18
1986-NRS	56	-
1990-NRS	44	7
1995-NRS	46	76
1997-NRS	45	78
2000-NRS	45	78
2002-NRS	54	-

Source: **Press Trust of India Report, Vidura, Vol. 40, Jan-March 2003, p. 36.**

The trend calls for a breakthrough to come out of a slow phase since the growth potential is many times more. In the last couple of years the overall readership of newspapers has increased by about four per cent both in rural and urban areas.

Table–2.23
CIRCULATION OF HINDU FROM 1978-2003

Year	*No. of Copies*	*Per cent of Growth*
1978	80	
1911	5,000	615.0
1938	31,000	520.0
1958	84,000	171.0
1978	2,81,000	234.5
1988	4,24,000	50.9
1998	6,97,000	64.4
2003	9,33,000	33.9

Source: The Hindu, September 13th, 2003, p. 7.

From 1996-1999, there is a 20.2 per cent increase in readership. From 1996-2000, readership has risen up to 28.7 per cent. In 1996, the readership is 100 millions and in 2000 it is 130 millions. In 2000; 6.87 million more newspaper readers than in 1996. In 2001 (June) there is an increase of 383 per cent readers compared to 1999.[62]

Table–2.24
NEWSPAPER CIRCULATION (1999) AND READERSHIP (2000)

		Circulation (2000)	*Readership (1999)*
National	Times of India	1,376,000	4,752,000 (Urban)
	Hindusthan Times	975,332	
	The Hindu	697,976	
	Economic Times	534,215	
Regional	Malayalam Manorama	1,111,000	9,299,000
	Indian Express	361,378	3,491,000
	Malayala Karnataka	1,044,352	
	Gujarat Samachar (Gujarati)	861,225	
	Anand Bazarpatrica (Bengal)	846,637	

(Contd.)

	Circulation (2000)	*Readership (1999)*
Punjab Kesari (Hindi)	777,805	5,644,000
Dainik Jargan (Hindi)	750,647	9,643,000
Aaj (Hindi)	718,248	
Matrubhoomi (Malayalam)	712,372	7,080,000
Eenadu	688,916	8,567,000
Sandesh (Gujarati)	658,624	
Daily Thanti (Tamil)	509,886	9,097,000
Bartaman (Bengali)	369,807	
Prajavani (Kannada)	325,310	
Statesman (English)	180,026	
Kerala Kamudi (Malayalam)	1,720,000	

Sources: Audit Bureau of Circulation Report 1999.

National Readership Survey Report, 2000

Appetiser effect of viewership to television news on newspaper readership: According to the study conducted by Centre for Media Studies (CMS) it was found that in the case of 60 per cent or more the time spent on their newspaper reading was more and that has attributed to viewing television news earlier in the day or the immediate previous night. This is because of higher readership, credibility and extensive coverage of the *The Hindu* in Chennai and *Eenadu* in Hyderabad. Another finding from the survey is that the period when Television news channels have proliferated is, that credibility of mainline newspapers has improved over the previous year (1999-2000).[63] Newspaper circulation directly proportional to literacy levels and standard of living.

Table–2.25

NEWSPAPER CIRCULATION IN 1997 AND 1999

Year	*Per cent of Adults in India Who Read Newspaper and Magazine*	*Per cent Increase in from 1997-99*
1997	45	
1999	49	4

Source: National Readership Survey 1999 by National Readership Studies Council, an autonomous division of Audit Bureau of Circulation, Mumbai.

Table–2.26
CIRCULATION OF PRINT MEDIA (2000)

	1999	*2000*	*Percent Increase*
Daily Newspapers	5,88,04,203	5,91,29,183	0.55
Tri & Bi Weeklies	5,62,778	7,84,144	39.34
Periodicals	7,07,20,512	6,70,50,436	-5.19

Source: Registrar of Newspapers for India Report, 2000.

Table–2.27
CIRCULATION OF NEWSPAPERS IN 2000

Name	*Circulation*
Times of India (seven editions)	16,87,099
Malayala Manorama (eight editions)	12,08,001
Dainik Jargan	11,38,035
Hindusthan Times	8,47,346
The Hindu	7,79,851
Anand Bazar Patrica	7,54,348

Source: Registrar of Newspapers for India Report, 2000.

Table–2.28
LANGUAGE-WISE CIRCULATION OF NEWSPAPERS IN 2000

Language	*Newspapers*	*Dailies*
Hindi	5,44,39,135	2,55,77,406
English	2,29,62,607	78,51,426
Malayalam	76,59,962	

Source: Registrar of Newspapers for India Report, 2000.

Table–2.29
TOP FIVE ENGLISH NEWSPAPERS RANKED SINCE 1999 BASING ON READERSHIP

Name of Newspaper	*Rank (Up to 2002)*	*Rank (in 2003)*
The Times of India	1st	1
The Hindu	2nd	3
The Hindusthan Times	3rd	2
Indian Express	4th	7
The Telegraph	5th	4
Deccan Chronicle	–	5

Source: National Readership Survey 2002, 2003 Reports by National Readership Studies Council, an autonomous division of Audit Bureau of Circulation, Mumbai.

Table–2.30

READERSHIP OF NEWSPAPERS (1999-2002)

Year	*Readership (Million)*	*Percent Increase*
1999	131	
2001	136	
2002	156	20
2002 (June)	180	(1999-2000)

Source: *The Hindu,* June 23rd, 2002, Sunday Magazine, p. 3. (National Readership Survey, 2002).

Table–2.31

READERSHIP OF NEWSPAPERS (2001)

Name of Newspaper	*Total Readers (In Millions)*	*2002 (In Millions)*
Dainik Bhaskar	11.26	13.16 (1st)
Daily Thanti	10.43	
Dainik Jargan	10.00	12.67 (2nd)
Eenadu	9.80	
Malyala Manorama	9.30	10.03 (3rd)
Lokmat	7.30	
Matrubhumi	6.80	
Rajasthan Patrica	6.50	
Amar Ujala	6.40	
Times of India	5.90	
Total	83.69	

Source: IRS 2002 published in *The Hindu Businessline,* Wednesday, April, 30th 2003, p. 6.

Literacy growth from 1999-2002 is 13 per cent increase based on National Readership Survey. IRS 2002 points to dip in print media readership. Among dailies, *Dainik Jargan* topped the list, followed by *Dainik Bhaskar* and *Malayala Manorama.* For the financial year 2002-03 and details newspaper circulations adding upto 142,005,543 copies daily. This circulation of more than 142 million represents a 24 per cent increase over the previously reported calendar year of 2001 in which 115 million copies daily were recorded. Among multi-edition dailies, *Dainik Bhaskar,* with 18 editions in Hindi claimed the largest circulation at 1.717 million copies and the next highest was *The Times of India* in English with 1.394 million copies. Among "single edition" dailies, *The Hindustan Times* in English claimed a circulation of 1.112 million copies while *The Hindu,* also in English came second with a figure of 0.922 million copies.[64]

Readership of Magazines

Magazine readership is 16.25 crores readers. Loss of 10 per cent from 2001-02. For *Outlook,* five per cent increases from 2001-02. For *The Week,* 6.5 per cent increase. 4.2 per cent increase for *Women's Era.* The top three magazines *The Week, Outlook, India Today* lost one per cent readers. The readership of these three magazines is 47.66 lakhs in 2002. Women readership (Women/Life style/Film magazines) lost by nine per cent from 2001-02. Business Standard 12 per cent from 2001-02. Total readership, 10 per cent loss from 2001-02.

Table–2.32

TOP ENGLISH NEWSPAPERS IN URBAN INDIA IN 2003

Newspapers	*Readership (Figures in '000)*
The Times of India	6925
The Hindusthan Times	2983
The Hindu	2733
The Telegraph	1312
Deccan Chronicle	1032
The Economic Times	966
The New Indian Express	888
Midday	846
Deccan Herald	832
Indian Express	668

Source: National Readership Survey, 2003 by National Readership Studies Council, an autonomous division of Audit Bureau of Circulation, Mumbai.

According to Indian Readership Survey, 2001 Reach of press is 33.4 per cent (same as last year that is in the year 2000), Reach of Television 49.4 per cent (same as last year) and Reach of Radio is 15.8 per cent (2.7 % down from last year). Internet have 4.19 million users.[65] Press reach is Maximum in Kerala., Second Tamilnadu, Third Andhra Pradesh, Fourth Maharastra, Fifth

Table–2.33

READERSHIP OF BUSINESS NEWSPAPERS AND MAGAZINES IN 2001-02

Newspaper/Magazine	*2002 Year (Lakhs)*
Business Today (3.5 per cent gain from	7.05 lakh readers 2001-02)
Business India	(12.6 per cent decline from 2001-02)
Business World	4.17
Economic Times	10.00
Business Line	3.00

Source: National Readership Survey 2001-02 by National Readership Studies Council, an autonomous division of Audit Bureau of Circulation, Mumbai.

Table–2.34

COMPARISON OF MEDIA IN 1999 AND 2002

Media	*1999*	*2002*
Reach of Magazines	93.8 million	86.2 million
Reach of Radio		28 per cent increase from 1999
Reach of Television		42 per cent increase from 1999
Reach of Internet		6 million

Source: National Readership Survey 2001-02 by National Readership Studies Council, an autonomous division of Audit Bureau of Circulation, Mumbai.

Table–2.35

TIME SPENT ON MEDIA (PER DAY) IN 2002

(Figures in Minutes)

Press	18
Television	82
Radio	12
Internet	1

Source: *The Hindu*, Tuesday, June 18th, 2002, 8th page (NRS Council).

Table 2.36
MEDIA REACH IN 2003

Media	*Per cent Penetration*
Print	52
Television	90
Radio	45
Cinema	6
Internet	8

Source: National Readership Survey, 2003 by National Readership Studies Council, an autonomous division of Audit Bureau of Circulation, Mumbai.

Karnataka and Sixth Punjab. Hindi dailies have 18.7 per cent growth. In 2001-02 and Marati dailies have 18 per cent growth in 2001-02. The penetration of print media dropped from 58 to 52. The penetration of dailies dropped by five per cent. *The Times of India* readership increased to 33 per cent when compared with the previous year. Among Times of India readers, more than 75 per cent belong to the highest socio-economic class 'A', and more than half the readers belong to households with a monthly income of Rs.10,000.

Competition in Newspaper Industry

The circulation of newspapers is certainly flat and not keeping up with the population increase. People are getting news increasingly from television.[66] Print is becoming less of a vehicle for bringing the news first. That role will go to Television broadcasters. The only mass buy today is in the super bowl. That is by picking demographics and addressing specifically to a particular segment. With the opening up of the media industry the new economy scenario has opened up a number of avenues that have contributed to the changing face of segment. At the *Indian Newspaper Society* (INS) convention held in Banglore on Friday (September 17th, 2000), Jaitely[67] said, "the commercial survival of newspapers was important especially in view of increased competition from the electronic and internet media. Content and credibility of media are two important factors that papers need to look at and maintain," he said, "content is now technology driven, and more people across the country are taking to gathering as much information as possible, which is evident from the rise in the number of pink papers in the country" he said. Surveys have also shown an increase in young readership levels and newspaper advertising incomes have also gone up.[68] The president of World Association of Newspapers, Roser Parkinson commented about newspaper competition at INS convention as follows. "No other medium can ever come close in terms of credibility and trust."[69] Murali decried "the tendency on the part of newspapers to indulge in price wars to gain circulation. This will only lead to monopolistic situations and will destroy the plural fabric of Indian Newspaper Industry." Speaking at the Indian Newspaper Society (INS) convention 2000 on "Reinvesting the print medium in new economy today" Arun Jaitly said, measures should be taken to improve overall quality increase the reach and expand advertisement revenues. Arun Jaitely voiced caution against "extensive price wars" among dailies leading to "monopolies."[70] In Confedaration of Indian Industry (CII) media Unconvention Arun Jaitely said "Media has become increasingly dependent on advertisements for survival. Editorial credibility, protection of intellectual property and libel laws have been neglected. Expansion of media needs to be monitored carefully." Information, entertainment and advertising to merge seamlessly so that viewer does not lose interest. Hence for a programme for children, it can be education for youth, career opportunities for adults, health and for rural audience, agriculture and others. Think consumer, link technology to consumer benefit. Build new business models for niche audience like home shopping, mass customisation. New skills for communication. But in India the issue is divergence than convergence.[71]

Price Wars in Newspaper Industry

Average price of a daily newspaper in 1983 was about 55 paise. Fifteen years later, because of price wars between certain newspapers in several metros the average price of dailies, has hardly increased by four times, considerably lower than the inflationary trend. However, advertising tariff has been revised more often than the price of newspaper fearing adverse impact on circulation. Today the average price of newspaper is around two rupees, irrespective of the number of pages and circulation.[72] The price wars in the newspaper industry would create monopolies leading to elimination of smaller newspapers. The print media is facing challenges within the industry and also from the multimedia television and Internet. Because of the Freedom of Press the government is not intervening matters related to price wars or reducing the size of newspaper (newsprint case). Monopolistic Restrictive Trade Practice (MRTP) law is not applicable to the newspaper industry. The newspaper industry was under seige and facing pressure on advertisement revenue and competition from Television and the Internet. Wage board for journalists and non-journalist employees had also recommended big increase in wages. The press was not able to free itself from shackles. The increase in the number of newspapers raising question about their being factual. There was a tendency among some of the younger newspaper reporters to accept the phenomenon of convergence among them in the matter of coverage of news. The changes being witnessed in the newspapers were the result of competition. However, there was no complaint about the overall credibility of newspapers in the country. The circulation of newspapers, particularly those in the regional, was increasing despite the expansion of the electronic media and the entry of Internet. Though the coverage of the Radio had not increased, its entertainment value increased once FM band was introduced. The Hindi newspapers had recorded significant increases and become multi-edition ones, even though the regional Television networks were expanding. The newspaper industry faces the problem of rising costs besides that of competition. There was a phenomenal increase in the price of newsprint in the last two decades. The free expression of views had been challenged by the business of running a newspaper. Circulation and advertisement revenue were growing. Newspapers were reporting an increase in traffic on their websites. Entry of Internet is not at the cost of newspapers but at the cost of Television. Today even though two million have access to net, 75 per cent internet users had given up viewing television, whereas only 12 per cent had given up reading newspapers. The readers wanted a medium whose source of news they could trust. It had also been found that an increasing number of youth were taking to reading newspapers. The newspapers themselves were becoming a portal for news.[73]

Cross Media Monopolies in Print Media

Cross-media monopolies could be a reality one day. But now it is in the beginning stage. The Ramojirao owned Eenadu group has become the de-facto power centre in Andhra Pradesh. Its daily newspaper along with Eenadu Television and Eenadu Radio commands a lion's share of readership, viewership and listenership. Eenadu Group companies, Usha Kiran movies and Mayuri Audio straddle the film and audio market. A broadband portal, Eenadu.com is the default home page on millions of computers and Television screens as *Eenadu* owns the Internet Service Provider (ISP) and cable company with the highest penetration in Andhra Pradesh bottomline. *Eenadu* has about 80 per cent of the state's Telugu-speaking population under its influence. How they vote, where they shop, the advertisements they see-everything is shaped by the news, information and entertainment coming from *Eenadu*. We could choose a different newspaper, television channel or ISP, but the network effect has kicked in. If we are locked out of the Eenadu net work, we pay more, service quality could be unreliable. It is routine for Eenadu operators to block out other Telugu channels and its ISP makes it difficult to access other sites. *Zee* and *Star* have interest in Cable companies. Zee is also into ISP, portal and till recently, print media business. Print media heavy weights like *Midday* and *The Times of India* are getting into FM radio. *The Times of India* is into music and has a popular portal Indiatimes.com. However, the move towards media conglomerates is hesitant. First, because cross-media restrictions are not yet clean. Second, cross media ownership does not constitute a strangle hold at the national level but at the local level. "In the US cross-media rules apply most to local radio stations and newspapers etc.," says Sevanthi Ninan, largely because competition is fierce at the national level. Third, the experience of newspapers that branched into TV or magazines shows that, traditionally each media market also has its own heavy weights. Print has *The Times of India* and *Hindusthan Times*. "What worries me is if a broadcaster, who also owns a cable distribution venture, blocks out channels of competing broadcasters" says Ninan.[74] With the plethora of newspapers available in each town in India and the restrictions on broadcasting for local markets, the concept of cross-media holdings is not relevant in the Indian continent at the moment," says Aroon Purie.[75] Considering the current frenzied growth and competition at the national and regional levels in newspaper industry, there seems little danger of monopolies forming democracy's worst nightmare, if it even comes, is a long way off.[76]

Newspapers vs Television

In the coverage of space shots, national conventions, sports events, and other spectacles which the public can view at first hand, Television is superb. But television cannot give all the news, with suitable interpretation and background, during the course of an average network newscast. Television can cover 10 per cent, perhaps less, of the news in a good newspaper on any given day. The essentials of governmental budget problems and taxes, of complicated programmes like medicare and other aspects of security, the work of urban renewal, housing, public health and road-building, the fight against air and water pollution, the daily tabulation of stock and bond markets and similar statistical material, can be only touched in a television news programme. Some of it, for obvious reasons, cannot be covered at all unless the newspapers do it. As Brinkley say: "It is impossible physically and otherwise to cover news in complete and voluminous detail on Television. It just cannot be done, nor is it possible to effectively deliver any kind of commentary on Television."[77] Television is a pictoral medium essentially, and if there is no movement if there is nothing happening, nobody is going to listen. It is clear therefore, that television is unlikely to drive the bulk of newspapers, out of business any more than Radio or the movies did. And despite all the worrying about the tendency of Television to pull people away from the printed world, reading has not exactly gone out of style. In addition to the rise in newspaper and magazine readership, the paperback book has boosted sales and readership in the book publishing industry during the period coinciding with televisions' greatest growth.[78] While the mass public relies on Television the better educated public, without any doubt, tends to depend more on a good newspaper and in recent years to have diminished its television viewing on the first breaks in the news, Radio has been the prime source of public intelligence, for two generations in the last generation or so, television has come along to share the honours. But for complete news, reported in depth and interpreted with honesty and good judgement, there is still no substitute for a good newspaper. In the competition with the electronic media and the news and picture magazines, newspapers have made numerous changes to build greater interest. There has been a substantial swing toward the six column newspaper, instead of the familiar and narrow eight columns. Some of the oldest and most famous have begun to use larger body type as a concession to the eyesight of their older readers. With few exceptions, all leading newspapers are well-entrenched in public esteem and without serious rivals in their field, the press has overreacted to the challenge of television. Some papers have gone overboard on comics, features, advice to the lovelorn and similar temporary attention-getters. Others have gone in for circulation contests that procure new readers, but generally only until the contest is over. The successful newspaper, more than any other news medium must specialise in news. That is its principal offering, with its advertising second. It cannot compete with television in entertainment, although this scarcely means that a newspaper can afford to be dull. Nor can it compete with the schools as source of instruction, although that has always been a by-product of an independent and intelligently conducted press News-learning-division; these are all proper newspaper functions, to them must be added the ingredient of interpretation, which is more important to the press today than event before.[79] The television and newspapers are furiously dumbing down after the emergence of Net.[80]

Newspapers and Radio

In July, 2001 the Rupert Murdoch became the first to launch a privately owned radio station in independent India. When government decided in 1999, to open up F.M. radio station to the private sector it chose not to open up frequencies for the community to use. In November, 2001, when a new organization called Gyanavani launched its first FM radio station from Allahabad. The first transmitter was commissioned in November, followed by Lucknow, Visakhapatnam and Bhopal by January, 2002. This F.M. radio is (Unique Selling Proposition) U.S.P.[81] Before the entry of private players there was no much competition between newspapers and radio. But with the entry of private players on F.M. radio, the race to attract listenership has begun. However, the low advertising spends on the Radio, High license fees and the lack of credible audience monitoring system will make things tough for these companies. Market share of All India Radio may increase from 1.5 per cent to 3.5 per cent. The advantages are, radio offers to retailers, a low cost, focused local reach and high speed of production. Radio can act as a pursuader. Advertising rates are also low. Radio may not be clubbed with television because of huge gaps in rates. But radio plus print deal may work. Cross media deals may only be to attract advertisers to try the medium for the first time.[82] Promotion through radio is more focused as it helps in targeting people of a particular city or geographical location. Advertising in radio is much cheaper than advertising in print. The reach of radio was as much as that of television. Currently radio share in the total advertisements is only two per cent and is slated to grow to 10 per cent.[83] The amount of time spent on Radio could rise average of 30 min per day three hours per day. Radio advertising pie is 2.25 per cent of total advertising. Problem in Radio broadcasting is high licensing fee.[84] Indian newspapers generate revenue by beaming international signal. The newspapers published daily in Tamil, has seen its growth in readership slow as more Tamil speaking Singaporeans click on Indian related news websites to read the latest headlines from their homeland.[85] The Indian Newspaper Society (INS) has launched a programme to showcase the effectiveness of advertising in print, which has been intacted by aggressive competing media like Television, Outdoor and Internet. Dubbed 'project press', it seeks to demonstrate the 'Media Multiplier" effect of print when used in conjunction with Television.[86] The rapid spread of television is another reason for the woes of the print medium. Over the last decade there is a massive growth of the Television medium. Tamil has the largest number of channels i.e. ten. There is a massive shift of consumer product advertising and corporate image building to this medium. This is because of so many channels and large amount of advertising spend. It also reaches to a large mass of not so literate people. It reaches to women folk.[87] To meet the competition Bennett and Coleman's *The Times of India* set to launch an afternoon newspaper in Mumbai focussing on entertainment and leisure to attract the younger crowd. It wil be in the crowd and it will be in the style of a tabloid. The newspaper will be completely pricd at Re. one per copy when compared to *Mid-Day* and afternoon despatch and courier which sell for Rs. 2.50 paise each.[88]

Newspapers — Size Reduction

The recent slimming of newspapers size is essentially a response to terrible economic pressure. Weight reduction will help in bringing in handsome cost savings. The recent changes in the width of major Indian dailies were not exactly unprecedented.

(i) If the size is slimmed then it is easy to handle.
(ii) It looks sleeker and more contemporary.
(iii) It is easier to navigate and read the paper, especially for those on the tread mill called time.

The Hindu trimmed the width of the paper from 16 inches to 15 inches. The saving is 6.25 per cent and newsprint saving is around nine tonnes/day. Multiply this with an average cost around Rs. 25,000 per tonne to get a saving of anything above Rs. 225 lakh/day or around Rs. eight crore per year. The traditionally strong Kasturi

Table–2.37

NEWSPAPER SIZE REDUCTION IN 2002

Name of Newspaper	*Width*	*Height* (*Figures in cms*)
The Economic Times	35	54.5
The Times of India	35	54.5
The New Indian Express	35	56.5
Financial Express	35	56.5
The Hindu	38	56.0

Source: Industrial Economist (30 May-14 June, 2002), p. 18.

and sons, Publishers of the *The Hindu* for close to 125 years, has suffered a 40 per cent drop in advertising revenues and a consequent loss in 2001-02 for the first time several years. *The New Indian Express* has been tottering even more due to the even bigger cut in its advertising revenue. In the last three years, international prices of newsprint hardened reaching dizzy heights. They started increasing from around 425 dollars per tonne to close to 710 Dollars per tonne. Adding to this the additional cost of depreciation of the rupee by nearly 10 per cent during this period.

The Times of India was dominant in the west, *The Hindu* in the south, *The Hindusthan Times* in North and the *Statesmen* in the East. Until about the Eighties by unwritten agreements, newspapers barons respected each other's territorial suzerainty. G. Narasimha Rao and G. Kasuri brothers contributed immensely to the upgradation of technology. So hot metal typesetting switch to computerised type setting.

Malayala Manorama and other large papers moved to 15 inches. Since the move towards the trimming began, there has been a 25 per cent in width alone, plus several of these have also trimmed to the length. So saving over a period will be close to 30 per cent. The newspapers have been clever in maintaining advertisement tariff even on the trimmed sizes. A 20 × 3 advertisement in *The Economic Times*, for instance, today would give only an area of 240 sq. cm as against 280 sq. cm earlier. *The Hindu* cut 32 to 40 paper edition to 24 pages. Special supplements get absorbed into a single pack. Major newspapers also leveraged their special regional strengths to hike their advertising rates so as to maintain current advertising revenues. Vernacular papers have also been adopting this trend and have a much higher pricing per page and much less cost on staff and production, even though the quality of printing is poor in political, film and crime news.

Now-a-days cost reduction techniques are employed by most of the newspaper organizations Some of them are as follows:

(i) Trimming of newspapers.
(ii) Reducing the number of pages of newspaper edition.
(iii) Keeping advertising tariff same inspite of trimming.
(iv) Increasing the advertising tariff.

Role of Newspapers in Society

The news is not a mirror of social conditions, but the report of an aspect that has obtruded itself. The news does not tell us how the seed is germinating in the ground, but it may tell when the first sprout breaks through the surface. The newspapers, in other words has come to be an organ of direct democracy, charged on a much wider scale, and from day-to-day, with the function often attributed to the initiative referendum and recall. It is like the beam of a search light that moves restlessly about, bringing one episode and then another part of darkness into vision. Men cannot do the work of the world by this light alone. They cannot govern society by episodes, incidents and eruptions. It is only when they work by a steady light of their own, that the press, when it is turned upon them, reveals a situation intelligible enough for a popular decision.[89] The main function of media is to create ideology and it moulds people's mind.[90] The scope and opportunity for the newspapers at present to perform its societal role are tremendous. One of the significant ways in which it can assist is in the protection and promotion of human rights. Indeed it is then that it can be truly called the "Ark of covenant of Democracy."[91] The press should play important role in safeguarding the interests of farmers, employees, workers.[92]

If we observe the history of the press from 1911-1947, that is during the National Movement in India, the rise and growth of the press in Bihar indicates the importance of newspapers which has affected all aspects of human life. It appears that newspapers are a component part of our social, political and cultural life. The *Prajabandhu* (Hindi) was a popular nationalist weekly in 1921, owned by Pandit Jeevanand Sharma.[93] Today newspapers are becoming so independent of public policy, so immune to the public needs, so scornful of governmental regulations, and so dependent on profit, that they have become one of the most powerful business on the face of the globe. They have become more powerful than the very governments in which they operate, for they hold unique combination of both political and economic power. Instead of advertised and sold, if it continuously caters the tastes of those who constitute the largest segment of the market, the financial stability of the system can be maintained. But low taste content is the key element in the social system of newspaper media. In the process of cross – commercialisation entering the portals of media edifies, issues and non-issues are getting mixed up. News with a commercial angle, news with a political fall-out, scandals and scams, get priority as issues rather than major concerns and needs of the society. "Women, wampum and wrong doings are always the news." Real issues like illiteracy, health, cancer of curruption that is pervading, all are ignored and media seems to be preoccupied with politics, politicians, celebrities from the tinsel world or the ramps. Almost inevitably anything that threatens people's peace, prosperity or well-being is news and likely to make headlines. Because of unglamorous, unsensational issues like drinking water, untouchbility, public health concerns, civic awareness are from media.[94] When five kilograms of heroin is recovered, newspapers carry banner headlines carry saying that five crore rupees worth heroin has been seized whereas about voluntary workers who counsel and treat and rehabilitate five or ten heroin addicts, there is no mention even if organisations dealing with such rehabilitation send across a press release.[95] Some issues are getting more attention than they actually deserve. Indian newspapers took Kargil as a national crisis. Many Delhi newspapers filled almost all their pages with stories, pictures of the fighting and other developments relating to Kargil. Human interest stories and conditions of present and former soldiers who felt neglected for years occupied prime newspaper space.[96] Tribals who lived on nature and forest produces for generations are now being threatened or hounded out of their natural habitats by both activists who are essentially city dwellers and the media in the name of environment protection. They talk to the emaciated tribal population about global warming, green house effect or depletion of ozone layer ignoring the ground realities of such tribals. It is only rarely that stories about commercial felling of trees by the political or city mafia get noticed in some corner of newspaper. Pressures of space and time, readership and audience ratings, often act as deterrents in getting issues, like the plight of the tribals or the deprived ignored in the media prime attention.[97] The Indian newsroom does not reflect the country's social diversity. It is observed that two categories are grossly under- represented. *(i) Dalits:* With urban sophistication, owners and editors claim lack of interest in the caste origin of the staff. They constantly look to the west for ideas on everything from newspaper title to stories to pictures. *(ii) Women:* Many newspapers recognise that women constitute an important market segment that need to be tapped. Consequently they are more inclined to employee women than before.[98] In newspapers the Muslim community voices are not heard. The moderate muslim who condemns terrorism has hardly been heard following the World Trade Centre (WTC) attacks on 11th, September 2001, the newspaper people generally have opinion that Muslims were not proactive enough in Indian society, only reacting when something was done either to them or in their name. But also that when Muslims did speak up, the media completely failed to reflect the voice.[99] If we examine some of the news stories like Tehelka defence scam, massacre in Nepal, Vajpayee-Musharaf news on terrorism, panchayat elections, collapse of World Trade Centre (WTC), in all these cases the unimportant events are given preference. In panchayat elections violence is more covered than real voting for lower castes etc. These news stories are not covered or less covered in newspapers.[100]

Womens' pages in newspapers are a relatively recent phenomenon. For example, *Eenadu* came out with a women page, 'Vasundhara' and *Vaartha* has come out with 'Cheli'. Newspapers influence society and women in a major way. It affects all aspects of womens' lives including their self-image. It influences most regarding women's development. It is important that we recognize the manipulative role and the class and gender bias of newspapers. In January, 1983, a committee was formed to write letters to the editors of national dailies on offending advertisements and articles in newspapers make sometimes and advertisements in newspapers stopped appearing.[101] Instead of remaining a tool in the hands of men and the elite, newspapers should be increasingly controlled by those who want to challenge and change the present system like in 1980's when *Indian Express* geared to raising awareness among the readers and also to disseminate ideas.[102] Only one-third of women portrayed as lead characters are depicted as managing enterprise, working as lawyers, journalists, advertising executives, doctors etc. Working women are depicted as ambitious, neurotic, ecentric in appearance or mannerisms, incapable of coping with their relationships and saddled with children problem. Women are portrayed stereotypically. In advertisements portraying good-looking, intelligent and confident women is appreciated whereas those depicting them as frivolous or without any purpose are not liked by women.[103] News Media played a remarkable role in a coverage of Gujarat carnage. The News Media tend to homogenise 'calamities' which are seen increasingly to differ only in quantitative terms.[104] Most newspapers inadvertently reveal a bias. The bias also come to play even among credible and professional media organizations. For example, an article that looks at recent coverage of Israel's military campaign in Palestine illustrates this bias. The suicide bombing of a bus, in which eight people were killed predictably made headline news on April 10th. But the same story also reported that atleast one hundred palestianians were killed in Jenin as a consequence of Israeli attack and that many "still lie where they fell."[105] In Gujarat communal clashes and the violence was carried by newspapers. The *Asian age* named Muslim victims. Some newspapers in Uttar Pradesh are fairly provocative, naming both communities and victims. Other Hindi newspapers however, refrained from being communal in editorial tone, *Janasatta, Punjab Kesari* and *Nav Bharat* are some examples. The *Dainik Bhaskar* had a banner headline describing Bapu's Gujarat as going up in flames. Another paper thought up the headline, 'Battering Ram' to describe the situation at Ayodhya. The *Hindusthan Times* published in a front page close up photograph of a child with 90 per cent burns and added in the caption that the picture had been taken just before the child died. The danger with the newspaper media is that, willingly or unwillingly, it promotes those whom it condemns.[106] The news media focus on the Gujarat communal clashes but do not investigate what happened on the Sabarmati Express at Godhra with equal fervour. But we are also guilty of blatant communalism. Similarly, in the Bombay *The Times of India* there was no need to write about the problems of Dharavi because the paper readers did not live there.[107] Coming to Children and newspapers, newspaper media occasionally report on just one or two industries that employ child labour. But it is common to see small boys serving tea even in government offices which is not covered by media. The Indian study found that unless something important event is there, news on sport, education or human interests, news coverage about children is a minor component of social issues.[108]

Newspaper Media and Tourism

The newspaper media has proved to be an enemy of the tourism industry in its time of crisis. The sensational war related stories appearing in some newspapers around the world were responsible for the disproportionate panic gripping foreign countries regarding the safety of their citizens of India. People in India may not be unduly alarmed by such articles as they are closer to ground reality, but when such articles appear in the foreign newspaper media, things change. Nobody would like to keep their citizens in a place where, such a situation occurs. It causes lot of damage to tourism industry when the number of foreigners visiting the country get reduced. Some people cancelled the ticket which were already booked. So tourism industry gets affected because of newspaper media.[109] Sometimes newspaper media is playing a negative role by debunking stereotypical depictions of India which is not a healthy trend for newspaper media.[110] Abroad enough research has been done to show that reading too much disaster coverage can induce post traumatic stress disorder in children. Most repeated news is bad news.[111]

Intolerence of the press among politicians, the police and government officials is growing, even though all three find the Fourth Estate occasionally useful. The Tamil Magazine, *Nakeeran* and its editor were used by the Tamilnadu and Karnataka governments during negotiations to secure the freedom of actor Rajkumar from the clutches of Veerappan. But subsequently the magazine' reporter Sivasubramanyam was arrested and continues to alternate between police and judicial custody. Gopal himself is suspect and facing severe questioning by the Tamilnadu police. In Gujarat, the State Government had tried to tame the press even before the events of February-March in 2002. In August, 2001, it had initiated a move to bring the press in the State under the purview of the Consumer Protection Act. Belonging to the media in India is a truly unique experience. They can be wooed and kicked at the same time. They can be elevated into positions for which they have no qualification if our journalistic politics of right colour, they can also be hounded for simply practising their profession if they are not of the right colour. Now public attention should be better safeguards for press freedom.[112] No one should be surprised at what happened in Gujarat on 7th April, 2002 (Sunday) when a peace meeting at Sabarmati Ashram led to a dozen journalists being beaten up by police earlier in the week, Sonal Kellog, a women reporter from *The Asian Age* and a male reporter from Surat based newspaper, were pounced upon by the police when they went into the walled city to interview women who had been attacked. Kellog was hit with a stick and the man was thrashed. When they went to the Police Commissioner to complain, they were told he had no time for them. Since February 27, there have been innumerable attacks on members of the press in Gujarat. Here is an incomplete list of attacks that have been recorded just last month (March, 2002): Rajul Chiniwala, a photographer from the Gujarat newspaper *Sandesh* in Surat, was caught by a mob. They poured kerosene and petrol on him and were about to set him on fire when a police van came on the scene. Reporter of *The New Indian Express* in Rajkot, was pushed around by a mob, the roll in his camera was removed and his camera smashed. Sudhir Vyas of the *The Times of India* in Rajkot was beaten by the police. Tanvir Siddique, senior reporter of *The New Indian Express* and Javed Raja, a senior photographer of with the paper, could not go out to report because of anti-muslim mobs on the streets. Apart from these instances, numerous other reporters have narrated how their press credentials were demanded by mobs. So far, when reporters cover riots, they have been confident that their press pass, or press sticker, would protect them and tell their story. And that the police will protect them. But when a group or a political party, using state force, prevents them from recording the story, then clearly the concept of freedom of the press stands threatened.[113] Now the news media organizations are facing the problems of concentration of ownership and creation of monopolies. Increasing tendency of multimedia conglomerates to use news resources to promote commercial interests. The emergence of media conglomerates and intense market competition are creating new organizational priorities in which profit growth often requires reducing the resources for news gathering, thereby diminishing the role of news media as public trust. Business priorities are encouraging the blending of news and entertainment as a strategy to build readers and ratings.[114] Newspapers are useful in highlighting the unity of culture. What we have to achieve is to focus on the wonderful co-existence of culture and tradition that has made ours a continuing civilization. All over this far flung land there is such a variety of experiences of people intermingling, of traditions and customs that are not exclusive but encompassing. There must be honesty and impartiality in the presentation of news. The best ones have always endeavoured, within the limits of human frailty, to present the news fairly and honestly in the news columns, leaving persuation to the realm of the editorial page and featured columnist.[115] It is time to do away with intellectualizing that does little except widen the gulf between the readers and newspaper and we have to make the newspaper both responsible and popular even though it is difficult to make the newspaper responsible as well as popular.[116] Media is responsible for development, progress, unity and harmony of the country.[117] It is only through its ability to serve the widest possible cross-sections of the people that a newspaper could succeed. To do it, it would need good business management and sound editorial guidance so that the news coverage is varied and occurate as well as comprehensive and objective and different points of view are presented and allowed to be expressed.[118] The press should take the lead in the nation building activities. The main challenge is save freedom which had been attained after great sacrifice and in turn to save democracy.[119] Accuracy and truthfulness must be there in news reporting and requires mature and sensible handling.[120] As the world rejuvenates itself with time, so must the newspaper media with one publication trying to outsell the other, this increasing freedom not always free from misuse. The sacredness of facts cannot diminish because the importance of comments has increased. A news item should not be ill presented with a bias or prejudice. Unfortunately, this is what we find happening—whether it is Godhra, Gujarat, Ayodhya, Chennai debate, POTA, Tehelka tapes, exodus of minorities from Bangladesh, Nobel Prize to Sir Naipaul etc.[121]

Problems and Prospects in Newspaper Industry

In October 1996, the government had levied a 10 per cent custom duty on the import of newsprint despite protest from the newspaper industry. But they assured that custom duty on import of newsprint would be withdrawn if the international price touched U.S. $ 575. Now they are not honouring their commitment and are going to add more duty on the import of newsprint. The newspaper industry would then be forced to buy poor quality newsprint produced by the domestic market. The quality of Indian newsprint manufactured by some private entreprenures is poor and it is also expensive. The foreign paper is cheaper and of better quality but it have customs and anti-dumping duties.

Sometimes artificial scarcity created in the international market and prices of newsprint shot up for instance in 1995 end and early 1996 there was an artificial scarcity created in the international market and the prices of newsprint shot up to 1000 U.S. dollars and even the indigenous manufacturers hiked their prices more than 50 per cent in four months. But when the international market rates fell, the domestic manufacturers did not reduce the prices.

Problems

(i) Rising of the newsprint is important obstacle for the growth of newspaper industry. (In 1997, it has been down from 10 per cent to five per cent.)

(ii) Competition from other media that is both Intra media and Inter media competition.

(iii) Vernacular newspapers are very poor in upgradation of technology. They have not been able to invest in training or in technology. So one can notice a vast lag in the quality and quantity of coverage between an English daily and the vernacular newspapers.

(iv) Liquidity is also another problem for newspaper industry that is the newspaper industry now-a-days is not having enough money to purchase newsprint and to give wages and salaries to workers as well as employees in the organization.

(v) Advertising revenues are reducing because of sluggishness in the economy, liquidity in the market and diversion to the ever-expanding electronic media.

(vi) The erosion in the value of rupee vis-à-vis the dollar had further affected the price of imported newsprint and increased the burden on the newspaper.

(vii) If 33 per cent anti-dumping duty is imposed on newspaper industry then that would result in premature death of newspaper industry.

(viii) Lack of research data—One of the biggest problem for managers of newspaper business is the absolute lack of research data, other than half-yearly NRS and IRS data. So there is a lacuna in newspaper research data.

Prospects

The exemption of five per cent customs duty on newsprint is an advantage for the Newspaper Industry, which is rising hopes of newspaper industry to get more profits. Companies like Ballapur Industries Limited (BIL) develops a "Machine-friendly paper" with specifications for high speed copying without any jamming, misfeeds or curling on the machine which is positive sign for the prosperity of newspaper industry. In newspaper industry now a days there is an opportunity for technological upgradation, modernization of plant and equipment (Fassimail). Substantial expansion of newspaper units at par with global standards to provide a platform for machinery (Eg. *The Hindu*). Rising advertising revenue and declining newsprint costs accounted for the improvement of operating performance by which the Industry will get more profits. Improvements in better staffing promotion, zoned editions, greater uses of colour and higher quality editorial products will leads to increase in core circulation thereby the industry will get more profits. The Newspaper Industry will also flourish if it focus on localization of news which helps in increasing the circulation The increase in the circulation of newspapers attracts the advertisers to allot more budget on advertising there by the Industry will get more revenue.

Newspapers in Andhra Pradesh

The advent of newspapers in Andhra Pradesh was when the Telugu Journal *Satyadoota* was published in 1836 for the propagation of Christianity. It was challenged by *Tatwabodhi* in 1864 by the Veda Samaj from Madras. The *Hitwadi* which was published weekly ceased to exist after a few years. Rao Bahadur K.Veeresalingam Pantulu, Scholar, educationalist and social reformer made a beginning in Telugu Journalism with his weekly the Vivek Vardhani devoted to social and Language reform.[122] The newspaper readership developed in Andhra Pradesh after independence. Late Tangaturi Prakasam Pantulu started a paper called *Swarajyam* in Madras, which became very famous during the independence struggle and it served the peoples' causes even later. The first political news weekly in Telugu was *Andhra Prakasika* published in 1886 by A.P. Parthasarathi Naidu. It was published from Madras.[123] The *Deshabhimani*, the first daily was published from Guntur in 1886 by Devagupta Seshachalarao first as fortnightly, then as weekly and bi-weekly and finally as daily newspaper.[124] *Krishna Patrica* was started by Konda Venkatappyya and Dasu Narayanarao in 1902. Andhra's first successful daily paper was *Andhra Patrica* was started as weekly from Bombay in 1908 by Desodharaka Nageswara Rao, who was a freedom fighter.[125] It was a prominent Telugu regional paper for the people of Andhra region. It gave fillip to the patriotic people of Andhra, who contributed a lot towards attaining Independence. Editorials and articles on politics and informing the political development in the country in Telugu became very effective to fight for freedom. The founder and the editor D. Nageswara Rao is a political luminary who made the *Andhra Patrica* very popular among all the areas of Andhra like Vijayawada in general and coastal areas in particular. *Andhra Prabha* was started in 1939 and edited by Khasa Subba Rao and after by Narla Venkateswara Rao.[126] Another Telugu daily called *Golukonda Patrica* was started in Hyderabad. It was popular in the Telangana area which was also known as "Nizam Area." The paper fought for the freedom of the country and served the people of Telangana region and critisizes the autocratic rule of the 'Nizam' who was then the ruler of the state. This paper spread political awareness in the backward areas of Nizam dominion. It became the mouth piece of intellectuals and reforms for bettering the life of the down-trodden. It fought many battles against the autocratic rule, due to some financial crisis it was wounded up. Another Telugu paper was started which was called *Andhra Janata* in 1960s. It was the organ of the Congress Party and was helpful in spreading the ideology of the Indian National Congress Party. Due to lack of capable management its doors were shutdown during 1970s.

Another Telugu daily the *Andhra Bhoomi* which emerged from Secunderabad is a sister concern of very popular english daily in Deccan area called *Deccan Chronicle.* This paper became quite popular particularly during the time of Gorra Sastry who was one of the prominent editors of the paper. Mr. Gorra Sastry's editorials attracted a large number of Telugu readers. *Andhra Bhoomi's* editions were started in 1985 from Visakhapatnam and in 1989 from Vijayawada. Now it has many branches in Rajahmundry, Tirupati, Ananthpur etc. all over the state. Another Telugu daily *Andhra Prabha* a sister concern of *The New Indian Express* group of newspapers launched in Madras. Later the editions were opened in Vijayawada, Hyderabad, Vijayanagaram etc. *Andhra Jyothi* is another Andhra's prominent

Telugu daily started from Vijayawada in 1967. It spreads its wings to three more centres and started publishing from Hyderabad, Tirupati and Visakhapatnam. Now it has many branches. It was stopped for some time because of certain problems and it started again under a new management. Vasavi group of companies took over this organization on January 1st, 2003, under the management of Vemuri Radhakrishna. *Vaartha* is the latest Telugu newspaper that started Publications from various centres in Andhra Pradesh simultaneously in 1996. *Eenadu* started printing from Visakhapatnam in 1974 and later it developed into seven editions including Vijayawada, Hyderabad, Ananthpur, Tirupati, Karimnagar and Rajahmundry. Now it has 23 editions within the state and editions also published for Non-Andhrites and Non-Resident Indians also. This Telugu daily started a new trend in Telugu journalism. Technically superior *Eenadu* is ruling the Telugu newspaper industry at present. It has been doing many experiments now. *Vasundhara* supplements, introducing seven features for weekdays one in each day, special page are few examples of that. It enjoys largest circulated title barring the other dailies from the picture. It prints nearly 10 lakh copies per day in Andhra Pradesh. It captured this position because of effective management and its politics. It also enjoys greater patronage from the advertisers. It has fully dominated the Andhra Pradesh newspaper market. Another prominent newspaper *Udayam* was started in Vijayawada in 1984. Later it extended its branches to Hyderabad, and Tirupati. By introducing latest technology it clicked in the market. But due to lack of sound and capable management it was closed. Now in 2003 again NRIs are planning to take over this organisation and they want to restart its operations. The entrance of English newspapers in Andhra Pradesh was also early. The first prominent newspaper in English started its publication in Andhra Pradesh was *Deccan Chronicle* in 1938. In 2001 in Hyderabad, *Deccan Chronicle* print order was 6,00,000 copies every day. *The Times of India* stood second with 40,000 copies even though it launched its edition in 2000 year in Hyderabad. *Indian Express* started its operations in Andhra Pradesh from Vijayawada in the year 1959. In 1991 *Indian Express* is divided in to groups that is *Indian Express* published from Bombay and *Indian Express* Chennai. Later on *Indian Express*, Chennai was renamed as *The New Indian Express*. *The Hindu* started operations in Andhra Pradesh from Hyderabad in the year 1980. *The Hindu* has one more publishing center at Visakhapatnam.

Most of the newspapers whether English or Telugu are operating from more than one centre so as to cater to the needs of the customers. There are also many local newspapers that have limited areas of operations.[127] In Visakhapatnam the prominent local published evening newspapers are *Leader* and *Vijaya Bhanu.*

Table–2.38

CIRCULATION OF NEWSPAPERS IN INDIA

Name of the Newspaper	*Circulation (Number of Copies)*		
	(July-Dec. 2001)	*(July-Dec. 2002)*	*(Jan.-June 2003)*
The Hindu	9,04,654	9,25,257	9.33.458
The New Indian Express	2,51,895	2,22,080	2,22,080
Deccan Chronicle	2,33,139	2,77,960	2,96,430
Andhra Bhoomi	65,869	48,137	39,528
Eenadu	8,41,890	9,11,966	9,19,721
Vaartha	2,00,000*	2,20,000*	2,25,000*
The Times of India	19,93,645	20,71,870	21,62,865

Source: Audit Bureau Circulation Reports (2001-03).

* Approximate figures as exact figures are not mentioned in ABC Report.

REFERENCES

1. B.N. Ahuja (1993), *History of Press, Press Laws and Communications,* Surjeet Publications, p. 9.
2. Desai, A.R. (1993), "Social Background of Indian Nationalism (second edition)", Bombay: Popular Prakashan., p. 237.
3. K.S. Pandey, Sahu. R.N., "*The Press in India, Perspective in Development and Relevance,* Kanishka Publishers, New Delhi, p. 6.
4. *Second Press Commission Report,* Vol. I.
5. B.N.Ahuja (1993), *History of Press, Press Laws and Communications,* Surjeet Publications, p. 73.
6. B.N.Ahuja (1993), *History of Press, Press Laws and Communications,* Surjeet Publications, p. 73.
7. J. Natarajan (1995), *History of Indian Journalism,* Publications Division, Ministry of Information and Broadcasting, Government of India, p. 245.
8. Styles: Two popular styles were employed in Telugu Journalism. They were Simple and Classical styles. Simple style means the style that could be understood by even school boy. Classical means the style which is not easy to understand.
9. Pothuri Venkateswara Rao (2002), *History of Telugu Newspapers,* Kesava Memorial Educational Campus, Hyderabad.

10. *Press Information Bureau Reports*, 1992.
11. N. Bhaskara Rao, *Vidura*, Vol. 40, January-March, 2003, p. 35.
12. N. Bhaskara Rao, "Opportunities and Challenges", *Vidura*, Vol.40; January-March, 2003, p. 36.
13. N. Bhaskara Rao, "Opportunities and Challenges", *Vidura*, Vol.40; January-March, 2003, p. 36.
14. *Business India*, January 30–February 12, 1996.
15. *Registrar of Newspapers for India Report*, 1990-1996.
16. *Registrar of Newspapers for India Reports*, 1999 & 2000.
17. Viren Chabra, "A Technology Driven Industry", *Vidura*,Vol. 40, Jan-March, 2003, p. 31.
18. Registrar of Newspapers for India Report 2000.
19. Mahesh Vijapurkar, "Newspaper Readership up, says Study", *The Hindu*, Tuesday, June 18, 2002, p. 8.
20. N. Bhaskara Rao, "Opportunities and Challenges", *Vidura*, Vol.40; January-March, 2003, p. 37.
21. Baistow, T. (1985), *Fourth-Rate Estate: An Anatomy of Fleet Street*, London: Comedia Publishing Group.
22. "Newspaper Size Reduction", *Industrial Economist* (30 May-14 June 2002), p. 18.
23. *India Today*, August 3, 1991.
24. Chaturvedi, J.P. (1992), *The Indian Press at Crossroads*, New Delhi: Media Research Foundation.
25. *Registrar of Newspapers for India*, 2002-03 Report.
26. Krishna Murthy. D. (1996), " Media and Social Responsibility" Paper Presented at a Seminar held between February 3 and 5 at Osmania University, Hyderabad 1966; Parthasarathy, R. (1991), *History of Journalism in India*, New Delhi: Sterling Publishers.
27. Yadava, J.S. (1985), The Changing Social Role of the Indian Press, *Media Asia*, 12(3):111-119.
28. Lal Sham (May 22, 1994), "Marking Change", *Indian Express*, New Delhi.
29. Nayar, Kuldip (July 11, 1994), "Niminy-Piminy Press: The Fourth Estate has Deviated from Principles", *Indian Express*.
30. Shobha De (January, 1988). "The Glam Press", *Inkworld*, New Delhi.
31. D.V.R. Murthy (February, 2002), *Newspapers: It's a Credibility Question*.
32. *The Hindu*, June 23, 2002.

33. *India Today,* June 8 2002.

34. *Financial Express,* Wednesday, June 26, 2002, p. 13.

35. EFE Bureau, New Delhi, "Green Signal for FDI in Print Media Draws Mixed Reactions", *Financial Express,* Wednesday, June 26, 2002, p. 4

36. Nivedita Mookerji, "Print Media Opened to Foreign Funds", *Financial Express,* Sunday, June 30, 2002, p. 2.

37. Arthabodh Gangadhar Darbar, "Who is Afraid of FDI: No Fears for Opening up Print Media", *Financial Express,* Monday, July 1, 2002, p. 6.

38. P.N.Vijay, "Print Opens up Finally, no Longer Middle Classes Suffer Undemocratic Policies and Monopolies", *Financial Express,* Thursday, July 4, 2002, p. 6.

39. Subhash Agraval, "Foreign Media in India: Sensible, but are we Hyping up its impact", *Financial Express,* Thursday, July 4, 2002, p. 6.

40. Sumit Mitra, "Swadesi Times", *India Today,* December, 2001, p. 59.

41. PTI, New Delhi, "I&B ministry to Move Cabinet with Proposal on FDI in print", *Financial Express,* Friday, April 26, 2002, p. 14.

42. Anita Joshua, "Cabinet Clears 26 per cent FDI in Print Media", *The Hindu,* Wednesday, June 26, 2002, p.11.

43. INS Chief Pawar, "FDI will Wipe Out Newspapers", *The Hindu,* Monday, July 15, 2002, p. 6.

44. Sumit Mitra, "Swadesi Times", *India Today,* December 3, 2001, p. 59.

45. M.P.Veerendra Kumar, "Formula for Disaster", *The Week,* December 3, 2001, pp. 78-79.

46. UNI, "Committee says, no to FDI in Print Media", *The New Indian Express,* Saturday, March 23, 2002, p. 9.

47. The Hindu Special Correspondent, "Report Against FDI in Print Media tabled", *The Hindu,* Saturday, March 23, 2002, p. 13.

48. The Hindu Bureau, "Panel Against Foreign Investment in Newspapers", *Business line,* Saturday, March 23, 2002, p. 13.

49. PTI, "I&B Ministry to Move Cabinet with Proposal on FDI in Print", *Financial Express,* April 26, 2002, p. 14.

50. Eenadu Editorial, "Picchi Kudirindi", *Eenadu,* Thursday, June 27, 2002.

51. Sevanthi Ninan, "High Pitch", *The Hindu,* Sunday Magazine, June 30, 2002.

52. K.K.Katyal, "India and the Foreign Press", *The Hindu,* Thursday, July 2, 2002, p. 10.

53. The Hindu Special Correspondent, " Journalist Union Oppose FDI", *The Hindu,* Sunday, July 7, 2002, p. 11.

54. Nivedita Mookerji, " Print Media Opened to Foreign Funds", *Financial Express,* Sunday, June 30, 2002, p. 2.
55. Express Bureau, " Guidelines for FDI in News Category of Print Media", *Financial Express,* November 21, 2002.
56. *A&M Agency Report,* 1997.
57. Registrar of Newspapers for India (2002-03).
58. National Readership Survey 2000 by National Readership Studies Council, an Autonomous Division of Audit Bureau of Circulation, Mumbai.
59. Vanitia Kohli, "Regional Print", *Business World,* January 1, 2000, pp. 46-49.
60. *The Hindu* , Friday, September 20, 2002, p. 9.
61. National Readership Survey Council, September, 2002.
62. "World Association of Newspapers", *Businessline,* Tuesday, June 5, 2001, p. 6.
63. *The Hindu,* Wednesday, July 4th, 2001.
64. Registrar of Newspapers for India, 2002-03.
65. Indian Readership Survey, 2001.
66. Peter, S. Prichard, "The Only Mass buy Today is in Super Bowl", *The New Indian Express,* February 18, 2000.
67. Arun Jaitely : Union Minister for Law and Company Affairs in the Year 2000.
68. INS Convention 2000 held by Indian Newspaper Society, "Newspapers have to Concentrate on Credibility and Content", *Indian Express Newspapers* (Bombay) *Limited,* Sunday, September 17, 2000.
69. *Industrial Economist,* 30th September–14th October, 2000, p. 14.
70. N. Murali, "Newspapers must Imbibe New Technology", *The Hindu,* September 16, 2000.
71. V. Sangeeta, "CII Media Unconvention:too Little; too Much", *Industrial Economist,* 15-29 November, 2000, pp. 30-31.
72. N. Bhaskara Rao, "Opportunities and Challenges", *Vidura,* Vol. 40, Jan-March, 2003, p. 38.
73. The Hindu Newspaper Bureau, "Newspaper Industry must Imbibe New Technology", *The Hindu,* September 16, 2000.
74. Sevanthi Ninan-Eminent Media Columnist (*The Hindu).*
75. Aroon Purie-Chief Executive Officer, Living Media.
76. Vanita Kohli (2001), "It is time for cross media monopolies", *Business World,* 22nd January 2001, pp. 44-47.

77. B.N. Ahuja (1993), *History of Press, Press Laws and Communication,* Surjeet Publications, p. 204.

78. B.N. Ahuja (1993), *History of Press, Press Laws and Communication,* Surjeet Publications, p. 204.

79. B.K. Ahuja (1993), *History of Press, Press Laws and Communication,* Surjeet Publications, p. 205.

80. Sevanti Ninan (2002), "Do-gooders on the Net", *The Hindu,* Sunday, July 21, 2002, p. 3.

81. Sevanti Ninan (2001), "Radio Revolution", *The Hindu,* Sunday, November 18, 2001, p. 3.

82. Harsha Subramaniam (2002), "Resurgent Radio?" *Hindu Businessline, Catalyst Supplement,* Thursday, June 13, 2002, pp. 1-2.

83. Nitya Subramanian, "T.V.Channels use Radio for Promos", *The Hindu Businessline,* Wednesday, July 17, 2002, p. 1.

84. Reuters, "The Radios Back to Rock", *The Hindu Businessline,* Wednesday, July 10, 2002, p. 18.

85. Neel Chowdary, "Indian Media Generates Revenue by Beaming Internationsignal", *Financial Express,* Friday, June 21, 2002, p. 4 (Supplement).

86. INS, "INS Campaign to Promote Print", *Financial Express,* Monday, March 11, 2002.

87. *Industrial Economist* 30th May-14th July, 2002, p. 18.

88. *Business India,* October 21, 2000.

89. Doris A Graber (1994), *Media Power in Politics,* University of Illinois at Chicage, p. 37.

90. Kamla Bhasin, "Girl Child and the Role of the Media", Reprinted by J.S.Yadava, Pradeep Mathur (1998), *Issues in Mass Communication* Kanishka Publishers with IIMC.

91. B.N. Ahuja (1993), *History of Press, Press Laws and Communication,* Surjeet Publications, p. 143.

92. Vernacular Newspaper Report in Bihar and Orissa (Patna, 1914), p. 251.

93. Basnathi Sinha (1994), *Press and National Movement in India* (1911-1947), p. 4.

94. E.S. Isac (1998), *Fifty Years of Challenges,* A Presentation in the Conference on Christians in Journalism on January 14-16th, 1998, Chennai.

95. E.S. Isac (1998), *Fifty years of Challenges,* A presentation in the conference on Christians in Journalism on January 14-16th, 1998, Chennai.

96. Indian Institute of Mass Communication (1999) Report, *Media and Kargil War.*

97. E.S. Isac (1998), *Fifty Years of Challenges,* A Presentation in the Conference on Christians in Journalism on January 14-16th, 1998, Chennai.

98. Robin Jeffery (2000), *Indian Newspaper Revolution,* Oxford University Press, New Delhi, 2000.

99. Sevantininan (2001), "Unheard Voices of Reason", *The Hindu, Sunday Magazine,* October 28th, 2001, p. 3.

100. Sevantininan (2001), "Resorting to Hype", *The Hindu, Sunday Magazine,* December 23, 2001, p. 3.

101. Kamla Bhasin and Bin Agarwal (1984), *Women and Meida: Analysis, Alternatives and Action,* pp. 110-11.

102. Illa Pathak, "Ahemedabad's Battle Against the Media", Reprinted by Kamla Bhasin and Bin Agarwal (1984), *Women and Meida: Analysis, Alternatives and Action,* p. 76.

103. Press Trust of India (2002), "Women How Free, How Equal", *The Hindu Businessline,* Wednesday, August 6, 2002, p. 17.

104. Prabhat Patnaik (2002), "Market, Morals and The Media", *The Hindu,* Friday, July 5, 2002, p. 12.

105. Kalpana Sharma (2002), "Gujarat and Freedom of Press", *The Hindu,* April 9, Tuesday 2002, p. 3.

106. Sevantininan (2002), "Media on Rampage", *The Hindu, Sunday Magazine,* March 10, 2002, Media Pulse, p. 3.

107. Sevantininan (2002), "Media and Civil Society", *The Hindu,* March 31, 2002, *Sunday Magazine,* p. 3.

108. Arul Aram, I.(2002), "Children and Media", *The Hindu,* Tuesday, July 2, 2002, p. 17.

109. Amitisen (2002), "Tour Operators Blame Media for Scare Talk", *Financial Express,* Saturday, June 8, 2002, p. 14.

110. Press Trust of India (2002), "Women How Free, How Equal", *The Hindu Businessline,* Wednesday, August 6, 2002, p. 17.

111. Sevanthininan (2002), "Media Ethics", *The Hindu,* Sunday, April 28, 2002, Sunday magazine, p. 1.

112. Sevantininan (2002), "A Free Press", *The Hindu Sunday Magazine,* July 7, 2002, (Media pulse), p. 3.

113. Kalpana Sharma (2002), "Gujarat and Freedom of Press", *The Hindu,* Tuesday, April 9, 2002, p. 3.

114. Salzberg, Austria (2002), "Journalism as Public Trust", *Hindu Sunday Magazine*, April 28, 2002, p. 5.

115. B.N. Ahuja (1993), *History of Press, Press Laws and Communication,'* Surjeet Publications, p. 159.

116. Everette E. Dennis, *Reshaping Mass Media: Mass Communication in Information Age.*

117. Sevantininan, "Western overdrive", *The Hindu*, June 9, 2002, p. 10.

118. Bhatt, S.C. (2000), *Indian Press Since 1955*, Publications Division, Ministry of Broadcasting of India, p. 141.

119. Press Council of India, "Media must Guide to Nation", *The Hindu*, Friday, April 26, 2002, p. 11.

120. Hindu Special Correspondent (2002), "Press should Play the Role of Peace Maker", *The Hindu*, Friday, May 17, 2002, p. 13.

121. Balbir K. Punj (2002), "Media Fact and Fiction", *The New Indian Express*, Wednesday, May 15, 2002.

122. J. Natarajan (1995), *History of Indian Journalism*, Publication Division, Ministry of Information and Broadcasting, p. 244.

123. J. Natarajan (1995), *History of Indian Journalism*, Publication Division, Ministry of Information and Broadcasting, p. 244.

124. *Ibid.*, p. 244.

125. *Ibid.*, p. 245.

126. J. Natarajan (1995), *History of Indian Journalism*, Publication Division, Ministry of Information and Broadcasting, p. 245.

127. Pothuri Venkateswara Rao (2002), *History of Telugu Newspapers*, Kesava Memorial Educational Campus, Hyderabad.

3

Profile of Newspaper Organisations

Profile of Visakhapatnam City

Visakhapatnam is the second largest city in Andhra Pradesh. It is on the east coast of Andhra Pradesh with a major natural harbor and seashore. The city is unique in its beauty and landscape. The city is as old as mankind. However, its earlier history is not traced fully. The earliest reference to the name of Visakhapatnam was found in an inscription dated A.D. 1068 and it had come from Bhimeswara Temple from Draksharamam in East Godavari district. The local belief was that a king of Andhra in the IV century was going on a pilgrimage and stayed at Visakhapatnam for few days. Having been very much impressed by the scenic beauty of the place, he built there a temple for God 'Visakha'. Since the king was interested in some of his subjects, he constructed their houses around Visakha temple, soon it grew and emerged in to a big city. Since the city's name is after God Visakha, some people called the town as Visakhapatnam which was later registered in the government records.

Visakhapatnam was made the district headquarters under the British regime in 1803. Since the population of the town was considerably high, the British rulers upgraded the town to that of a Municipality in 1859. The town is rapidly growing and keeping in view the size, population, etc., of Visakhapatnam in 1981, it was made a Corporation.

There are different names to the city. Some people call it as Visakhapatnam. Some other shorten it to Vizag. In some quarters the city is called as port city. The youth call it as Steel City. During the British regime it was named as Waltair. The same was registered in the records of Indian Railways. Later it was changed as Visakhapatnam in the early 1990s of this century, due to political pressures. The dynamism of this city's growth in recent decades was such that late C. R. Reddy, the then Vice-Chancellor of Andhra University visualized it as "The City of Destiny" in 1921. The population was just 32,000 in 1871. The rate of increase in population has been rising enormously after independence, due to the national government industrial policy. As a result, several industrial units both large and small were set up both in formal and informal sectors. This resulted in the growth of population on account of migration from other districts of Andhra Pradesh and from other states of the country. As a result, the population which was a little over one lakh in 1951 has gone up to six lakhs in 1981. The same crossed the one million mark in the census survey of 1991. On average the population of Visakhapatnam City has grown at the rate of 5.2 per cent per annum during 1951 to 1981.

As already stated, Visakhapatnam is not only the second largest city in the state, it is also the city which contains a large number of key industrial units. There are about 20 major industries in the town. The Visakhapatnam port was built way back in 1933. The city has a vast hinterland comprising of Andhra Pradesh, Madhya Pradesh and Orissa states. In the early seventies, the outer harbor had been constructed to facilitate loading and export of iron-ore to other countries. In the early forties (1941), Hindusthan Shipyard had been established in Visakhapatnam. In 1956, Caltex the oil refinery was started. During the sixties several large, medium and small industries such as Bharat Heavy Plate and Vessels, Indian Oil Limited, Coromandal Fertilizers, Hindusthan Polymers, Hindusthan Zinc limited etc., were established both in the public and private sectors.

During the seventies, the major stress was on strengthening the defense with huge outlays on the Eastern Naval Command, Naval Dry Dock by the Director-General of Naval Projects. Extensive export of marine resources on the East Coast with Visakhapatnam as the base, gave a new dimension, contributing though in small way to the emancipation of the weaker section. Several industries were started to manufacture floating cranes, cement, marine communication equipment and a host of chemical, electrical and engineering goods. In the early eighties, the Government of India started the first phase of construction of one of the biggest integrated steel plants in the country with a massive outlay of over Rs. 4,000 crore in Visakhapatnam. This has a great impact on the structure and economic profile of the city. In the face of all these, the sample respondents employees, business people and professionals represent proportionately to a fair study.

Visakhapatnam is a fast growing industrial city. It has now a population of 13.2 lakhs approximately, with a growing literacy rate. The number of newspaper readers are also increasing enormously. Now, attention is being paid by the newspaper managements to attract the readers by improving both quality as well as the finished product, as readers now-a-days are more quality conscious than price conscious. As such, priority is being given to make use of the latest technology in printing and using qualitative newsprint.

Table–3. 1

BIG NEWSPAPERS PUBLISHED FROM VISAKHAPATNAM (1995)

Dailies	*Total Circulation*	*Local Circulation*
English		
The Hindu	4,97,650	20,196
Indian Express	3,87,426	13,772
Deccan Chronicle	1,24,176	2,012
Newstime	9,812	1,090
Telugu		
Andhra Jyothi	NA	17,822
Eenadu	5,46,478	64,228
Andhra Prabha	56,588	3,471
Andhra Bhoomi	NA	9,081

Source: Audit Bureau of Circulation Reports, 1995.

Organisational Profiles of Newspapers Published from Visakhapatnam City

Profile of *The Hindu* is a national daily, published simultaneously from ten centres, viz., Chennai, Coimbatore, Madurai, Bangalore, Hyderabad, Gurgoan, Visakhapatnam, Tiruvanathapuram, Cochin and Vijayawada. The paper is known for its seriousness and has a reputation for objectivity and credibility, in the coverage of news. It was the first to introduce a facsimile edition in the country while

Table–3.2
CIRCULATION (JULY-DECEMBER, 2001)

Name of Newspaper	*Publishing Centres*	*Circulation*
The Hindu	Chennai, Banglore, Coimbatore, Hyderabad, Kochi, Madhurai, New Delhi, Vijayawada, Tiruvananthpuram, Visakhapatnam.	9,04,654
The New Indian Express	Banglore, Manglore, Belgaum, Bhuvaneswar, Chennai, Coimbatore, Hyderabad, Kochi, Kozikode, Madurai, Shimoga, Vijayawada, Thiruvananthpuram, Visakhapatnam etc.	2,51,895
Deccan Chronicle	Hyderabad, Karimnagar, Rajahmundry, Vijayawada, Ananthpur, Visakhapatnam.	2,33,139
Andhra Bhoomi	Ananthpur, Visakhapatnam, Hyderabad, Karimnagar, Rajahmundry, Vijayawada.	65,869
Eenadu	Ananthpur, Cuddapah, Guntur, Hyderabad, Karimnagar, Kurnool, Nellore, Rajahmundry, Srikakulam, Suryapet, Tadepalligudem, Tirupati, Vijayawada, Visakhapatnam, Warangal.	8,41,890
Vaartha	Ananthpur, Cuddaph, Hyderabad, Kurnool, Rajahmundry, Nizamabad, Tirupati, Ongole, Vijayawada, Visakhapatnam, Warangal.	Under Consider-ation*

- The Circulation figures of Vaartha are Under Consideration by ABC. Vaarthas' Circulation in 2000 (Jul.-Dec.)is 2,81, 417 copies.
- Vaartha Circulation in Visakhapatnam District in 2000 is 22,114 copies. In Visakhapatnam City is 9,691 copies (ABC 2000, Jul.-Dec. figures).

Source: Audit Bureau of Circulation 2001 (Jul.-Dec.) figures.

Table–3.3
CIRCULATION OF SELECTED NEWSPAPERS IN VISAKHAPATNAM CITY IN 2003

Dailies	*Total circulation (India)*	*Circulation in Andhra Pradesh*	*Local Circulation (Visakhapatnam City)*
English			
The Times of India	14,49,828*	80,014	252
The Hindu	9,81,565	2,26,852	35,001
The New Indian Express	1,97,374**	33,000***	3,500***

(Contd.)

Dailies	*Total circulation (India)*	*Circulation in Andhra Pradesh*	*Local Circulation (Visakhapatnam City)*
Deccan Chronicle	3,42,053	3,42,053	12,793
Telugu			
Eenadu	9,56,088	9,26,182	48,320
Vartha	2,50,000***	2,50,000***	12,000***
Andhra Bhoomi	33,641	33,641	1,114
Andhra Prabha	15,000***	15,000***	500***

Source: Audit Bureau of Circulation Reports, 2003 (July-December).

* Except circulation figures of New Delhi, Chandigarh, Patna which are under consideration.

** These figures exclude Circulation in Andhra Pradesh. (The Circulation figures of Andhra Pradesh are not mentioned ABC Report).

*** Approximate Figures, as exact circulation figures are not mentioned in ABC Report.

launching its Coimbatore edition. *The Hindu* was also the first newspaper in the country in the early 60s to avail of a chartered plane service to reach its readers in far-flung areas. The saga of the development of the 'business' of *The Hindu* over 125 years of its existence has been one of having to continuously strike a fine balance between two seemingly competing considerations – the public mission or larger societal purpose encompassing the credible information providing, educational, opinion building and watchdog role of *The Hindu*, the newspaper, versus the commerce part of conducting its operation as business. Throughout the first quarter century of its history, fired by the ideals and public spiritedness of its six young founders and reflecting the times, the newspaper was run primarily as a public mission, without too much concern for commercial considerations. Like the other native papers of that era, *The Hindu* has to struggle its way through vicissitudes. Starting as a weekly in 1878 and subsequently becoming triedly, it turned into a daily in 1889. The great partnership between G. Subramania Ayer and M. Veeraraghavachariar which gave birth to *The Hindu* in 1878 had nurtured and sustained it through a long period of struggle and conflict, broke up in October 1898. Its circulation was barely 800 copies. In 1901, one of its founders and then its sole proprietor, M.Veeraraghavachariar, failed in his attempt to make *The Hindu* a limited company by inviting public subscription for Rs.1,20,000 in order to give the paper stability and strength as well as permanent footing. On 1st April, 1905, *The Hindu* was taken over by S. Kasturiranga Iyengar and for the last four generations the paper remained in the family. All the top executive positions are held by the members of the family. In 1905, Kasturi Ranga Iyengar died. In 1923, the circulation of *The Hindu* was 17,000 copies with good advertising support and it had already become a force to reckon with, Kasturi Ranga Iyenger had also installed the first Rotary printing press in South India and modern linotype composing machines. *The Hindu* was a pioneer in newspaper technology even then, *The Hindu* continued to progress. Run by a partnership firm of Kasturi Srinivasan and Kasturi Gopalan, the sons of Kasturi Iyenger, it was converted to a private limited company in 1959 when debentures and redeemable preference shares were issued to finance its modernization. These were redeemed in due course and Kasturi and sons limited, the company publishing *The Hindu* and its sister publications, became a totally family owned company. *The Hindu* launched the Visakhapatnam edition on May 10th, 1990. At the same time of launching this edition, The Hindu wrote:

> "In addition to its comprehensive coverage of national and International news, *The Hindu* will provide from its new base more extensive reportage of news on the political, economic, social and cultural activities in the different districts and regions of the state."

Table–3.4

CIRCULATION OF THE HINDU FROM 1878-2003

Year	*Number of copies*	*Per cent of Growth*
1978	80	–
1911	5,000	615. 0
1938	31,000	520. 0
1958	84,000	171. 0
1978	2,81,000	234. 5
1988	4,24,000	50. 9
1998	6,97,000	64. 4
2003	9,33,000	33. 9

Source: Audit Bureau of Circulation figures (1878-2003).

Table-3.5
CIRCULATION OF THE HINDU IN STATE AND CITY IN 1997-2001

Period	*Circulation (Andhra)*	*City (Visakhapatnam)*
January-June 2001	26,815	27,804
January-December 2000	15,449	19,452
January-June 1999	10,549	13,963
January-December 1998	11,524	14,029
January-December 1997	11,334	13,418

Source: Audit Bureau of Circulation Reports (1997-2001).

- Product mix of *The Hindu* group are: *The Hindu, The Hindu Business-line, The Hindu* International edition, *Sport Star, Frontline, Survey of Indian Industry,* Survey of Indian Agriculture, Survey of Indian Cricket. As on June 2001, *The Hindu* circulation crossed five lakh.

Contents of The Hindu: Description of the Main Edition

Local News: It gives happenings of the city, advertisements in relation to the city regarding educational institutions, shopping, weather forecasts of the city, list of various engagements in city and a special column by 'name around the city' is present containing various welfare activities, medical camps, awards etc. in relation to the city.

Regional News: It gives district-wise presentation of happenings, a column containing a brief coverage of various aspects called 'Briefly', Regional appointments.

State News: It covers news from mainly the southern states Tamilnadu, Karnataka, Kerala. It occupies about one to two pages depending on the news.

National News: It gives information regarding political happenings, social events, Government policies and decisions. This day that age, *The Hindu* crossword, a complete guide for Radio and Television, Classifieds mart-appointments, Letters to the editor, Tenders etc.

International News: It covers in-depth news from around the world, pictoral coverage of latest happenings etc. It consists of an important column called Globe Scan. Two pages are generally allotted to cover this news.

Business News: It gives Corporate news, Stocks, Finance, Share India, Commodities, A column by name 'barometer' consisting of

Bombay stock exchange, exchange rates and bullion rates. It consists of one column known as 'Monitor' consisting of recent business changes.

Sports News: *The Hindu* newspaper give wide and exclusive coverage, in-depth analysis about national, regional and International news. It covers news about Cricket, Tennis, Bridge, Snooker, Golf, Billiards, Football, Racing, Athletics, Hockey, Chess, Squash, Basketball, Weightlifting and so on. Three pages are allotted daily to the sports news. Photographs of all sports are taken up by their own team of photographers.

Along with all this, the main paper also consists of tenders, advertisements, national weather forecast, readers mail, death column, daily entertainments and engagements, notifications, digest column which acts as an index for readers to go through the news they are interested in. Cartoon by Keshav, a special page which highlights the life of Hyderabad. Announcements, religion news, consumer notes, campus notes etc. are also there in *The Hindu*.

Description of Supplements: *The Hindu* main edition is accompanied with a supplement on all the weekdays. The supplements are printed keeping in view different areas of interest, different categories of people and different age groups. The supplements are:

Monday

- *(i)* *Monday mart:* This is a special feature about scientific industries (in Chennai only),
- *(ii)* *Metro Plus* a four page feature supplement focused on features relating to the city, and
- *(iii)* An exclusive feature on your city (in Chennai, Banglore, Hyderabad, Delhi and Tiruvanantapuram).

Tuesday

Open page, Education and Book review: It consist one of the most popular of Review of the latest literature, articles on education, special reports. One of the most popular features appearing in Tuesday supplement is 'Know Your English'.

Wednesday

- *(i)* *Opportunities:* It acts as a guide to better positions and better performance. It consists of focus which gives in-depth details about a particular field like technical, business, literature, fine arts etc., helps the readers to know the prospects of that particular field. It helps them in planning their career,

(ii) *Job columns:* These are the advertisements based on functional segments. This makes it easy for the unemployees to search for job opportunities related to their functional segment. The various segments are General, Marketing/Sales, Overseas, Information Technology, Engineering/Production/Technology, and

(iii) *FAQS:* This is the question and answers column where a suitable career guidance is given depending on the questions posed. This helps to open the knots of trouble some issues regarding the readers' career.

Thursday

(i) *Business/Science:* This part of the supplements is related to science that is helpful in business, the various scientific aspects that have been developed recently in business. This contributes to the knowledge of not only to the business people but also to the common man. Various aspects covered are Net speak, Out of the box, New products which help the companies in developing the market for their new products, questions and answers, and

(ii) *Science/Technology:* This is the other part of the supplement which gives knowledge about the recent development in the field of science and technology which is helpful to all categories of and age groups of people. This part makes itself attractive by giving photo features of various scientific events. Various columns presented are Hotline, Question corner, Mediline, Agriculture, Farmers notebook, etc.

Friday

Friday review is a special guide on entertainment. It consists of Cinema, T.V, Film highlights, On location, Radio review, Heritage, TV highlights/The week ahead etc.

Saturday

Young world supplement consists of Kitty corner which contains cartoons and Kaleidoscope, Events, Voices, Forsaken friend, Animal time, Crayon corner, Funtrack, Quiz time, News scan, Word squares, Jumble for kids, Quest, School zone, Sports special, Letter to the editor, What's on this week.

Sunday

Sunday magazine supplement which is a weekend colour newspaper for the entire family consists of Art, Experience, Review, Celebrity watch, *The Hindu* cross word, Bridge, Astro-focus, Health watch, Literary review, First impression, Eye catchers, Social history, Preview of movies, Sociology, Classifieds, Matrimonial, Automotive, Business offers, Educational, Sunday mart, Situation vacant, Real estates, Rental etc. Recently a feature that is added to this is 'world of women.'

Brief Description of The Hindu

The most popular newspaper in South India and first go to International, *The Hindu* enjoys the second largest readership in India after *The Times of India* with 9,33,000 readers in the year 2003. The newspaper is regarded as the national newspaper and carries the inherent drawback of not catering to the local news as it covers the national news. The decisions taken are all centralized. The marketing staff is highly qualified and professional in their approach. A bulky newspaper, it is generally preferred by the older generations and people who have a flair for professionalism. It is also regarded as the paper for the well off.

The Constituents of the Newspaper are in the Following Percentages:

News	57. 56
Information	02. 94
Advertisements	37. 81
Entertainment	01. 68

Source: The newspaper has an awareness of 60 per cent.

In a 24 pages issue the *page layout* is as follows:

Page 1: Consists of 2/3 of National news and remaining 1/3 of main sheet consists of local news which is different in different editions.

Page 2: Consists of 'Life' and advertisements.

Page 3: Consists of more Local news (District news and City news in district and city editions respectively).

Page 4: Consists of State news.

Page 5: Consists of Local news.

Page 6:	Consists of Southern States News i.e., Tamil, Karnataka, Kerala, Andhra Pradesh.
Page 7:	Consists of News from States.
Page 8:	Consists of Television and Radio programmes, 'Variety', Religious news.
Page 9:	Consists of Hindu crossword puzzle which is very popular.
Page 10:	Consists of Editorial news.
Pages 11-12:	Consists of National and International news.
Page 13:	Consists of National news.
Page 14:	Consists of International news.
Page 15:	Consists of Business news.
Page 16:	Consists of the feature 'Markets' contains stock exchange information.
Pages 17, 18 &19:	Consists of Sports Information.
Page 20:	Featured 'Land scope' consists of some interesting photographs.
Pages 21-24 :	Consists of supplements which cover different types of news on different days.

Pricing Policy Adopted by The Hindu

The Hindu had been enjoying monopoly till the end of the year 2000. Until then, there was no competitor for it in South India. But in late 2000, *The Times of India* tried to capture the South Indian market with its market penetration strategy. *The Times of India* has charged very low price on its paper, one can say the price is nominal. *The Hindu*, one of the leading newspapers in South India, has always kept an eye on its competitors activities. Due to this forethought, *The Hindu* has not given any chance for the competitor to skim into the market. As soon as *The Times of India* entered the South Indian market, *The Hindu*, has itself shifted from cost-plus pricing to competitive pricing. *The Hindu* has adopted this policy to withstand itself in the market. In this competitive pricing strategy, the price of *The Hindu* newspaper is fixed keeping in view *The Times of India*. Due to this, *The Hindu* has drastically decreased its price. Though, The Times of India adopted market penetration strategy, it has failed in its effort.

The Hindu however had an increase in the number of subscribers. *The Hindu* group is thus a centrally controlled organization. All its Publications are edited by the members of the family who are also the members of the Board of Directors and they also undertake the responsibility of policy formulation for the entire organization. The branch offices are under the control of the Head Office and have merely to execute the policies and plans formulated by the Head Office.[2]

Profile of Vaartha

Vaartha is the latest newspaper that has entered into the market. Before the initial release of the paper there was huge promotion and is presently occupying the second position. The newspaper is a division of the Sanghi group which itself has a high industrial presence. The investment is huge when compared to the other newspapers but has not achieved the intended goals. The newspaper is deficient in the aspects of the newsprint quality and printing. The marketing activities are also not professional in nature. The newspaper is presently publishing a Hindi newspaper also by the same name *Vaartha*. If the present trend of Vaartha continues an English newspaper from the same organisation would not be a surprise.

The constituents of the newspapers are in the following percentage:

News: 78.97, Information: 05.11, Advertisements: 14.20, Entertainment: 01.70.

The newspaper has awareness of 60 per cent.

Vaartha one of the upcoming Telugu newspapers was started on February 1st, 1996. The founder of the organization is Girish Sanghi. He is the Chairman and Managing Director of the Company. *Vaartha* stands next to Eenadu in Telugu newspaper industry in Andhra Pradesh. *Vaartha* covers Visakhapatnam, Hyderabad, Vijayawada, Rajahmundary, Cuddapah, Ongole, Nizamabad, Warangal, Tirupati, Ananthpur, Kurnool and Karimnagar. Apart from these areas in Andhra Pradesh *Vaartha* also covers Bhubaneswar in Orissa. Despite heavy competition from *Eenadu* and other newspapers this newspaper still has a favourable image in the minds of the public.

Organisational Structure of *The Hindu*
Branch Office (Visakhapatnam)

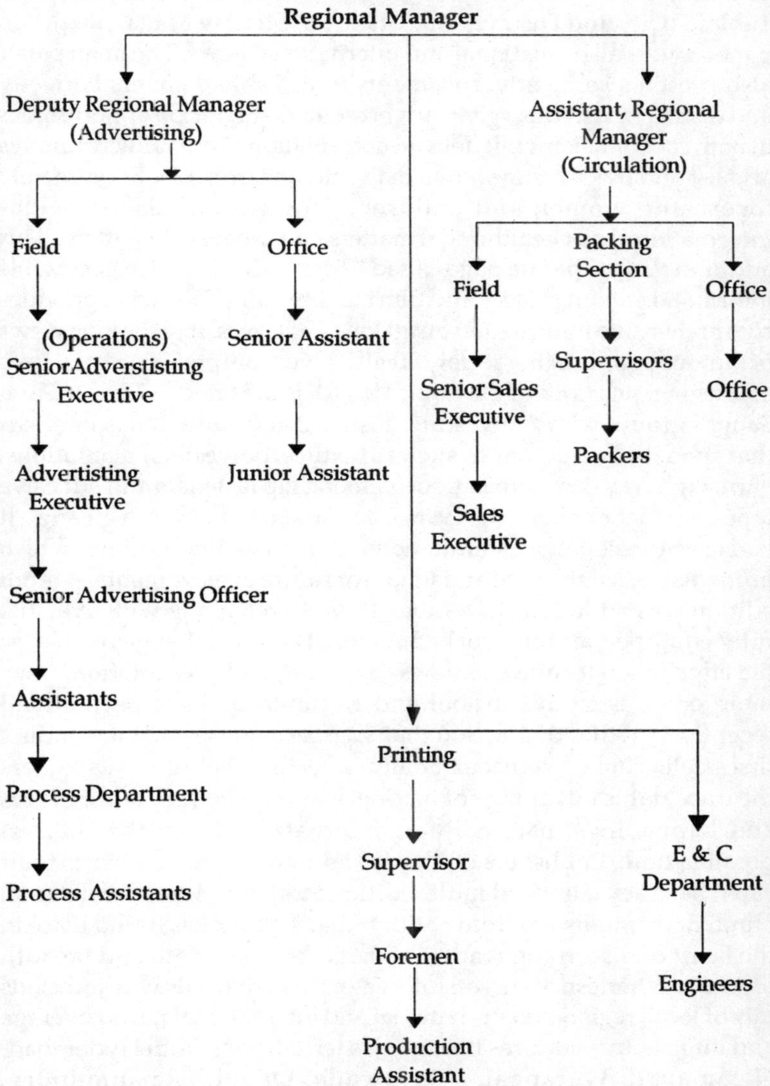

Source: Organisational Manuals of *The Hindu*.

Product of the Company

The newspaper has the following divisions. *(i)* Main paper, *(ii)* Tabloid (City and District), *(iii)* Cheli, *(iv)* Sunday Magazine. Main paper covers all the national and international news. The main paper also presents some advertisements in it. Tabloid covers both city and district news. It also gives advertisements about job opportunities in both city and district. It delivers information about railway timings and list of movies being shown in the city theatres. Cheli completely focuses on women and children. This edition also provides information about health, legal matters and other such matters. This addition has a separate page called "Tera" where we can get sizable information about movies and film stars. Sunday magazine provides comprehensive information on all kinds of topics. It gives interviews of famous people in the society. It also gives comprehensive analysis of burning questions of the hour. *Vaartha* is the brainchild of, a Gaint Sanghi group, whose investment is Rs. 2,400 crore. It has interests that span diverse activities such as textiles, polyesters, plantations, yarn, high way communications, cement, zip fasteners and adhesive tapes. In fact in February 1996, *Vaartha* started off with a bang. It had an unprecedented simultaneous launch of nine editions, which immediately set the tone and tenor for future achievements. A tenth edition was added in November 1997, which along with over 100 fully equipped and networked regional centres, that gave *Vaartha* the edge when it comes to news gathering and presentation. Two more editions from Kurnool and Karimnagar have been added recently. Another distinction that *Vaartha* enjoys is that it is India's first satellite linked vernacular daily. A feature that allows its readers the unbeatable advantage of having access to the very latest events and happenings, nationally or internationally, in the shortest possible time. Publishers of *Vaartha* added another feather to their cap when they launched multi-edition *Swatantra Vaartha* a national Hindi daily published from South India. *Vaartha* has found place in the heart of discerning readers right across the length and breadth of Andhra Pradesh. It successfully caters to their needs with judicious mix of local, regional, state, national and international news coverage and informative features through it's ten editions from Hyderabad, Nizamabad, Warangal, Vijayawada, Ongole, Rajahmundry, Visakhapatnam, Cuddapah, Tirupathi and Ananthpur. Two more are on the anvil, Kurnool and Karimnagar which will add to the strength. The network of multi location printing centres, which is linked to over 100 regional offices via satellite, is *Vaartha's* major strength. Tabloids containing local news pertaining to each of the 22 districts from part of everyone of the editions, apart from eight main pages of news and a four page feature in colour. Moreover, three city editions each for Hyderabad, Vijayawada and Visakhapatnam with ten zonal editions are instrumental in fulfilling the need to focus on locality specific issues and topics. In response to the demands of the Telugu reading population residing in the adjoining districts of Karnataka and Tamilnadu, *Vaartha* also comes out with two interstate editions especially for this segment. *Vaartha's* bouquet of features includes: 'Cheli' – A woman's best friend. This everyday feature provides her with everything that would allow her to be the best she can. Important issues that affect women are covered along with a plethora of special interest information, personality development, beauty secrets, recipes, household tips, child care, fashion, career, success stories and so on. In short, *Cheli* offers the inspiration and motivation for women to emerge from shadows.

Mogga

This is where young talent is spotted and encouraged. Young and budding writers are encouraged to write stories, articles and personal experiences. The feature includes everything of interest for the all round growth of a child; puzzles, general knowledge, art, sports, science, history, places and personalities.

Naadi

A daily feature that is devoted to health and medicare. Here information can be gleamed about the various advances being made in the medical world, research being conducted for finding cures, articles by experts on common health problems, guidance on how to stay fit and take care of the body and responses to readers' queries on various health related issues. Alternate medicines like Unani, Ayurveda, Naturopathy, Acupuncture get equal importance.

Tera

Daily curtain rises on the exciting, glamorous world of films. Everyday of the week exclusive interviews, shooting news, sneak previews, reviews, and hottest gossip to do with films it will finds its way into the pages of *Tera*. A spicy masala mix of entertainment to rival and celluloid production.

Palle

A weekly column that focuses on agricultural and rural issues, possibly a first for any newspaper in the country. Horticulture, flori, pisci, sericultures, cottage and rural industries are covered, analysed and tips offered to improve performance. Finally, this vital but often ignored sector gets the right importance it deserves.

Vanijya Vartha

The world of business and finance is comprehensively covered in this daily two page section. Corporate news, information, interviews, in depth analysis of stock market trends, policy matters, new issues etc. A virtual workout for those who believe in fiscal fitness.

Vruthi

For those looking for a bright future, 'Vruthi' provides the right direction. It offers youth the opportunity for all round development of their personality through effective counselling on education, career prospects, general knowledge, competitive exams and necessary guidance. Indeed young readers are given confidence to face the challenges of tomorrow.

Aata

Sports coverage was never so exhaustive or informative. Action from all over the world is brought home to the sports enthusiasts together with interviews, comments, articles and excellent photographs. No wonder *Vaartha* readers always have their eyes on the ball and keep track of all events on the playing fields.

Aadhyatmicam

A much needed feature in today's world of increasing religious intolerance. It promotes unity and upholding of values with inspired writings of prominent religious leaders cutting across communal lines. Perhaps nobody looks forward to Sundays more than *Vaartha* readers. A special 48 page colour supplement keeps the entire family glued till it is read from cover to cover. *Vaartha* broke new ground in harnessing this all-pervasive technology. It has the distinction of being the first Telugu daily to have Internet edition that has proved to be a boon to the homesick Non-Resident Indians who eagerly await for news from back home. The Vaartha internet edition has more than 300 pages of news from India and particularly from all districts of Andhra Pradesh. Updated every half-an-hour, the internet edition is a veritable gold mine of the latest information and events.

Organisational Structure of *Vaartha* Branch Office (Visakhapatnam)

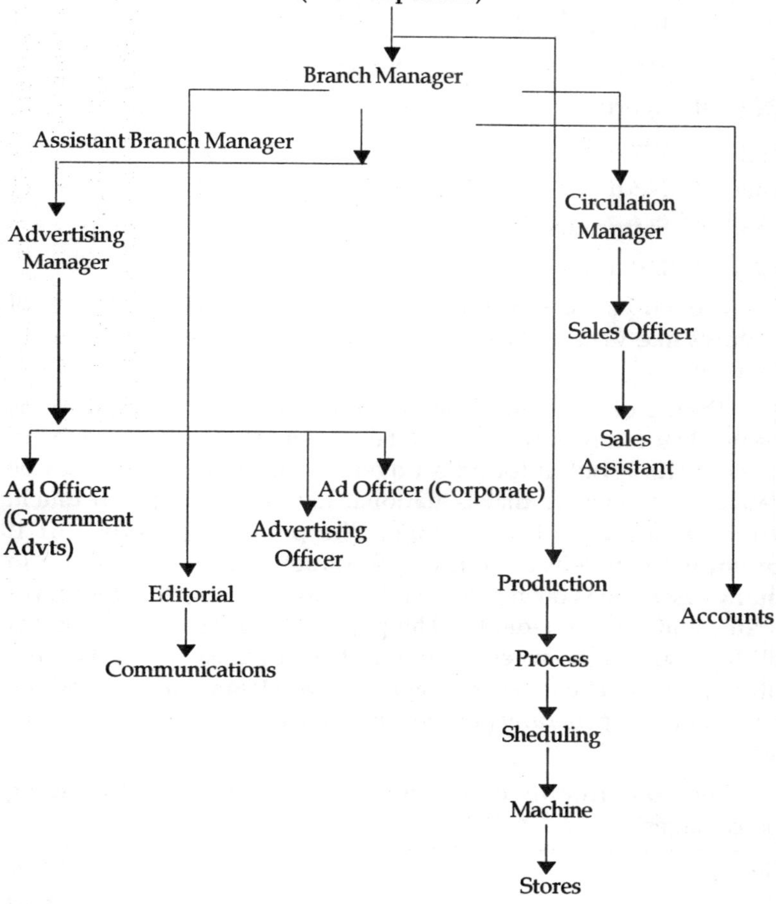

Vaartha: Layout of newspaper:

Page 1: International, National, Regional (General)

Page 2: State, National

Page 3: National

Page 4: Editorial, State

Page 5: State, Regional

Page 6: National and State news

Page 7: Business news

Page 8: International

Page 9: State news

Page 10: Sports

Page 11: Cheli, Mogga

Page 12: Nadi

Page 13: State news

Page 14: Entertainment

Tabloid consists of Local and Regional news. It consists of features like Vruthi, Raitu, Srama and also gives news relating to local sports.[3]

Profile of *The New Indian Express:The New Indian Express* is probably the only newspaper that does not enjoy a high readership or circulation but is found all over India. In one way it can be called a newspaper that is national having the regional touch, which is an added advantage. The paper is popular for it promptness in delivering frank, sensational flash news. Also in many cases, it has been responsible for the investigators reports of scams and other incidents. The paper publishes colour editions all throughout the week. The number of pages is less than the other papers. The marketing activities are team oriented and the customers are generally people who have migrated from the other states.

The constituents of the newspaper are in the following percentages:

News	57. 97
Information	04. 63
Advertisements	35. 36
Entertainment	02. 02

The Newspaper has an awareness of 40 per cent.

History of the Organisation

The New Indian Express (NIE) is the single largest chain of newspaper in India, published from 19 centres viz., Ahmedabad, Baroda, Banglore, Belgaum, Bhubaneswar, Chandigarh, Coimbatore, Delhi, Hyderabad, Cochin, Kozikode, Chennai,

Maduri, Mumbai, Nagpur, Pune, Thiruvananthapuram, Vijayawada and Visakhapatnam. *Indian Express (The New Indian Express* previously called as *Indian Express*)[4] is owned by Ramnath Goenka who was the first to start a chain of newspapers in India known as 'Express Group' of newspapers. With the death of Ramnath Goenka in 1991, his two grandsons Vivek Goenka and Manoj Kumar Sonthalia shared the ownership of the paper. *Indian Express* was found in 1931 by P. Varadarajulu at Chennai and was later taken over by S. Sadanand of the free press journal. When Sadanand was unable to run the newspaper on account of financial problems, he sold the paper to Ramnath Goenka. Throughout the freedom struggle, *Indian Express* played a key role in disseminating news about the national struggle. K.Swaminathan was the first editor of the newspaper between 1932 and 1939. Later, he was succeeded by G. Ramachandran who served the paper as its editor from 1945-47. Goenka put forth all his energies in making the paper one of the finest dailies. Prominent editors such as Khasa Subba Rao, Pothan Joseph, J. Natarajan, Prem Bhatia, H.Y.Sharada Prasad and S. Mulgoankar worked for the paper and shaped it to earn a prominent place among the English dailies in the country. The Visakhapatnam edition of *Indian Express* was launched in 1984 with the aim of reaching the readers in Visakhapatnam and the neighbouring state, Orissa. At present, the editor of the paper is Shekar Gupta. *The New Indian Express* holds the second place in circulation in all its publication centres. It had a net circulation of over five lakhs by the end of December 1995. Today, *Indian Express* group has printing facilities at 19 publishing centres across India, bringing out 29 Publications (dailies, weeklies, fortnightly, monthlies and quarterlies) in five languages English, Hindi, Marahi, Gujarati and Tamil. It has over 50 branch offices spread throughout the length and breadth of India, more than any publishing group in India. *Indian Express* group has led the way when it comes to addressing social problems such as loneliness of the aged, the problem of dowry, the evil of female feticide, Aids awareness etc.

Readership and Circulation

Circulation and readership are very important for a paper. Higher circulation and readership signify the popularity of the paper. It indirectly indicates the standard of the paper in view of the readers. Higher circulation naturally attracts the advertisers though the rates are higher than other papers. The following figures give us an idea about the readership and circulation of different papers and *The New Indian Express* in different sources. The figures are compiled from corporate office of Chennai.

In the survey conducted it is found that many of the earlier clients of *The New Indian Express* have shifted to other papers. They complain that the standard of the paper is not the same as before. At the same time they say that the Editorial has its own image and is very good.

From the above figures it can be seen that *The New Indian Express* has a decline in readership while its competitor, *The Hindu* has a one per cent increase. The highest growth rate is *Eenadu,* which has the highest circulation in Andhra Pradesh. The other publication of Express (Madurai) group *Andhra Prabha* has a growth rate of 40 per cent. The decrease in growth rate of readership implies that the readers' interest in the paper is coming down.

Comparing the above figures it is found that *Eenadu* has highest circulation. The figures show that the circulation has come down significantly. It has come down by 60 per cent.

The New Indian Express Newspaper Layout.

18 *Page Issue*

Page 1	General (International, National, Regional news)
Page 2	Leisure (TV Information and Horoscope etc.)
Page 3	Local news.
Page 4	Local news
Page 5	State/region
Page 6	State
Page 7	Nation
Page 8	Tenders
Page 9	Nation
Page 10	Editorial
Page 1	General (International, National, Regional news)
Page 11	Turn page
Page 12	Ads/ Tenders/ National news.
Page 13	World news.

***The New Indian Express:* Organisational Structure (Visakhapatnam Branch)**

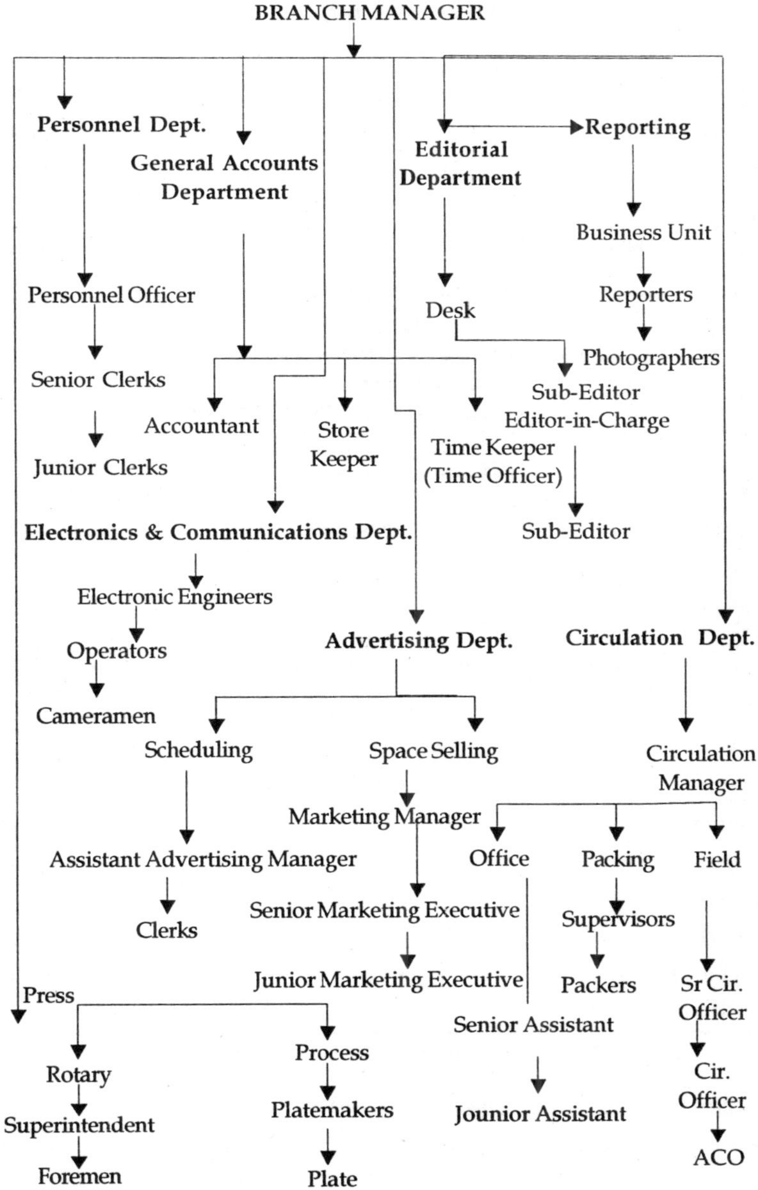

Table–3.6

COMPARISON OF READERSHIP OF THE NEW INDIAN EXPRESS WITH OTHER NEWSPAPERS (2000)

(Fig in 000's), (All adults)

	NRS 97	*NRS 99*	*Growth*
The New Indian Express	281	275	-2.13
The Hindu	450	455	1.09
Deccan Chronicle	728	864	30.20
Eenadu	4096	8199	100.00
Andhra Prabha	344	483	40.40

Source: National Readership Survey Reports (1997-99).

Table–3.7

COMPARISON OF CIRCULATION OF THE NEW INDIAN EXPRESS WITH OTHER NEWSPAPERS (1999-2000)

	Circulation July-Dec. 99	*Readership (in 000's)*
The New Indian Express	3,10,786	1,695
The Hindu	7,20,549	2,328
Deccan Chronicle	1,39,057	864
Eenadu	24,147	483
Andhra Prabha	8,06,109	8,355

Source: Audit Bureau of Circulation, (1999), National Readership Survey, 2000.

Table–3.8

READERSHIP FIGURES OF THE NEW INDIAN EXPRESS IN VISAKHAPATNAM FROM (1997-99)

January-June 97	16,041
July-December 97	11,880
January-June 98	12,312
July-December 98	12,331
January-June 99	11,841
July-December 99	6,924

Source: National Readership Survey by NRSC. (1997-99).

Page 14 Market news.

Page 15 Market news.

Page 16	Tender
Page 17,18	Sports news.

16 Page Issue

Page 1	General (International, National, Regional News)
Page 2	Leisure (TV Information and Horoscope etc.)
Page 3	City news.
Page 4	City / regional news
Page 5	State news
Page 6	Tenders
Page 7	National/ city news.
Page 8	Editorial news.
Page 9	Turn Page (National or international)
Page 10	Advertisements, National news.
Page 11	International news.
Page 12	Ads/ Tenders/ National news.
Page 13	World business news.
Page 14	News relating to Travel.
Pages 15-16	Sports news.

(i) *Supplements:* Sunday Express consists of Sunday magazine, sports, leisure. It covers sports, cinema etc. Art include books, literature, 'then and now', insight living etc.

(ii) Monday consists of excel which related to education, opportunities columns etc.

(iii) *Tuesday:* It produces supplements called Health and Women Life at alternative weeks. Women life consists of fashion, home and away, health parenting etc.

(iv) *Wednesday:* Consist of science express supplement which consists of information relating various sciences like Physics, Chemistry, Botany, Zoology etc.

(v) *Friday's:* Supplement name is Youth Express which contain news relating to youth, teenagers fashions, preferences etc.

Profile of Andhra Prabha

Originally it was a Telugu paper belonged to *The New Indian Express* group, Chennai. But on September 16th, 2002, it was taken over by the Vasavi group of companies with its chairman Muttha Gopalakrishna. Andhra Prabha is now being published from Hyderabad, Vijayawada and Visakhapatnam, would start editions in Rajahmundry, Tirupati and Karimnagar initially and in Guntur, Kurnool, Ananthpur and Nalgonda towns later. Andhra Prabha publishes local, national and international news. There is a separate edition called Nagara Prabha everyday for cities and for each district there is separate tabloid which cover local news (News from that particular district). Sundays it has come out with Sunday Andhra Prabha consisting of Kadambam, Viseshalu etc.

Layout

Page 1	National, International
Pages 2, 3	Regional
Page 4	Editorial
Page 5	National
Page 6	State news
Pages 7, 8	Business news
Page 9	Sports
Page 10	Cinema

Description of Deccan Chronicle and Andhra Bhoomi

The *Deccan Chronicle* was established in Hyderabad in the year 1938. It was initially started as a local newspaper but soon become a very popular regional newspaper in Andhra Pradesh. C. K. Rajgopal, a businessman by profession started it and was managed by his sons. In 1971, the management changed hands. It was taken over by industrialist turned politician, T. Chandrasekhar Reddy who became the Chairman of Deccan Chronicle group and started divisions in other prominent cities also. In Visakhapatnam it was started in 1985, in Vijayawada in 1992 and in Rajahmundry in 1994. The *Andhra Bhoomi* also ran parallel to the *Deccan Chronicle.* It was started in Hyderabad in 1968. In Visakhapatnam it was started in 1985, Vijayawada in 1992 and Rajahmundry in the year 1994. The initial investment for the Visakhapatnam unit was about rupees six crore. The capacity of the press was high. The machines had the capability of printing 40,000 copies per hour and 30,000 copies per hour respectively. The circulation in the initial stages was 38,000 copies of *Andhra Bhoomi* and 5,000 copies of *Deccan Chronicle.* The work force was about 232 employees. The initial number of agencies were 184. The various departments in the organizations were:

(i) Editorial Department,
(ii) Advertising Department,
(iii) Computer Section,
(iv) Camera Section,
(v) Routing Section,
(vi) Page making Section,
(vii) Plate making Section,
(viii) Packing Section,
(ix) Dispatch Section,
(x) Marketing Department ,
(xi) Account Department,
(xii) Security.

Due to the improvements in the technology and the need for faster delivery of news, some sections had nothing significant to do and hence disappeared:

Deccan Chronicle has become a family member to most of the people living in and around Hyderabad. The paper enjoys a total monopoly as far as the circulation in Andhra Pradesh is concerned. Established in 1938 it has gone a long way by upgrading its technology and features provided in the newspaper that gives features that are very close to the lives of the various sections of the society. The marketing activities are target oriented and effort is team oriented. The paper has to do justice to the regional role that it is playing. The constituents of the newspaper are in the following percentages:

News	48. 55
Information	03. 36
Advertisements	46. 15
Entertainment	01. 92

The newspaper has an awareness of 20 per cent.

Andhra Bhoomi newspaper is the sister concern of Deccan *Chronicle*. It is the first newspaper that had once got an edge over the other newspaper due to its rural coverage. The newspaper enjoys the third position among the urban population and second position in the rural areas. The newspaper is simultaneously publishing weekly and monthly magazines also. There have been instances when the paper increased readership due to coverage of the election reports, politics etc. The marketing activities are generally seen in the semi-urban and rural areas. The paper has separate local supplements for each and every district. The average net paid circulation of *Deccan Chronicle,* the largest circulated English newspapers in Andhra Pradesh, grew by over 83,600 in the January-June, 2004 over the same period of 2003. An Audit Bureau of Circulation,[7] report certifies that *Deccan Chronicle* had an average net paid circulation of 3,80,093 copies during the corresponding period of 2003, an increase of 83,663 copies. The growth over July-December 2003 was 38,040 copies, when the average net paid circulation was 3,42,053. The National Readership Survey has certified *Deccan Chronicle* as the fifth largest read English newspaper in the country.[8]

The constituents of the newspaper are in the following percentages:

News	75. 86
Information	06. 00
Advertisements	15. 86
Entertainment	02. 28

The newspaper has an awareness of 50 per cent.

Monday, Tuesday, Wednesday, Thursday the *Andhra Bhoomi* come out with Priyadarshini supplement. On Fridays the supplement published is Vennela. Saturdays along with that Priyadarshini supplement Sadhana supplement is also published by Deccan Chronicle group. Sundays along with Priyadarshini Sunday magazine is being published. Visakhaptnam *Andhra Bhoomi* contain four district supplements. They are Visakhapatnam city, Visakhapatnam district, Srikakulam, Vijayanagaram. The district supplements consist of eight pages. Sadhana magazine is related to education. It consists of study material, guidance for learners, world round up etc. Tabloids consist of local news, local advertising etc. Sunday magazine consist of cover stories, real stories, astrological information, crime stories, expert advice etc. Vennela consist of entertainment news, cinema news etc. Priyadarshini consist of women issues, fashions, style, preference, puzzles for children, entertainment, jokes, study materials, literature, cartoons etc.

Layout of Deccan Chronicle

Page1 Consist of National and International news.

Page 2	Consist of National news.
Page 3	Consist of Editorial
Page 4	Consist of State news.
Page 5	Consist of International news.
Page 6	Consist of Business news.
Page 7	Consist of State news.
Page 8	Consist of Sports news.

Marketing of Deccan Chronicle and Andhra Bhoomi

Product: The product from the newspaper industry is the newspaper, which itself carries features like news, information, advertisements and entertainment. Each newspaper covers these four important aspects in varying proportions. The *Deccan Chronicle* and *Andhra Bhoomi* unit at Visakhapatnam publishes two newspapers in two different languages. The *Deccan Chronicle* in English and *Andhra Bhoomi* in Telugu.

Price: The sales of any product are based on price compared to other factors. It plays a major role in buying a product. The prices were reduced in paper industry in October 2000 when *The Times of India* reduced its price Rs 1.50. With this all the English newspapers in the industry were forced to cut down their prices in order to survive in the competition. Even though the prices were reduced all the papers were maintaining the same number of pages and supplements in spite of reduced prices. With the reduction the circulation of all the newspapers also increased tremendously. When compared with the last two decades, readership percentage increased abnormally within a time span of 12 months. Even though the company had spent lots of money on publicity earlier, growth percentage increased just above 10 per cent. After the price slash, even without publicity, the market has seen a tremendous growth rate of 400 per cent in its circulation. In 1980, the price of the paper in weekdays was 30 Paisa and for Sunday it was 40 Paisa. In January 2000, price of the paper in weekdays was only one rupee and for Sunday it was Rs. 2.50 Paisa. From March these prices were increased to Rs. 2.50 Paisa for weekdays except Sunday and Rs. 3.00 for Sunday. After the reduction of the price by *The Times of India, Deccan Chronicle* also reduced its price from Rs. 2.50 Paisa to Rs.1.50 Paisa in weekdays and Rs. 3.00 to Rs. 2.00 on Sundays. It is also found in the survey that the circulation of the paper has increased because readers were subscribing only one paper before the price cut. After reducing the price people are subscribing to more than one paper. Circulation of *Deccan Chronicle* after reducing prices in city is 16000 per day and in district it is 6,000 per day.

Promotion: Newspaper is a media that promotes other business. Naturally, it does not require excessive promotion of itself. But now-a-days, in the changing market scenario, it is imperative to opt for aggressive promotional activities. At the *Deccan Chronicle* and *Andhra Bhoomi* unit, Visakhapatnam, the market is divided into Urban, Rural and Semi Urban areas. Basing on this segmentation various promotional activities are being undertaken. In Urban areas, they mostly depend on an aggressive door-to-door sales canvassing, besides operating promotional campaigns like hoardings, cross promotional activities. In the rural areas, slides are being exhibited in cinema theatres. They also use stickers, wall paintings etc., for promoting the product.

Place: *Deccan Chronicle* and *Andhra Bhoomi* are regional newspapers. Their operations are limited to the states of Andhra Pradesh and to the border districts of Orissa. The international presence for both the newspapers is done through the help of Internet.

Table-3.9

THE CIRCULATION OF ANDHRA BHOOMI AND DECCAN CHRONICLE NEWSPAPERS IN 2003

	Andhra Bhoomi	*Deccan Chronicle*
Urban	1200	12000
Semi Urban	2000	3000
Rural	1800	3000

Source: Organisational Manuals of *Deccan Chronicle* (Holdings) Limited, Visakhapatnam.

The organization has a good network of transport system in order to deliver the newspaper to the respective agents. The agents take the responsibility of delivering the newspaper to the final customer.

Layout of Deccan Chronicle Newspapers

Deccan Chronicle carries a variety of features everyday and there are special items for each day of the week. In order to study the features, the study can be divided into the study of features that are covered daily and the other for the features that come on a specific day. The topics covered by the newspaper for all days of the week are as follows:

Page 1: In the first page of the newspaper news that is of greatest interest is published. The latest news, flash news etc., appear on the first page. The first page covers the news in the National, International and Regional levels depending on the importance. It also contain cartoon, weather report, advertisements etc.

Page 2: Contain classifieds. Classifieds are advertisements that are charged according to the words in advertisements. In the classified advertisements, there are general, employment, real estate, automotive, matrimonial, rental, business offers, finance, education advertisements. In the newspaper the second page is completely dedicated to the classified advertisements that are collected at the Hyderabad unit. It also contains 'Stars Today' for the astrologically sensitive and 'Show Time' which contains various television programmes. It contain train timings also.

Page 3: Contain City/Regional News and Advertisements. City/Regional news is the news from the city and local areas in and around Visakhapatnam which is covered in this page. The news pertaining to politics, infrastructure, reports of regional festivals, functions etc. are given importance. The topics like city note and crime briefs are also printed in this page.

Page 4: Contain Regional News.

Page 5: Contain state news. The news pertaining to the state as a whole are published in the page.

Page 6: Contain Articles, Editorial, Letters to the editor, Final word, Fifty years ago, Why do we say this.

'Articles' are published in the centre pages of any newspaper. This facilitates easy reading. Articles written by prominent authorities from the concerned field are selected for publishing. The articles pertain to the present scenario are taken for printing. 'Editorial' for any newspaper is like the heart and voice of it. It is the editorial where the editor expresses his views and ideas. 'Letters to

Editor' is the correspondence where any citizen or reader can express his/her views about the articles and editorials published in the newspapers. 'Final word' is generally a line of wisdom told by some great person. In 'Fifty years ago' column the most important news that had been published in the newspaper fifty years ago is reprinted. This helps the reader being in touch with the past happenings. In 'why do we say this feature' a saying or word is taken and is discussed for its usage in the day to day life. This improves the skills in the usage of words while one is talking.

Pages 7 and 8: Contain 'General' news. News from National, Regional and International level is printed on this page.

Page 9: Contain state news.

Pages 10, 11,12: Contain news at National and International level and it also contains advertisements.

Page 15: This pages is dedicated to the news from the other southern states of the country. The business news is sometimes printed in the 18th page when there is more news to be carried from the business mart.

Pages 16 & 17: Contain Business Chronicle. Business news from all the business centres is published in this page. The stock market news is also given due importance. It also contain the information regarding the bullion market and commodity rates. The advertisements regarding tenders are published here.

Pages 18, 19, 20: Consist of sports and entertainment news. It carries cross word puzzles, 'believe it or not column', and Cartoon for fun filled folks. Supplements : *Sunday:* Sunday Magazine. It contain books and literary works, Perspective, Your luck this week, Quote, Health, People, Comics and Gossips etc. It also contain Interview of the week, Internet, Delhi durbar, Cinema-Cinema., *Monday:* Vizag Chronicle, *Tuesday:* School Chronicle, Teen Chronicle, *Wednesday:* Vizag Chronicle, *Thursday:* Cinema-Cinema and Career chronicle, *Friday:* Vizag Chronicle and Life style, *Saturday:* Entertainment and TV. Guide and Career Chronicle.

Organisational Structure of *Deccan Chronicle* and *Andhra Bhoomi* (Visakhapatnam)

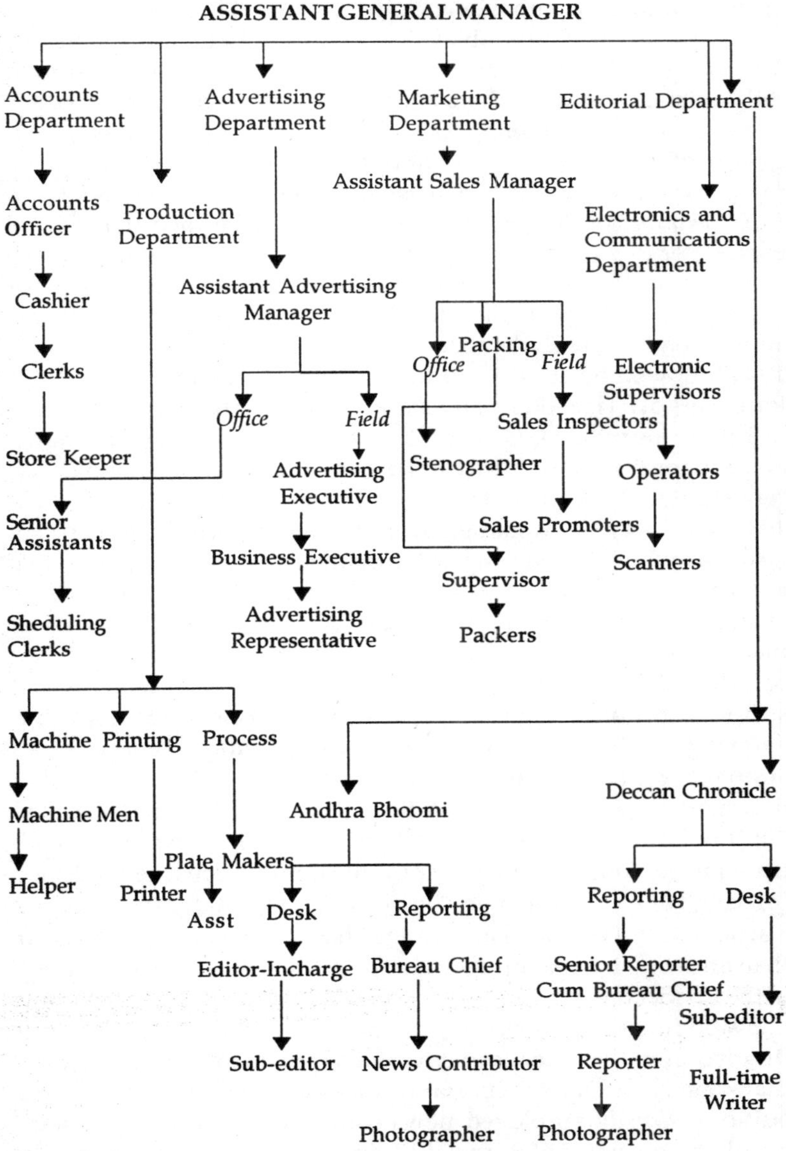

Profile of Eenadu

Eenadu is the largest circulated Telugu newspaper which has the largest number of publishing centres. The publishing centres are Visakhaptanam, Hyderabad, Vijayawada, Tirupati, Anantpur, Karimnagar, Rajahmundry, Suryapet, Guntur, Nellore, Kurnool, Srikakulam, Tadepalligudem, Warangal, Cuddapah. The chief editor of the paper is Ch. Ramoji Rao, also the proprietor of the *Eenadu* group of Publications. *Eenadu* is popular for its innovative presentation and coverage of news and experiments with its layout. *Eenadu* started on August 10th, 1974 with initial print order of 4,500 copies per day and its first edition started from Visakhapatnam. With the success of the Visakhapatnam edition in 1974, *Eenadu* expanded its base in the state by establishing many editions subsequently. The Hyderabad edition was set up on December 17th 1975 followed by another edition at Vijayawada in 1978. Within four years of its inception, *Eenadu* carved a niche for itself in the field of Telugu journalism. On June 20, 1982, *Eenadu* launched its fourth edition from Tirupati. With this new edition, *Eenadu* appointed staff reporters at all the district headquarters with Teleprinter lines. Till 1982, the Telugu newspapers were giving importance to national news by publishing news agency dispatches on the front page while the state and district news was confined to inside pages. *Eenadu* changed the trend and focused on state news by giving it a prominent place on the front page. On January 25th, 1989, Eenadu introduced the district supplement called "Mini" edition. Each district supplement consisting of 8-12 pages, is published in tabloid size, catering to the needs of local people. Today, these district supplements have become so successful in the state that the other newspapers have started imitating it. Each of the 25 districts in Andhra Pradesh is supplied the 'Mini' edition in colour along with the main edition. Most importantly, the mini editions are published for the Telugu readers in the neighboring states-Tamilnadu, Karnataka and Orissa. These 'minis' have been successful in more than one way. For readers they give detailed news about happenings in the districts. In Hyderabad and Visakhapatnam, *Eenadu* has gone one step further by providing zonal news in the city. Each city is divided in to three zones and a mini supplement is published for that zone in the city, concentrating on local news. Because of these editions, *Eenadu* employed news contributors all over the state, numbering over 1,400, in addition to the staff reporters. The distribution network of Eenadu is so large that it has 4,800 news agents to supply the newspaper to every nook and corner of the state. In order to cater to the segmented audience (readers), *Eenadu* started various features. Pratibha (talent), a weekly feature for the benefit of the students was introduced in 1989 to discuss topics related to education. Many weekly features, 'Ryte raju' (a farmers column), Good Health (health column), Real estate (on housing), 'Computer chit-chat' (on computer), 'Melu kolupu' (consumer column), and 'Business section' (a commerce page) and 'Pellipandiri' (a matrimonial column) were introduced.

A daily four paged broadsheet pullout for women, 'Vasundhara' was introduced on September 24, 1992 which discusses issues exclusively related to women. In 1991, *Eenadu* pioneered the cause of prohibition in the state of Andhra Pradesh, supporting the womens'agitation for the same. Now, that is in October 2003, the circulation is nearing ten lakhs. *Eenadu* currently established itself as the largest circulated daily not only in Andhra Pradesh but also in the country. Its name is included in first hundred dailies all over the world. In India it occupied the 10th place. It consist of internet website also. Now it has 22 editions. Before July Ist, 2002 it had 15 editions. On July 1st, 2002 it launched seven editions at a time. It also participated in many social welfare activities like Sukhibhava. *Eenadu* is having product diversification also. Those are E-Television Channel, Ramoji film city, Textiles, Kalanjali, Priya pickles, Oils, Margadarsi, Films etc. On July 1st, 2002, the print order was 9,19,989 copies.

Eenadu recently introduced various features in 'Vasundhara' supplement. The special features are Chaduvu - Monday (Relating to education)

Sukhibhava – Tuesday (Health aspects)
Champion – Wednesday (Sports information)
Eenadu – Thursday (About electronics and technology)
Siri – Friday (About money matters)

Eetaram – Saturday (About youth)

Bujjai – Sunday (Information relating to children) in week days and one feature on each day.

Eenadu is the only newspaper brings out Vasundhara supplements on all days of week. It covers women issues, recipes etc. Besides that it brings city editions everyday covering local news.

Business news is published all days of week. Regional, National, as well as international news is also published in *Eenadu.*

Eenadu layout

Page1	General
Page 2	National
Page 3	National
Page 4	Editorial, International and National
Page 5	State, National, International
Pages 6,7	Business news
Page 8	National, State news (Pelli pandiri on Sundays)
Page 9	Regional, State, National news
Page 10	Sports and advertisements
Page 11	Vasundhara
Page 12	Vasundhara (women news)
Pages 13, 14	Special features like Siri, Bujjai etc.
Page 15	Entertainment

Tabloid contain Local news, Regional news, T. V. Information, Classifieds, Local ads, Local and Regional sports information.[10]

Profile of Andhra Jyothi

Andhra Jyothi is one of the premier Telugu dailies published initially from four centres in Andhra Pradesh Viz., Hyderabad, Tirupati, Vijayawada and Visakhapatnam. Now it has 12 publishing centres all over Andhra Pradesh State. The paper was launched on July 1, 1960 at Vijayawada under the editorship of Narla Venkateswara Rao, the Doyen of Telugu Journalism. Venkateswara Rao shaped the newspaper and carved a niche for Telugu journalism. The paper served the cause of Telugu literature by running special supplements. It was a forum to discuss and debate for literatures and opinion pieces in the columns of the newspaper were published as long as Narla Venkateswara Rao was editor. He continued to be the editor of the paper till 1977. During the emergency in 1975, the paper accepted the government guidelines on censorship.

With the retirement of Venkateswara Rao in 1977, Nanduri Ram Mohan Rao who was an assistant editor then, became the editor of the paper. During his editorship, the newspaper pursued the same editorial policy as outlined by his predecessor. Significantly, during his tenure, the paper started publication from new centres. The new editions were launched from Hyderabad (1986), Tirupati (1987) and Visakhapatnam (1991).

N. Ram Mohan Rao resigned from the organization, on October 19th, 1994. He was succeeded by I. Venkata Rao, the present Chief Editor of the paper. The paper is owned by the Andhra Printers Limited of K. L. N. Prasad.

The paper publishes a weekly column, Cortulu-Chattalu (Courts-laws), 'Patrikeyam' (a critical evaluation of the state of Journalism), Law point (a counseling column on legal matters), 'Viswa Darpanam' (a view of the world), and 'Mukha-Mukhi' (face to face), a discussion column on general issues. 'Janavakyam' (Leters-to-the editor) is published daily except Mondays.

The paper also publishes an educational column for students and a column for women in its district supplement. The *Andhra Jyothi* also publishes an eight page supplement in colour for each district in the state on the lines of *Eenadu* another Telugu daily. *Andhra Jyothi* occupies the second position in circulation in the state. On January 1st, 2003, it was taken over by Vemuri Radhakrishna.[11]

Interviews with Newspapers Organisational Heads in Visakhapatnam City

Interview with Eenadu Unit Manager M. Rameshbabu in 2003

Opinion on allowing of FDI in newspaper *media:* it is not good. They not only enter into investment area, they enter into other areas also.

About Competition Like Price Wars: It is not a healthy competition. If they work hard and honestly, definitely they survive.

Future of Newspapers: Local as well as National newspapers are having a good future, if they provide better customer service. Now-a-days the people want to know about what is happening in each and every corner of society.

Intermedia competition: After telecasting news for everyone hour in some of the Television channels, surprisingly the sales of newspaper got a 20 per cent increase.

Cost of production: The cost of production for *Eenadu* newspaper is more than the selling price. Even then the newspapers are surviving today, because of advertising revenue.

About newsprint: Eenadu is using a mix of imported as well as indigenous newsprint.

Reason for becoming market leader: Eenadu occupies the largest market share in Andhra Pradesh because of updating, creativity and by knowing the pulse of readers.

Interview with General Manager of Deccan Chronicle Holdings Limited, A. C. Venkata Krishnan in 2003

Opinion on present day competition: There is cut-throat competition going on in Newspaper Industry. The jungle rule of 'Survival of Fittest' would apply to this industry. The competition among the newspaper industry as well as the competition faced from electronic media have to be taken in to account. Only Number one in newspaper industry can survive hereafter and there is no scope for others. Added to this, the price wars have started which is very common to newspaper industry. This war was started by a paper having command in North India because of its very good financial stability. This paper can afford to indulge in any such wars. As a matter of fact, it is a very bad trend in the industry and it has already corroded the finance of many medium and small-scale industries including regional papers that have to follow suit on account of the competition. As a matter of fact, the newspaper industry gets a very meager amount by way of cover price which does not even cover the cost of production.

Opinion on allowing 26 per cent of FDI in Newspaper Media: The Government of India has allotted 26 per cent FDI in newspaper industry recently. How far it is going to help the Newspaper Industry has to be seen. Those newspapers which are commanding very good circulation and getting good revenue by and large do not need any support from foreign investors. Whereas the other category who are not in a position to cope up both circulation-wise and advertisement revenue-wise on account of the competition need support. Even these people by meager financial support cannot improve their position. It is the image and other aspects that go a long way to make a newspaper popular. There is no dearth for financial assistance in India for any industry. But before investing, any investor whether Indian or a foreigner, would look for returns. He will definitely see the performance of the industry including its balance sheet for the last three years and the projections for the next three years before investing any money. In respect of foreign investors they are not only interested in the returns but also would like to have supremacy on the editorial board to gain control over the industry which the Government of India has curbed. So it has to be seen as to how far this relaxation by Government of India is really going to help the needy groups in the industry.

Opinion about future of Newspaper Industry: The future of newspaper industry in India is bleak. Only number one can survive with the tough competition, we are facing with electronic media. Other newspapers cannot survive under any circumstances. As a matter of fact, it is big question mark (?).

Suggestions: Only regional language papers have a future in this country than national newspapers or an English newspaper. It is clear that most of the language newspapers, commanding good circulation, have become more popular than English newspapers. As a matter of fact, papers like *Malayala Manorama, Eenadu, Dailythanti* etc., are selling even more than any English newspaper in their regions.

Interview with Vaartha Branch (Unit) Manager K.S.Krishna Mohan (2003)

Opinion on 26 per cent FDI allowance in Newspaper media: It is not a healthy sign. Once we welcome the foreign people into our industry they slowly spread their tentacles and they try to dominate. They can change our peoples' mindset and convert them as their followers. Newspaper media is different from other trade sectors. If FDI is allowed in trade and other service sectors it leads to healthy competition. But newspaper is one sector in which we cannot expect FDI to be beneficial because it affects the sovereignty and freedom of press. But if FDI is allowed it is beneficial to newspaper employees.

About competition and price wars: It is not a healthy competition. Actual cost of production and distribution per unit is Rs. 6. But it is given only for Rs. 2.30 paise for agents, which is less price than cost of production. They try to compensate this loss by increasing advertising revenues.

Future of Newspaper Industry: Even though F. M. Radio has large listenership, it will never become a competitor for newspaper media.

The people are not listening to the Radio at the cost of reading newspaper. Television is a competitor. But, newspaper is having its own advantage especially as documentary evidence, and also as future reference. It display prospectus, company profit and loss accounts, balance sheet etc. Newspapers are surviving because standardization, ethics, editorial, moral values, policy of newspaper quality, credibility, authenticity, bringing out scams, maintaining public relations. 'Because of this *Vaartha* occupies second position in Andhra Pradesh with annual circulation of 5,00,000 (2002)' he said. In 2001, it was 4,00,000 (in Telangana and Rayalaseema the Readership of *Vaartha* was more than *Eenadu*). In Visakhapatnam, *Vaartha* Circulation is 45,000 (2002) and, in 2001 it was 35,000 copies.

Problems of Newspaper Industry: Tough competition, perishability, and some printing and composing errors which are unavoidable and delay in distribution and newspaper delivery problems are quite common. Five per cent excise duty which is imposed on newsprint must be reduced.

Prospects of Newspaper Industry: Newspaper Organisations can enjoy profits if working conditions are improved and human resources are developed. Press people have got lot of recognition and they can bring many aspects into lime light which cannot be done individually.

***Interview with Venkata Ratnam, Deputy Regional Manager of The Hindu* (2002)**

Opinion on allowance of 26 per cent FDI: If FDI is allowed in newspaper industry then foreign people can interfere in the country's politics, culture and economy. The culture change occurs and they gradually interfere in the company's internal affairs also which is not good. If FDI is 26 per cent and less than that, then the foreigners do not have complete control. But if more than 26 per cent is allowed the foreigners will also get control over the company affairs which is not good sign. This newspaper industry unlike trade sector is enjoying freedom of press which would get disturbed because of FDI. Once the foreign people are allowed, they not only show interest in profits, but they also have desire to dominate and control the company matters.

Opinion on Competition in Newspaper Industry (About Price wars): The price wars first started when *The Times of India* reduced the price. The price reduction to some extent is good because, now-a-days the reading habit of people has come down. So price reduction is an advantage because people would buy a newspaper as it costs less. The price when reduced to one rupee, more people are willing to purchase newspapers. That increases the circulation of newspapers and slowly readers get habituated. So, *The Hindu* circulation gets doubled. But in another way, it is not good because, after the price reduction there is a large gap between price and cost of producing and distributing newspaper. But this can be compensated by advertising revenue, as increase in circulation leads to more advertisements and they generate more advertising revenue.

Future of Newspaper Industry: Future of the newspaper industry is good if it goes for regionalisation even though, it is a national newspaper. So, in *The Hindu* first, third, fourth, fifth, sixth pages contain more local and regional news. According to his view, money is not enough to manage the newspaper organizations. It requires a lot of competitive spirit, concentration. One should not go for multi-business where the people cannot find enough time to concentrate. While selecting the manpower also newspaper organisations must be very careful. Management must remunerate the employees properly so that they have improved job satisfaction and commitment. In order to survive and to develop, *The Hindu* matrimonial column was redefined. Instead of mentioning the box number of Chennai, now they are mentioning about the box number of regions.

Opinion on size reduction: Even though newspapers now-a-days are reducing the size, according to him there was no content loss. Quality and quantity remains unchanged.

Newsprint: The Hindu people are using a mix of imported and indigenous newsprint in 1:1 ratio.

Basing on above interviews, it can be concluded that the price wars were opposed by most of the newspaper organizations in Visakhapatnam City. *The Hindu* people said, even though price reduction leads to unhealthy competitive situation, by reducing newspaper prices, it slowly develops newspaper reading habit among readers. So it is beneficial to newspaper organisations because now-a-days there is declining trend in reading of newspapers. Allowing 26 per cent FDI in newspaper is not liked by more number of newspaper organisations because newspaper media is not just like other commodity. Here foreigners not only involve in corporate decision-making process, they also influence people which is not good according to more number of newspaper organisations. Most of newspaper organizational heads opined that, if newspaper go for localisation and regionalisation of news, newspapers have better future in coming days. Electronic media no way competitor to newspaper media, according to more number of newspaper organisations. Some Organisations' heads said, after telecasting news frequently and after emergence of F.M. surprisingly, the newspaper readership has increased. Majority of newspaper organisations are using a mix of imported and indigenous newsprint.

REFERENCES

1. Records of District Industry Centre, Visakhapatnam.
2. Organisational Manuals of *The Hindu*.
3. Organisational Manuals of *Vaartha*.
4. From September 1999, *Indian Express* is called as *The New Indian Express*.
5. Organisational Manuals of *The New Indian Express*.
6. Organisational Manuals of *Andhra Prabha*.
7. Audit Bureau of Circulation is a non-Profit, Voluntary Organization Comprising Publishers, Advertisers and Advertising agencies. It Vigorously scrutinizes accounts before certifying the number of copies actually sold.
8. *Deccan Chronicle* Bureau (2004), "Chronicle Climbs to 3.8 lakh," *Deccan Chronicle*, September 24, 2004, p. 1.
9. Organisational Manuals of *Deccan Chronicle* and *Andhra Bhoomi*.
10. Organisational Manuals of *Eenadu*.
11. Organisational Manuals of *Andhra Jyothi*.

4

Marketing System of Newspapers: An Analysis

Marketing: An Introduction

Peter Drucker says the purpose of a business is to create a customer.[1] "There is only one valid definition of business purpose: to create a satisfied customer. It is the customer who determines what the business is."[2] When customer is created, he is to be satisfied. Marketing includes all resources and a set of activities necessary to direct and facilitate the flow of goods and services from the producer to consumer. There are two main activities in marketing. They are matching the product or service with the demand and the transfer of ownership and possession at every stage in the flow of goods from producer to consumer. In simple terms, marketing comprises all activities involved in determination and satisfaction of customer needs at a profit. According to American Marketing Association, marketing means "A process of planning and executing the conception, pricing, promotion and distribution of ideas, goods and services to create exchanges that satisfy individual and organizational objectives."[3] W. J. Stanton defines the term marketing as "a concept emphasizes customer orientation and coordination of marketing activities to achieve the organisation's objectives."[4] "True marketing starts...with the customer...It asks, what does the customer want to buy? It does not say, this is what our product or service does. It says, these are the satisfactions that customer looks for, values and needs."[5]

Philip Kotler described marketing is "A marketing concept which is a customer orientation backed by integrated marketing aimed at generating customer satisfaction as the key to satisfy the organisational goals."[6] "The customer is the foundation of a business and keeps it in existence."[7] Thus, the marketing concept is more consumer oriented and the emphasis is mainly on the consumer— the kingpin in the marketing activity as against the product. Richard H. Buskirk felt that "if marketing efforts are to be successful they must at all times be consumer oriented." A close observation, analysis and understanding of the modern marketing concept reveals that consumer is the focal point and everything revolves around him. According to Rajan Saxena, Marketing is "Understanding and responding to customer needs."[8] By satisfying the consumer every seller can survive and pocket some profit. Hence, if the marketing efforts are to be successful, programme of every producer/seller should properly be planned and implemented. The producer/seller should chalk out proper strategies relating to the marketing mix consisting of four 'P's that is product, price, place and promotion. Philip Kotler has rightly pointed "Marketing Management is the analysis, planning, implementation and control of programmes designed to bring about desired exchanges with the target market for the purpose of achieving the organisational objectives."[9] Felton felt marketing to be 'a corporate state of mind that insists on the integration and coordination of all marketing functions which, in turn, are welded with all other corporate functions for the basic objective of producing maximum long-range corporate profits."[10]

Marketing relies heavily on designing the organisation offerings in terms of the target market needs and desires and using effective pricing, communication and distribution to inform, motivate and service the market. V.S. Ramaswamy and S. Namakumari opine that "Marketing is a total system of interacting business activities designed to plan, promote and distribute need satisfying products and services to existing and potential consumers."[11] According to Skinner 'Marketing involves a diverse set of activities directed at a wide range of products, and it stresses the importance of facilitating satisfying exchanges between buyers and sellers."[12] Out of the four elements in Marketing Mix product alone has the want satisfying capacity. "Marketing concept is customer-oriented philosophy that is implemented and integrated through an organization to serve customers better than competitors and achieve specified goals."[13] Every consumer measures the weight and want satisfying capacity of the product/service that he receives in exchange of money, hence the marketing concept, the idea of looking at the product from the consumers' point of view. In other words, instead of offering consumers what you think, one should find out what they really want. Wants operate close to the level of consciousness and reflect positive desires such as pleasure, approval, profit or negative desires such as loss, disapproval and convenience.[14] In studying consumer behaviour, we have to consider not only what people buy, but where, how often and under what conditions they make their purchases. Consumer Behaviour is "A process whereby individuals decide whether, what, when, where, how and from whom to purchase goods and services."[15] Consumer research is extremely important to marketing strategy, because knowledge of the factors that influence consumer purchases can help to increase market share. If marketers have thorough knowledge of the psychological and socio-cultural factors operating on consumers, it becomes much easier for them to predict how consumers will react to new products, price changes and promotional campaigns. Thus, knowledge of consumer behaviour makes it easier to analyze the market and plan appropriate strategies.

An understanding of the economic psychological and sociological characteristics of the consumers and their motivations, attitudes, recognitions and personalities can help to discover new market opportunities, provide a sharper segmentation of the market a meaningful product differentiation, and to formulate marketing strategies based on consumer responses as major variable. A human need is a state of deprivation of some basic satisfaction.[16] Alderson has aptly pointed out "wants spring from needs and are not something alien to be set-off in opposition to needs."[17]

In brief, an understanding of consumer preferences, beliefs, needs and wants, desires, emotions, habits and egocentricities are all important determinants for the success of the marketer and all can vitally influence his decisions relating to the identification of opportunities, product policy, channel of distribution, pricing, personal selling and promotional strategies.

Marketing Mix in Newspaper Industry

Marketing does not mean simply matching any product with the market. Fundamentally, the modern marketing concept rests on the fact that the marketing activities start and end with the consumer. It consists of blend of four 'P's which are controllable variables often described as product, price, promotion and physical distribution, together called as Marketing Mix. Neil H. Borden, described Marketing mix as "The combination of the four inputs which constitute the core of a company's marketing system: the product, the distribution system, the price structure and the promotional activities."[18] These are intended to satisfy the wants of the target market.

Product

Product is a bundle of utilities consisting of various product features and accompanying services.[19] According to Schwartz, "A product is something a firm markets that will satisfy a personal want or fill a business or commercial need."[20] It is a physical item or service or combination of the two. Product plays a central role in the activities of the organizations, for it is the medium through which they seek to achieve their dual objectives of maximizing both consumer and organizational satisfaction.[21] In newspaper organization the newspaper itself is a product. It is a physical item. It is highly perishable. In recent times, people are very educative. They like to subscribe only to those newspapers which are qualitative as well as quantitative. Now-a-days competition among newspaper organisations is very stiff. In order to capture the maximum market share, every newspaper organisation is trying to develop their respective products as per the tastes of the subscribers. For example, *Eenadu* introduced special features like Bujjai, Siri and so on to their special supplement called Vasundhra. After introducing the Vasundhara supplement *Eenadu* succeeded in winning of the hearts of lady subscribers. By constant upgradation and development of the product by adding extra features the readership and circulation of newspapers is increasing day-by-day. *The Hindu* improved the quality of its newspaper by new technology. Likewise the remaining newspapers are also adding news features, supplements for Saturdays and Sundays, some of them are offering week days supplements, giving information about television programmes, etc., to increase their market share. In this way competition among newspaper has become very sharp. This is a very healthy competition from the readers point of view, because readers are able to get diverse information apart from qualitative news for their price. Often, the newspaper organisations have been bringing out supplements on festival days and on the days when examination results are being announced. These are the occasions for grabbing a better market share. Not only that most of newspaper organisations are using qualitative newsprint even though newsprint costs are very high. This is because of severe competitive conditions prevailing in marketing of newspapers. Readers prefer qualitative newspaper that is having both quality of news as well as quality of newsprint which should be good. So the first and foremost 'P' of the marketing mix, the product is very important in getting good marketing results for any newspaper organization which becomes the basis for success.

Price

Price may be defined as the value of product attributes expressed in monetary terms which a consumer pays or is expected to pay in exchange and anticipation of the expected or offered utility.[22] Setting basic price for a finished product is called price. Recent times because of the tough competition prevailing in the newspaper market, the price of newspaper is decreased to a large extent and on some days most of the English newspapers are offering it for only one rupee. This price war had started when *The Times of India* launched its Hyderabad edition with reduced price and offered the newspaper only for one rupee. Because of the price war, almost all the English newspapers offered their papers to the readers for a less price and the price is less than cost of production. This pricing is known as 'Predatory pricing' which is quite common among newspaper organizations. It is not a healthy competition according to most of the newspaper organization heads in Visakhapatnam City. But they have to follow this pricing strategy because of the tough competition prevailing in the market. Otherwise they cannot retain present readership and circulation levels.

Place (Distribution)

The third and most important 'p' of the marketing mix is place. That is physical distribution. Weld regarded distribution channels as an identifiable, discrete and indispensable function of marketing.[23] Distribution plays a vital role in the newspaper marketing. The role of distribution is to make the product available to the final consumer through a network of middlemen (agent) in minimum time and as quickly as possible with minimum expenditure. A.W. Shaw defined distribution as the "Application of motion to materials as they move from the times, places, forms and conditions, where they have no value, to the times, places, forms and conditions where they have value."[24] American Marketing Association defines distribution channel as the structure of intra-company organization units and extra-company agents and dealers, wholesale and retail, through which a commodity, product or service is marketed.[25] The channel is therefore the vehicle for viewing marketing organisations' external aspects, and for bringing the physical and non-physical gaps which exist in moving goods from the producers to the consumers through the exchange process, including the determination of price. Vaile defined distribution channel as "The combination and sequence of agencies through which one or more of marketing flows move."[26] The Middlemen between the publisher and subscriber is the newspaper sales agent. The publisher appoints these agents by collecting deposit amounts in advance as per their existing terms and conditions of contract. The amount of deposit varies from publisher to publisher. The Middlemen that is the newspaper sales agent will be offered commission on the total copies sold. The publisher will bear the entire expenditure for sending paper parcels from office to the middlemens' agency point.

The Channels of Distribution for Newspaper Marketing is as follows:

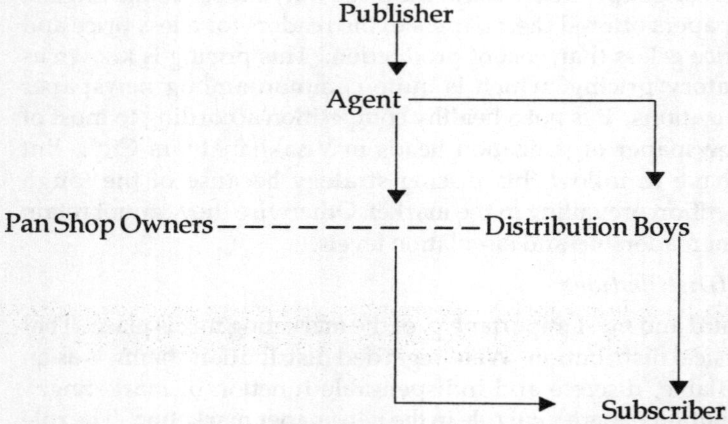

The printed publications to distant places will be sent through taxies. For example, Itchapuram town in Srikakulam district, the newspapers will be sent by taxi almost by all newspaper organizations. The total distance between Visakhapatnam and Itchapuram is 235 kms. The taxi is used to transport the parcels to all agency points existed in between Visakhapatnam and Itchapuram. The total expenditure for this taxi is Rs. 25,000 per month. The publisher bear the expenditure only for one side that is for carrying parcels from publishing centre to destination. The transport operator has to bear the return expenditure. Normally the transport operator opts for passenger service in return route to minimize the cost. Like this in Visakhapatnam city, the paper parcels of agents will be sent through taxies and autos. From the agency distribution points, distribution boys who are appointed by the agents, will distribute papers to the subscribers. The entire newspaper business depends mostly on the distribution boys only. If the distribution boy does not deliver the paper on time or properly, the subscriber will discontinue that particular paper and switchover to another one that has timely delivery. Thereby the circulation will be affected adversely of those newspapers which do not ensure timely delivery. Hence, the distribution boys play a key role in improving the circulation of newspapers.

Promotion

The role of selling has become more complex because the newspaper product is more technical, buyers are more sophisticated and the competition has become fierce. This necessitated the need for proper flow of communication from the producer to the consumer either along with the product or prior to the introduction of product into the market. Promotion is the fourth and final element of the marketing mix. Sales promotion moves the product towards the buyer, whereas the advertising moves the buyer towards the product. The committee on definitions of American Marketing Association offers the following definition of sales promotion. "In a specific sense sales promotion includes those sales activities that supplement both personnel selling and advertising, and coordinate them and make them effective, such as displays, shows and expositions, demonstrations and other non-recurrent selling efforts not in the ordinary routine."[27] Sales promotion plays an important role in newspaper marketing. Now-a-days almost all newspaper organisations are conducting sales promotion campaigns regularly without interruption. Some of the newspapers like *The Hindu, Eenadu* and *Deccan Chronicle* are conducting door-to-door campaigns through personal selling process. The personal selling process is "oral presentation in a conversation with one or more prospective purchasers for the purpose of making sales."[28] The Publishers of the newspapers appoint some candidates in the capacity of sales promoters and divide them into teams. Each team will consists of five to six members. They will be trained under the supervision of sales supervisors and development officers. After the completion of training period they will operate in the field under the supervision of a team leader. Everyday they start work at 6.00 a.m. and work till 11.00 a.m. They meet people in person and explain about their newspaper and motivate them to subscribe. Normally each sales promoter will make 50 to 60 calls in the area allotted per day and enroll new subscriptions to the tune of not less than five per day. In recent times this type of sales promotion work is done regularly by all newspaper organisations. The subscriptions enrolled in this system hardly stands for one month due to change in tastes of subscribers. This is one of the most important and dependable promotional activity. Besides this, there are some other promotional activities by different newspapers to increase the sales of newspapers. To grab the new readership a free copies scheme was introduced. This is exclusively for attracting new subscribers. Under this scheme the publisher supplies his Publications to the people in a selected areas for a week or for ten days at free of cost as a sample to provide an opportunity to know the quality features of the newspaper. In this scheme the reader has a choice, whether to subscribe or not. If the reader is satisfied with a particular newspaper he may continue subscribe and continue to take it. This scheme has yielded positive results. Some Publishers introduced another scheme and this is mainly meant for agents. If any agent enrolls new subscription on his own he will be paid commission of ten rupees on each such new subscription, apart from his commission, provided that subscription for a particular copy should stand at least for two months. This scheme also yielded positive results. Publicity of some of the newspapers like *The Hindu, Deccan Chronicle* is given by having small plastic boards to each stalls and hanging the newspaper in front of stalls. Direct marketing is in the form of direct mail and internet marketing etc.[29] Most of the newspaper organisations follow internet marketing through websites.[30] Through websites readers get up-to-date information and they can have it whenever they require.

Marketing Practices of Newspaper Organisations: A Review

Strengths

Newspaper media has following strengths when compared with other media. Newspapers can reach remote areas also where it is not possible for other media.

Nowadays people are very much interested to know about the happenings surrounding them. So publishing of local news and localisation of news can be possible only through newspaper media. Growth of *Eenadu* is because of the intense exploitation of the potential of the countryside through district supplements, varied techniques to employ readership. Because of this localisation of news, readership improved a lot.[31] Sensational news can be covered in newspapers in a detailed manner. For example, the growth of *Malayala Manorama* of Kerala was because of coverage of naxalite adventures. It can cover more news stories. Readers can skip items, in which they are not interested.[32] Not only that readers can read the newspaper at any convenient time. Newspapers can publish news for small sections of readers also. In newspapers, it is possible to publish more columns relating to women. Today more women have already entered into lime light, writing news items relating them definitely increases readership. *Eenadu* with that view, introduced 'Vasundhara' a special supplement for women and succeeded. Newspaper media is the cheapest media available to readers and it is having its own strengths like documentary evidence and publishing of company balance sheets, and other type of financial statements etc. Lengthy application forms can be published in this media, which is not possible in other media like Television and Radio. It can be expanded in terms of pages to accommodate more news, give extra supplements and other features. Readers can read different news according to their requirement. It is handy in places like offices, hospitals shops etc. Another strength for this media is its accessibility through internet, where synergy of two different media is possible, which is not possible in other media.[33]

Weaknesses

One of the important problem for newspaper organisations is the cost of newsprint as that is manufactured indigenously is very high. The tariffs and customs duty on imported newsprint is also high. So most of the newspaper organisations are using newsprint which is not qualitative, in order to reduce cost of production. Some newspaper organisations reduce the size of newspaper to reduce the cost of newsprint. As a result readers get dissatisfied because of degradation in quality of newsprint and quantity of news gets reduced because of size reduction. Another weakness for newspaper media is only literates can read and understand the news. Not only that hot news cannot be published immediately. In order to attract readers, some statements given by politicians and leaders can be altered and published as there is no control on newspaper media like a censor board. As a result, credibility is adversely affected.

Opportunities

Technology upgradation is an opportunity for newspaper media and they can use advanced technology like *facsimile* (Eg: *The Hindu*) and greater use of colour is possible. Another opportunity for newspaper media is increase of advertising revenue. Advertising expenditure in India which has increased by nearly 30 per cent in 2003 when compared to four per cent in 1998. So advertisers are interested to invest in newspaper organisations whose circulation is high which is a positive sign for newspaper organisations. Newspaper media can utilize this opportunity to increase advertising revenue. Rise in literacy levels increases hopes for newspaper oranisational people to increase readership. Increase in purchasing power of people is also a positive sign for newspaper industry. On Tuesday 25th June, 2002 government opened doors to allow 26 per cent of FDI in print media, with which newspaper organisations can produce qualitative newspapers.[34] Exemption of five per cent customs duty on newsprint is an opportunity for newspaper industry because it can import more newsprint, which is more qualitative than indigenous newsprint. Companies like Ballapur Industries Limited (BILT) have developed machine friendly paper which avoids jamming, misfeeds or curling on machine. This makes newspaper printing good and can attract readers and ultimately there is a chance for increasing readership. Better staffing definitely improves readership. Newspaper organisations can utilize abundently available manpower in India at a cost advantage because of more population and less employment opportunities.

Threats

Even though advertising spending by investors is increasing, the advertising revenue for newspaper organisations is very less when compared with other media because the investors are preferring other media like television, internet and FM radio which are more appealing, attractive and interesting.[35] Government controls the price and quota of news print given to newspaper organisations. Not only that, rise in newsprint costs, imposition of more tariffs, customs duties, anti-dumping duties (33 %) makes the production of newspaper more costlier which is a threat for newspaper organizations. It is very difficult for small newspaper organisations to survive and some small newspaper organisations have already closed down because the newspaper business is in no way profitable for them. Another threat for newspaper organisations are absence of proper research data. Only NRS (National Readership Survey) and IRS (Indian Readership Survey) are conducting survey for every six months. Except that there is no proper research data to know about reader preferences immediately. So newspaper organisations are not following adaptive culture that is not changing according to changed circumstances and they still prefer only defensive culture and very rigid which is a threat for newspaper media. So by continuous research, they must understand the tastes and preferences of readers and add new features every time by constant innovation. Price wars are very common in newspaper industry. Because of price wars, the newspaper organisations are reducing prices of newspapers, even less than the cost of production (which is known as predatory pricing) in order to survive. Ultimately this is a big threat for these organisations. So the price wars are not healthy and sometimes can create monopoly situation.[36] Surveys shows that, the reading habit of readers is declining day-by-day because they are more interested in viewing of Television and Internet browsing rather than reading. So time spent on reading newspaper is decreasing, which is a threat for newspaper organisations because, it has an impact on readership. Construction of apartment buildings is a big loss for newspaper circulation because, the people who are staying in apartments generally share newspapers. So the number of subscriptions get reduced. The biggest threat for newspaper organisations is competition. Competition is both within and outside the industry.

Competition within the Industry

Circulation of newspapers in India had witnessed nil growth or negative growth from 1993-2003. Intense competition among newspapers has been centred on the factors of circulation and cover price. Better staffing, promotional methods like gifts, prize schemes and related activities, use of colour, zoned editions (District or local editions) are methods generally followed by news organisations to increase circulation. This ultimately increases more production and promotional costs. The newspapers are designed to appeal to a wide range of interests and to address as many population groups as possible, which means more features and sections and thus more pages and ultimately increase in cost of production.

Threat of Competition from Electronic Media (TV Satellite/Cable)

After the introduction of cable, satellite television, the newspaper readership declined because, the people are watching television at the cost of reading newspaper. Not only that the advertising market scenario presents a highly competitive picture with television intruding into newspapers' advertisement share, newspapers are no longer able to fuel their advertising revenue by increasing the advertisement rates.[37] Though the cost of advertisement has doubled over the last eight years, the advertisement volume/share of newspapers in the advertisement market has not correspondingly increased. The growth of newspapers had been abysmally low when compared to the Television viewership growth. Even in terms of reach, television has out performed newspapers. Television has the largest reach among media in India. According to Indian Readership Survey 2003, 90 per cent of people have access to Television as compared to 52 per cent to print media. Newspaper growth rate in India has not kept up with literacy growth rate. Literacy growth rate is more than 60 per cent from 1979-2002, whereas diffusion rate of newspaper increased to only 45 per cent. Satellite/cable connectivity had an exponential growth. There were one million households with satellite/cable television connections in 1992. This has increased to more than 18 million in 2002.[38] After the emergence of satellite and cable connections the newspaper readership declined enormously. New type of electronic media like Direct-To-Home (DTH) connectivity are also in the pipe line. From mid-August 2004, doordarshan is providing Direct-to-Home connectivity for viewers. This stunning growth of satellite/cable in a very short period of time has made newspaper market men sit up. With the government deciding to allow the connections of Internet through cable television, the spread of Internet is sure to grow by leaps and bounds. This rigorous growth of internet is not only because of telephone penetration which has direct relationship with the growth of internet, but also because of offering internet through cable television. This portends an ominous signal for the already suffering newspaper industry. The advent of private sector Internet Service Providers (ISP) will only hasten the spread of Internet usage with affordable rates and varied services. The new competitive media for newspaper industry is Internet, which is online in technology and interactive in nature, presents a threat to the traditional economies of scale of newspapers. In December, 2003 more than two million have access to internet. As more and more people use the electronic medium, the advertisers would migrate to them. Then the subsidy that supports the fixed costs of the print product that is advertisements revenue will be gone. So newspapers will cut content/ raise prices for readers and advertisers, speeding their migration/ defection. In spite of all these, though there is a threat from other media, newspapers may still continue to be a cheap and effective way to distribute information, if adaptive culture is followed. Today what the readers want are depth of substance and fizz. Newspapers must have to provide it in order to survive and grow in near future.[39]

REFERENCES

1. Philip Kotler (1998), *Marketing Management, Analysis, Planning, Implementation and Control,* Prentice Hall of India Private Limited, 1998, 9th edition, p. 38.
2. Peter F. Drucker (1954), *The Practice of Management,* (New York: Harper and Row,1954), p. 37
3. "AMA Board Approves New Marketing Definition"(1986), Marketing News, March 1,1986, p.1, Published by American Marketing Association.
4. William J. Stanton, M.J.Etzel, Bruce J.Walker (1994), *Fundamentals of Marketing,* Tata McGraw Hill Publishers, p. 10.
5. Peter F.Drucker (1974), *Management: Tasks, Responsibilities, Practices, People and Performance,* (New York:Harper and Row,1974), p. 64.
6. Philip Kotler (1995), *Marketing Management, Analysis, Planning, Implementation and Control,* Prentice Hall of India Private Limited, 6th edition.
7. Peter F. Drucker (1970), *The Practice of Management,* Allied Publishers Limited, p. 37.
8. Rajan Saxena (1997), *Marketing Management,* Tata McGraw Hill Publishers, p. 4.
9. Philip Kotler, (1994), *Marketing Management, Analysis, Planning, Implementation and Control,* Prentice Hall of India Private Limited, p. 13.
10. Felton A. P. (1959), "Making the Marketing Concept Work", *Harward Business Review,* July-August, p. 55.
11. V.S. Ramaswamy and S. Namakumari (1990), *Marketing Management,*

Planning, Implementation and Control, (2002 edition), Macmillan Publishers, p. 4.

12. Steven J. Skinner (1998), *Marketing,* All India Publishers, p. 7.
13. Cravens, Hills, Woodruff (1996), *Marketing Management,* Richard D. Irwin, Inc, p. 4.
14. C.B.Mamoria, R.L.Joshi (1996), *Principles and Practice of Marketing in India,* Kitab Mahal Publishers, p. 94.
15. Walter, C.G. and G.W.Paul (1970), *Consumer Behavior: An Integrated Frame work, Home Wood, III, Richard D. Irwin,* p. 7.
16. Philip Kotler (1994), *Marketing Management, Analysis, Planning, Implementation and Control,* Prentice Hall of India Private Limited, p. 9.
17. Alderson, W. (1955), "Needs, Wants and Creative Marketing", *Cost and Profit Outlook,* Vol. 8, September 1955, p. 2.
18. Neil H. Borden (1964), "The Concept of Marketing Mix", *Journal of Advertising Research,* Vol. IV, No.2 (June, 1964), pp. 2-7.
19. Alderson, W. (1957), *Marketing Behaviour and Executive Action,* III: Richard D. Irwin, p. 274.
20. Schwartz D. J. (1973), *Marketing Today: A Basic Approach,* New York: Har Court Brace Jovanovich, pp. 321-22.
21. Baker, M.J. and R.McTanish (1976), *Product Policy and Management,* London: Macmillan Press, Preface.
22. J.C. Gandhi (1995), *Marketing: A Managerial Introduction,* Tata McGraw Hill Publishers, p. 217.
23. Weld, L.D.H. (1917), "Marketing Functions and Merchantile Organisation", *American Economic Review,* June 1917, pp. 306-18.
24. Shaw A.W.(1915), "Some Problems in Market Distribution", Cambridge, Harvard University Press, 1915, pp. 4-28.
25. Committee on Marketing Definitions (1960), *American Marketing Association.*
26. Vaile, R.S. (1952), E.T. Grettrer and R.Cox., *Marketing in the American Economy,* New York: Ronald Press, p. 113.
27. V.S.Ramaswamy and S. Namakumari (1990), *Marketing Management, Planning, Implementation and Contro,* Macmillan Publishers, p. 562.
28. American Marketing Association (1960), *Marketing Definitions: A Glossary of Marketing Terms.*
29. Annual Reports, Records and Literature of *Deccan Chronicle* Group of Publications, *Indian Express* Group of Publications, *The Hindu* group of Publications, *Eenadu* group of Publications, *Vaartha* group of Publications.

30. *www.deccan.com* (Deccan Chronicle), *www.hinduonline.com* (The Hindu), *www.indexpress.com* (The New Indian Express), *www.eenadu.com* (Eenadu), *www. Vartha.com.* (Vaartha)

31. Robin Jeffery (2000), *Understanding Language Press*, University Press, New Delhi.

32. *Ibid.*

33. E. S. Isaac (1998), *Professional challenges in Journalism*, A Presentation in Conference held on January, 14-16, 1988.

34. Sabil Francis (2002), "Signal of Internet: FDI in the Print Media", 26th June, 2002, *The Hindu.*

35. Ervin White (2000), "Many Newspapers see Empty Pages as Firms Face Decline in Retail Ads", Thursday, 21 September, 2000, *Indian Express Newspapers (Bombay) Limited.*

36. Indian Newspaper Society (2000), "Price Wars in Newspaper Industry Deplored", *The Hindu*, 16 September, 2000.

37. Ervin White (2000), "Many Newspapers see Empty Pages as Firms Face Decline in Retail Ads", Thursday, 21 September, 2000, *Indian Express* Newspapers (Bombay) Limited.

38. National Readership Survey 2003 by National Readership Studies Council, an Autonomous Division of Audit Bureau of Circulations, Mumbai.

39. Gracia (President and CEO of Garcia Media, Redesignes more than 450 Publications from all Over the World Including Wall Street Journal and The Miami Herald (U. S. A.), Die Zeit (Germany), EL Tiempo (Colombia) and Liberation (France).

5

Distribution of Newspapers: Assessment of Intermediaries Role and Performance

Distribution and It's Role in Marketing Mix of a Firm

Distribution is one of the major aspects of marketing mix. Distribution is the the combination and sequence of agencies through which one or more marketing flows move.[1] It is only through distribution that public and private goods and services can be made available for use or consumption. Producers of such goods and services are individually capable of generating only form or structural utility for their products or services. They can organize the production capabilities in such a way that the products they have developed can, in fact, be seen, analysed, debated and by a few perhaps, digested. But the actual large scale delivery of the products to the consuming public demands different types of efforts that create, time, place and possession utilities. Consumers cannot obtain a finished product unless the product is transported to where they can gain access to it, stored until they are ready for it, and eventually exchanged for money or other goods or services so that they can acquire it. In fact, the four types of utility (form, time, place and possession) are inseparable, there can be no 'complete' product without incorporating all four into any given object, idea or service. As marketers continue to face hostile, unstable, and competitive environments, distribution will play an increasingly important role. Companies are already moving into new distribution channels that match up with market segments more precisely and effectively.[2] In newspaper industry marketing channels are newspaper agents, retailers and distribution boys. Undoubtedly, value utility is created by distribution channels. Both the market and distribution channel are often more crucial than product. They are primary, the product is secondary.[3] Distribution of newspapers forms a prologue to the analysis of the study as it plays very important role in marketing of newspapers and this chapter mainly divided in to four parts. The first part deals with physical distribution of newspapers. Second part deals with agents' views and perceptions about newspaper distribution. Third part explains retailers' (pan shop owners) views and perceptions about newspaper distribution. Last part mainly highlights distribution boys' views and perceptions, as these three sections of people that is newspaper agents, retailers and distribution boys are mainly involve in distribution of newspapers to readers.

Physical Distribution

Physical distribution is a term more appropriately applied to the out going product flow from the firm to customers through some defined network of transportation links and storage or distribution nodes called distribution network.[4] This network may tie the firm to an individual consumer or to the other firms that may either use the products produced in another stage of manufacturing, conversion or service generation or serve wholesalers or retailers in the distribution of products to another set of customers. Thus, the physical distribution cycle as viewed from the producer of the product is often likely to represent a cycle to the buyer of the product, and it is often repeated several times in a given marketing channel.

Perhaps the key to the methods used to manage transportation, storage, and inventory control in the physical distribution cycle of a firm is the nature of the materials management process of the buyer. Where the products or services are being distributed in a physical distribution network subject to customer demand, inventories are often decoupled. Both from production and from related inventories under traditional reorder point system. However, where products or services are distributed in a physical distribution network subject to demand, production, transportation and inventory control decisions can often be tied directly to the buyers material management process.[5] Physical distribution has economic significance as well as managerial significance. First many managers have realized that improving the efficiency of individual logistic operations such as production, warehousing or transportation is useless, if the efficiency of the individual function throws the total system out of balance. Second the system has become an important competitive tool and is the area where the struggle to control distribution takes place.[6] Many of the technological developments over the last 30 years have been system oriented and as such force consideration of the logistics of the system as whole. Finally, logistics is no longer just a part of business where cost can be minimized, but is seen instead as an important strategic consideration. The physical distribution not only controls visible distribution cost but it also controls some hidden costs like cost of lost sales, concealed orders and customers dissatisfaction, etc. The interdependence of customer service levels and these costs makes the job of controlling costs even more difficult.

Physical Distribution in Newspaper Organisations

Physical distribution the fourth 'P' in marketing mix plays a vital role in newspaper business. The newspapers can sustain only when it wins the readers' acceptance. Every reader whether he is urban or rural expects that the newspaper should be delivered at his/her doorstep early in the morning, before sunrise of everyday. In order to satisfy the readers, every newspaper organisation has its own physical distribution channels. All newspapers which are publishing Visakhapatnam are operating the modes of transportation such as: *(i)* Direct vehicles, *(ii)* Link vehicles, *(iii)* RTC buses, *(iv)* Milk vans, *(v)* Two wheelers and *(vi)* Trains. The main mode of operation is direct vehicles from the place of publication to destination. The area of operation is divided into several routes basing on the area of coverage. Most of the newspapers published from Visakhapatnam are mainly covering three districts of Coastal Andhra Pradesh namely, Visakhapatnam, Vizianagaram and Srikakulam and some parts of Orissa particularly Southern Orissa. The publications like *Eenadu* and *Andhra Jyothi* have their publication centres at Srikakulam to cover Srikakulam district and Southern Orissa from there. Their area of coverage from Visakhapatnam is limited to Visakhapatnam district and a part of Vizianagaram district. The newspapers published from Visakhapatnam are operating mainly identical direct routes namely:

1. Visakhapatnam to Itchapuram in Srikakulam district (distance: 235 kms).
2. Visakhapatnam to Gummalakshmipuram in Vizianagaram district (distance: 184 kms).
3. Visakhapatnam to Kotauratla in Visakhapatnam district (distance:100 kms).

4. Visakhapatnam to Payakaraopeta in Visakhapatnam district (distance:100 kms).
5. Visakhapatnam to Jami in Vizianagaram district (distance: 70 kms).

These routes are operated by private transport operators. These operators transport the paper bundles and drop them at the specific stages given to them. The concerned agents takes the bundles from the dropping point for making distribution. The bundles pertaining to distant places are given priority in dispatch from the place of publication. The direct transport vehicles not only carries the parcels of the route, but also the parcels of the link taxies, link mopeds, milk van parcels, Road Transport Corporation (RTC) bus parcels etc. The parcels pertaining to rural area especially of the interior places are dropped by the direct vehicle operator at the main place from where bus services are available for loop lines for onward dispatch. For example, the parcels pertaining to interior places around Srikakulam town are dropped at Srikakulam bus station from where the parcels will be sent in RTC buses to other interior destinations. Normally the publisher keeps a transhipment boy to dispatch the paper bundles to the interior places through buses. These interior parcels are called as sub parcels. The publisher spends a little amount on RTC buses by taking permits. RTC charges around Rs.16 per one kilogram of weight per month as transport charges for unaccompanied luggage. Besides this a little amount, around Rs.30 per parcel, will be paid to the transhipment boy per month. Likewise, some parcels are sent by link taxies. These routes are:

(i) Srikakulam to Parlakhimundi in Orissa state. (distance: 70 kms).

(ii) Vizianagaram to Kothuru in Srikakulam district (distance: 90 kms).

(iii) Vaddadi to Arakuvalley in Visakhapatnam district (distance: 100 kms).

In some of the loop lines the parcels are sent by milk vans by offering a small amount to milk vendors. This procedure helps the publisher to ensure proper delivery of paper parcels to the destination. Normally newspaper Publishers opt such type of operations where they cannot make their own operations. Publishers incur a nominal expenditure that is approximately Rs. 50 per paper bundle per month.

There is one more method that every publisher opts for. It is called the transportation by mopeds. The publisher allots contract to private operators basing on the condition of the mopeds. It is also finalised on monthly payment basis. Generally publisher pay for to and fro milage in the specific routes. Publisher pay the charges at the rate of three to four rupees per kilometre. The reasons for paying to and fro charges to mopeds are the moped run on petrol and the distance is short. But they pay only for one side to the taxi operators because taxies run on diesel through which the operations become less costlier than petrol. The moped operator takes the responsibility of carrying the enroute parcels and handing over them safely to the concerned agents promptly on time.

Some publishers send their paper parcels by trains to far away places like Orissa State. The entire sale of the newspaper depends on the arrival time of the newspapers into market. Hence all the Publishers ensure timely delivery of newspapers in to the hands of subscribers and readers by adopting appropriate methods.[7]

Distribution boys play a key role in the development of circulation of newspapers. If the distribution boys maintain good relations and rapport with subscribers, he may influence the subscribers to subscribe whatever the boy delivers rather than his/her own choice. Some of the distribution boys attract readers by offering delivery of magazines besides the daily papers. The readers need not go to shops for buying the magazine required. The distribution boy has a capacity to turn the readers' mind from subscribing to one paper to another by delivering the other paper which is new to the subscriber. The subscriber is normally accustomed to read the newspaper basing on the time at which the boy deliveres it.

Agents' Views and Perceptions

Newspaper Agents Basing on Gender

Table 5.1 reveals the distribution of agent respondents by gender. Out of total sample of 14 agents 12 (85.7 %) are males and two agents (14.3 %) are females. Analysis reveals that majority of newspaper agents in the area of study are males and very less percentage (14.3 %) of newspaper agents are females. In the case of females who were newspaper agents, only the ownership is with them and the actual business was carried by men (spouse) only.

Table-5.1
NEWSPAPER AGENTS – GENDER

Gender	*Frequency*	*Percentage*
Male	12	85.7
Female	2	14.3
Total	14	100.0

Source: Primary data.

Newspaper Agents Basing on Age

Table 5.2 shows distribution of newspaper agents age-wise. Out of 14 respondents as many as 12 respondents (85 %) are in the age group of 21 to 40. Age groups of 15 to 20 and 41 to 45 consists of one (7.1 %) respondent each. Analysis reveals that majority of the agents are middle aged persons. The mean value is 33 indicates the average age of newspaper agent is 33 years.

Table-5.2
NEWSPAPER AGENTS – AGE

Age	*Frequency*	*Percentage*
15-20	Nil	Nil
21-25	1	7.1
26-30	4	28.6
31-35	4	28.6
36-40	4	28.6
41-45	1	7.1
Total	14	100.0

Source: Primary data.

Publications Distributed by Newspapers Agents

Publications distributed by agents are as follows. *The Hindu* group of publications was distributed by two agents. *Deccan Chronicle* group of publications was distributed by five agents and *The New Indian Express* group of publications was distributed by five agents. Three agents were distributing *Eenadu* group of publications. Two agents were distributing *Vaartha* group of publications. As can be seen from the analysis that the *Deccan Chronicle* and *The New Indian Express* have more number of agents when compared with *Eenadu*, *Vaartha* and *The Hindu* group of publications.

Nature of Business

The nature of business varies from one agent to another. There are two different types of newspaper agents. One type prefer to do it on a full time basis whereas the other type prefer to do it as part time. Enquiry in this regard reveals that, out of 14 agent respondents, ten (71.4 %) agents were doing as full time, where as four (28.6 %) agents were doing it as part-time business. So majority of newspaper agents are doing full-time business only.

Number of Copies Distributed

Table 5.3 shows distribution of respondents basing on number of copies distributed by agents. As many as seven (14.3 %) newspaper agents were distributing up to 500 copies and only one agent (7.1 %) was distributing more than 2,000 copies. As can be seen from the analysis, a large number of agents are selling copies up to 500 range and very few agents were selling copies above 2,000 range. The mean value 764.8 indicates that on an average of 765 copies were generally distributed by each newspaper agent.

Table–5.3

NUMBER OF COPIES DISTRIBUTED BY AGENTS

Number of Copies	*Frequency*	*Percentage*
Up to 500	7	50.0
501-1000	2	14.3
1001-1500	4	28.6
1501-2000	Nil	Nil
2001-2500	1	7.1
Total	14	100.0

Source: Primary data.

Duration of Carrying Newspaper Business

Table 5.4 depicts distribution of newspaper agents basing on duration of carrying newspaper business. Out of 14 respondents, five (29.4 %) agents are doing business during the last five years and only two (11.8 %) agents are in business for more than 16 years. It is observed that large number of agents are doing business spanning between one to ten years. The mean value is 8.4. That means on an average the duration of carrying newspaper business by newspaper agent is 8.4 years, which reflects reasonably good experience in newspaper business.

Table-5.4
AGENTS BASING ON DURATION OF CARRYING NEWSPAPER BUSINESS

Duration	*Frequency*	*Percentage*
Less than 5 years	5	29. 4
5-10 years	5	29. 4
10-15 years	2	11. 8
More than 15 years	2	11. 8
Total	14	100.0

Source: Primary data.

Investment Made by Newspaper Agents

Table 5.5 reveals the distribution of newspaper agents basing on investment made by them. Out of 14 respondents who are doing newspaper business, four (28.6 per cent) respondents invested less than or equal to Rs. 25,000 and only one (7.1 per cent) agent invested Rs. 1,00,000—Rs. 1,50,000. It is observed that, out of 14 agents, more number of agents have invested the amount which is equal to or less than Rs. 25,000 and average investment made by total respondents is Rs. 75,107. On the whole, it can be concluded that less than or equal to one lakh rupees is sufficient to do newspaper business.

Table-5.5
INVESTMENT MADE BY NEWSPAPER AGENTS

(Rs.in 000's)

Investment	*Frequency*	*Percentage*
Up to 25	4	28.6
25-50	3	21.4
50-100	3	21.4
100-150	1	7.1
Above 150	3	21.4
Total	14	100.0

Source: Primary data.

Time of Receiving News Paper Bundles

Out of 14 respondents, three (20 %) respondents are receiving paper bundles in between 3.00 a.m. and 3.30 a.m. As many as ten (66.7 %)

respondents are receiving paper bundles in between 3.31 a.m. and 4.00 a.m. Paper bundles received by two (13.3 %) agents are at 4.01 a.m. to 4.30 a.m. Only one agent receives *The New Indian Express* bundle at 3.30 a.m. and the same agent receives *Vaartha* at 4.00 a.m to 4.15 a.m. So the total became 15, even though only 14 agents were responded. As can be seen from the analysis that majority of newspaper bundles reach to the destination in time that is between 3.00 a.m. and 4.00 a.m. So it is possible for newspaper agents to deliver the newspapers in time to the readers and satisfy the customer expectations of early morning delivery.

Return on Investment for Agents

Out of 14 respondents eight (57 %) agents have Rs. 5,000 return on investment. The return on investment by three (21 %) agents is in between Rs. 5,001 to Rs. 10,000. More than Rs. 10,000 was secured by three newspaper agents. Thus, the return on investment is very less for newspaper agents.

Salary Structure of Distribution Boys

Salary paid by newspaper agents to distribution boys is generally of two types. One is fixed salary per month irrespective of the number of copies distributed by distribution boys. Another type of salary payable to distribution boys is flexible in nature. That is basing on number of copies distributed by boys. Out of 11 agent respondents who are paying fixed salary to their boys, eight agents pay Rs. 300 to Rs. 400 as fixed salary and two agents pay Rs. 401 to Rs. 500 for the distribution boys. Only one agent pay Rs. 501 to Rs. 600 as salary to distribution boys. Another agent offer above Rs. 600 as a salary to distribution boys. Out of three newspaper agents who were paying variable salary to their boys, one agent offer Rs. 4.00 as compensation per each copy, another agent pay Rs. 5.00 per copy and Rs. 6.00 per copy was offered by remaining agent as a salary to distribution boys. If variable salary is paid to distribution boys then they get more motivated and they try to distribute more number of copies than their counter parts who are getting fixed salary.

Extra Remuneration to Distribution Boys

Sometimes the distribution boys have to perform some extra work like collecting money from newspaper subscribers. Some of the agents pay extra money for extra work done by distribution boys whereas some agents were not paying any extra remuneration for distribution boys. Here extra work for distribution boy means extra work done by the distribution boys other than distributing newspapers. Extra money means the money paid by the agents to distribution boys other than salary. Out of 14 respondents, nine (64.3 %) respondents are not paying any separate remuneration to distribution boys for collecting money from the subscribers. Five (35.7 %) agents pay separate remuneration for collecting money from subscribers. Out of five agents, three (60 %) agents pay Rs. 1.00 to Rs. 1.50 per subscription, one (20 %) agent pay Rs. 2.50 per subscription and one agent pay Rs. 5.00 per subcription, if collection work is completed on or before 10th of every month.

Reasons for Preferring a Particular Agency by Agents

There may be some reasons for every agent for preferring newspaper business. Out of 14 agents responded, three (21.4 %) agents are doing business out of interest. In consideration of the financial requirements one (7.1 %) agent prefered this newspaper agency. As he get habituated to it, one agent selected this business, where as two (14.3 %) agents opted this to get some experience. Five (35.7 %) agents are doing newspaper business because of unemployment whereas two agents are not so specific. (like spending of leisure time).

Unsold Facility for Newspaper Agents

Unsold facility means newspapers that were not sold out are allowed to return to newspaper organizations. This reduces the risk of newspaper agents who depend on newspaper organizations for their livelihood. If newspapers are not sold out they can return the newspapers to the newspaper organizations thus reduce the burden of newspaper agents. Many of the newspaper organizations now-a-days offering this facility to its agents in order to make the newspaper business more attractive. Out of 14 respondents, 12 (85.7 %) respondents have unsold facility whereas two (14.3 %) respondents do not have unsold facility. Out of 12 agents who have unsold return facility, three (25 %) agents have one per cent on total number of copies supplied to them where as two per cent return facility for two (16.7 %) agents. Four (33.3 %) agents have five per cent return facility and three (25 %) agents have 10 per cent return facility. On the whole, the agents have the facility of returning unsold newspapers although the per cent of return facility varied from one to five. This facility may be used as a trade promotion strategy in the light of fierce competition that exists today in newspaper market.

Opinion of Newspaper Agents on Newspaper Business

Out of 14 respondents, 10 (71.4 %) agents said that they are able to make profits from the newspaper business and four (28.6 %) agents opined that newspaper business is not profit making. However these four agents are continuing the same business as they get habituated to do newspaper business although there is no profit. Two agents continue to do newspaper business because there is no alternative despite the fact that they are not generating profits in newspaper business. One agent is continuing on the consideration that atleast it is providing employment for some other people if not profit to him.

Special Supplements Catching Attention According to Newspaper Agents

The newspaper agents were asked to state the special supplements that are catching the eye of readers and popular in newspaper market. The information furnished by the agents newspaper-wise is given in Table 5.6.

Vrithi: (Career), Cinema and Naadi (Health).

Vaartha

Vruthi: For those looking for a bright future, 'Vruthi' provides the right direction. It offers youth the opportunity for all round development of their personality through effective counselling on education, career prospects, general knowledge, competitive exams and necessary guidance. Indeed young readers are given confidence to face the challenges of tomorrow. *Cinema* consists of entertainment news relating to movies. *Naadi* is a daily feature that is devoted to health and medicare. Here information can be gleamed about the various advances being made in the medical world, research being conducted for finding cures, articles by experts on common health problems, guidance on how to stay fit and take care of the body and responses to readers' queries on various health related issues. Alternate medicines like Unani, Ayurveda, Naturopathy, Acupuncture get equal importance.

The New Indian Express: Sunday magazine, Vibes, Health.

Sunday magazine covers sports, cinema etc. Art include books, literature, 'then and now', insight living etc., *Vibes* supplement which consists of information relating various sciences like Physics, Chemistry, Botany, Zoology etc. *Health* supplement consist of information relating to research conducted for finding cures, articles by experts on common health problems, guidance on how to stay fit and take care of the body and responses to readers' queries on various health related issues.

The Hindu: Metro plus, Young world.

Metroplus a four page feature supplement focused on features relating to the city. *Young world* supplement consists of kitty corner which contains cartoons and kaleidoscope, events, voices, forsaken friend, animal time, crayon corner, funtrack, quiz time, news scan, word squares, jumble for kids, quest, school zone, sports special, letter to the editor, what's on this week.

Deccan Chronicle

T. V.and Entertainment Guide, Lifestyle, Career Cronicle.

Career chronicle contain information useful for youth to develop their career. Life style consists of fashions and preferences of people. T.V. and Entertainment Guide consists of news relating to movies, television programmes etc.

Eenadu

Vasundhra supplement is a daily four paged broadsheet pullout for women, which discusses issues exclusively related to women. *Eenadu* recently introduced various features in 'Vasundhara' supplement. The special features are:

- *(i)* Chaduvu – Monday (Relating to education),
- *(ii)* Sukhibhava – Tuesday (Health aspects),
- *(iii)* Champion – Wednesday (Sports information),
- *(iv)* Eenadu – Thursday (About Electronics and Technology),
- *(v)* Siri – Friday (About money matters),
- *(vi)* Eetaram – Saturday (About youth),
- *(vii)* Bujjai – Sunday (Information relating to children) in week days and one feature on each day.

Andhra Bhoomi

Vennela consist of entertainment news, cinema news etc. Priyadarshini consist of women issues, fashions, style, preference, puzzles for children, entertainment, jokes, study materials, literature, cartoons etc.

Table–5.6
CLASSIFICATION OF NEWSPAPER SUPPLEMENTS AND TARGET GROUPS

Name of the Newspaper	*Education*	*Entertainment*	*Health*	*For Women*
Eenadu	Chaduvu	Cinema	Sukhi Bhava	Vasundhara
Vaartha	Vrithi	Cinema	Naadi	Cheli
Andhra Bhoomi	Sadhana	Vennela	Sanjivini	Priyadarshini
The Hindu	Young World	Sunday Magazine		
The New Indian Express	Vibes	Cinema scope	Health	Women
Deccan Chronicle	Career Chronicle	T.V. and Entertainment Guide, Cinema Cinema	Health	Life style

Source: Primary data.

Classification of Newspaper Supplements

Table 5.6 shows comparitive analysis of supplements. Of all supplements relating to education, Young world of *The Hindu* became more popular as it contains more attractive features. In supplements relating to women, Vasundhara of *Eenadu* could catch attention of readers, particularly women readers in regional language (Telugu). This contains more interesting and innovative features relating to women when compared with other supplements in that category.

Problems of Agent Respondents

When newspaper agents are doing business, one or other time they definitely face certain problems. This analysis explains very well about the problems faced by newspaper agents. Out of 14 respondents, seven (50 %) agents are facing problems while doing newspaper business. Out of seven agents, three agents said that they do not have the facility of returning unsold newspapers. Two agents have problem with distribution boys because of their irregular attendance. One agent said that readers are not sticking to one newspaper and they frequently change the newspaper they are reading. One agent expressed that it is difficult for him to get up early in the morning as agents are required to do most of their job early in the morning in newspaper market. The analysis reveals that nearly half of the agents are facing problems either with the distribution boys or with the subscribers.

Ranking of Newspapers by Newspaper Agents

Table 5.7 shows information pertaining to selected newspapers ranking in terms of cost benefit analysis from the newspaper agents. *The Hindu* is given first rank by five agents (35.7 %), second rank by four (28.6 %) agents. *The New Indian Express* was given first rank by one (14.3 %) agent. *Deccan Chronicle* was given second rank by three (23 %) agents. *Eenadu* was given first rank by five (41.7 %) agents and second rank by three (16.7 %) agents. *Vaartha* was given as second rank by two (16.7 %) agents. *Andhra Bhoomi* was given third rank by one agent. From Table 5.6, it is seen that the first rankers are *The Hindu, Eenadu* followed by *The New Indian Express*. These are followed by *The Hindu, Eenadu, Deccan Chronicle, Vaartha* and *Andhra Bhoomi* in second ranking. The only third ranking is for *Andhra Bhoomi*. These rankings are based on the opinion of the agents in terms of their cost and benefit considerations alone although there are other factors such as circulation, income, popularity, etc., that influence rankings.

Table–5.7
RANKING OF NEWSPAPERS BY AGENTS

Name of the Newspaper	*I Rank (No. of Agents)*	*Per cent*	*II Rank (No. of Agents)*	*Per cent*	*III Rank*	*Per cent*
The Hindu	5	38.7	4	28.6	-	-
Eenadu	5	41.7	3	16.7	-	-
The New Indian Express	1	14.3	-	-	-	-
Deccan Chronicle	-	-	3	23.0	-	-
Vaartha	-	-	2	16.7	-	-
Andhra Bhoomi	-	-	-		1	100.0

Source: Primary data.

Opinion on Reading Newspaper through Internet

Out of 14 respondents, seven (50 %) respondents responded to the quest of reading newspaper through internet, one agent (respondent) expressed the opinion that ordinary newspaper is more flexible for reading than reading newspaper through internet. Another agent opined that internet gets news early and easily when there is internet at home. But most of the people may not have internet at home. According to four agents the normal newspaper is more preferred than internet newspaper when viewed from the cost point of view because of browsing charges. One agent opined that reading newspaper through internet is added advantage to normal newspaper business. Likewise majority of newspaper agents reacted positively about the surfing of internet by newspaper readers and its impact on physical readership. So agents are very positive towards future of newspaper business even though newspaper is available through internet. The analysis reveals that surfing of internet to read newspaper may not have adverse impact on normal newspaper business.

Opinion on Future of Newspaper

The future of newspapers in terms of their future prospects in the market is collected from the agents. Out of 14 respondents, Five (35.7 %) respondents have positive opinion towards the future of newspaper and seven (50 %) agents did not respond. Only two (14.3 %) respondents have negative opinion on future of newspaper. Though seven agents have not responded, from the response of the others it can be inferred that the newspaper business has bright future.

Retailers' Views and Perceptions

Retailer Respondents Basing on Age Group

Table 5.8, reveals distribution of retailer respondents basing on age. Out of 50 respondents, 11 (22 %) respondents are in the age group of 26 to 30. Only one (2 %) respondent is in 61 to 65 age group. From table, it is observed that majority of respondents are in middle age. There is inverse relation between age and number of respondents. As age is increasing, number of respondents are decreasing. The mean value is 33.6. That means average age of retailer respondents is 33.6 years.

Satisfaction Expressed Towards Time of Arrival of Newspaper by Retailers

Out of 50 respondents, 36 respondents are satisfied with time of arrival of newspaper and 14 respondents are not satisfied with the time of arrival of newspaper. So by and large, the time of arrival is satisfactory.

Table-5.8

RETAILER RESPONDENTS BASING ON AGE GROUP

Age	*Frequency*	*Percentage*
15-20	3	6
21-25	8	16
26-30	11	22
31-35	9	18
36-40	7	14
41-45	6	12
46-50	3	6
51-55	2	4
56-60	0	0
61-65	1	2
Total	50	100

Source: Primary data.

Ranking of Newspapers by Retailers basing on Fast Movingness of Newspapers

Out of 50 respondents *Eenadu* is given as first rank by 32 respondents. According to 11 respondents, *The Hindu* is in first position. For seven respondents, *Deccan Chronicle* is in first position. For three respondents, *Vaartha* is in first position. Analysis reveals that *Eenadu* is fast moving newspaper. Here fast moving means easily sold by retailers.

Number of Newspaper Copies Sold by Retailers

Table 5.9 shows distribution of respondents basing on number of newspapers sold. The average of respondents who are selling all types of newspapers up to 10 copies per day is 20.3 and the average of respondents who are selling above 50 copies per day is 2.35. It indicates majority of the respondents are selling 0 to10 copies per day. Average copies sold by the retailer is 8.33.

Commission Given to Retailers to Sell Newspapers

For *The Hindu, The New Indian Express, Vaartha, Andhra Bhoomi, Andhra Praba* the commission given is 20 paise per copy. For *Deccan Chronicle* and *Eenadu,* the commission given is 12 paise per copy. From this it is clear that the commission is less for *Deccan Chronicle* as well as *Eenadu.*

Table–5.9
RETAILERS BASING ON NUMBER OF COPIES SOLD

Number of Copies	*The Hindu*	*New Indian Express*	*Deccan Chronicle*	*Eenadu*	*Vaartha*	*Andhra Bhoomi*	*Andhra Prabha*	*Average*
0-10	6	35	18	2	11	50	-	20.30
11-20	27	6	18	16	26	-	-	15.50
21-30	7	3	5	19	3	-	-	6.20
31-40	4	3	4	5	4	-	-	3.30
41-50	3	2	3	3	3	-	-	2.35
> 50	3	1	2	5	3	-	-	2.35
Total	50	50	50	50	50	50	50	50.00
Average								8.33*

Source: Primary data.

* Weighted Average is caluculated.

Magazines Arrival Time to Retailers

Andhra Bhoomi weekly, *India Today* and *The Week* magazines are arriving on every Monday. *Outlook* magazines is arriving on every Sunday. *Swathi* magazine is arriving on Thursday. *Andhra Prabha* weekly is arriving on every Saturday.

Table–5.10
CIRCULATION OF MAGAZINES IN VISAKHAPATNAM

Name of Magazine	*Circulation (Number of Copies) (Approximate Figures)*
Swathi	12,000
Andhra Bhoomi Weekly	3,000
Andhra Prabha Weekly	1,000
India Today	4,000
Week	2,000
Outlook	2,000
Total	24,000 (Approx.)

Source: Primary data.

Number of Copies of Magazines Sold

Table 5.11 depicts distribution of respondents basing on number of magazines sold. Out of total 50 respondents, on an average 25.3

respondents are selling 0 to10 copies of magazines per week and only 1.3 respondents are selling 51 to 60 copies of magazines per week. As can be seen from the table, majority of respondents are selling copies from 0 to10 per week. Very less number of respondents are selling copies from 51 to 60. The average copies of magazines sold by the retailer is 6.8 per week.

Table–5.11

RETAILERS BASING ON NUMBER OF MAGAZINES SOLD

No.of Copies	*Swathi*	*Andhra Bhoomi*	*Andhra Prabha*	*India Today*	*The Week*	*Outlook*	*Average*
0-10	-	36	40	8	32	36	25.3
11-20	9	10	8	6	9	7	8.2
21-30	15	4	2	7	3	4	5.8
31-40	7	-	-	5	2	2	2.6
41-50	10	-	-	4	3	1	3
51-60	3	-	-	3	2	-	1.3
Above 60	6	-	-	17	-	-	3.8

Source: Primary data.

Commission Given to Retailers to Sell Magazines

Out of 50 respondents who are selling magazines, 19 (38 %) respondents are getting commission of ten per cent on total number of copies sold by them. Three (6%) respondents are getting commission of eight per cent. Twenty-four (48 %) respondents are getting commission of seven per cent. Four (8%) respondents are getting the commission of six per cent on sales. So majority of the respondents (48 %) are getting commission of seven per cent on sales.

Unsold Facility for Retailers

Out of 50 respondents 20 (40 %) retailers have returning unsold newspapers. That means on unsold newspapers, some concession is given by newspaper organisations to retailers. Unsold facility is not given to 30 (60 %) respondents who are covered under survey.

Classification of Retailers who Influence Buyers at the Time of Purchase

Out of 50 respondents, 20 (40 %) respondents influence buyers when the customer is purchasing the newspaper and 30 (60 %) respondents did not influence customers when they are purchasing a particular newspaper. Out of 50 respondents, no retailer is getting any type of incentive.

Retailers facing problem with newspaper organizations or with buyers Out of 50 respondents, 46 (92 %) respondents are not facing any problems by newspaper organisations or buyers and four (8 %) respondents are facing problems.

(i) *The problems are:* According to two retailers, the commission is very less.
(ii) *Andhra Bhoomi* and *Eenadu* do not have any unsold facility that returning of unsold newspapers.
(iii) During Sundays adequate copies are not made available by some of the newspaper organizations.

Distribution Boys' Views and Perceptions

Classification of Distribution Boys Basing on Gender

There exists some relationship between gender and distribution of newspapers. Table 5.12 shows distribution of distribution boy respondents basing on gender. Out 50 respondents, all 50 (100 %) respondents belongs to male group only and there is no female who distributes newspaper to subscribers. It is because of the reason that the distribution work start at early in the morning before 4.00 a.m. which is not convenient for females.

Table–5.12
DISTRIBUTION BOYS – GENDER

Gender	*Frequency*	*Percentage*
Male	50	100
Female	0	0

Source: Primary data.

Classification of Distribution Boys-Age

There may be some relationship between age and number of respondents. Table 5.13 shows distribution boy respondents-age wise. Out of 50 respondents, 21 (42 %) respondents belongs to 21 to 25 age group and only one (2 %) respondent belongs to 46 to 50 age group. Analysis reveals that majority of distribution boys are in 21 to 25 age group and few number of boys are in 46 to 50 age group. Study reveals that frequency of distribution boys is decreasing as age group is increasing. There exists inverse relation between age group and number of respondents. Mean value is 23.4. That means average age of respondents is 23.4.

Table–5.13
DISTRIBUTION BOYS – AGE

Qualification	*Frequency*	*Percentage*
15-20	17	34
21-25	21	42
26-30	6	12
31-35	5	10
36-40	0	0
41-45	0	0
46-50	1	2
Total	50	100

Source: Primary data.

Respondents Educational Qualification

There may be some relation between number of respondents and educational qualification. Table 5.14 reveals classification of distribution boys basing on educational qualification. Out of 50 respondents 27 (54 %) respondents belongs to up to 10th class category, only one (2%) respondent belongs to post-graduate category. As can be seen from the table, more respondents are in up to 10th class category and less respondents belongs to post-graduate category. As educational qualification is increasing the number of distribution boys who are distributing newspapers are decreasing.

Table–5.14
DISTRIBUTION BOYS – EDUCATION

Qualification	*Frequency*	*Percentage*
Up to 10th	27	54
Intermediate	8	16
Degree	10	20
Post-graduate	1	2
Others*	4	8
Total	50	100

*Others include I.T. I, P.U.C, S.L.S.C so on.

Source: Primary data.

Publications Distributed by Distribution Boys

Table 5.15 shows distribution of distribution boys basing on Publications distributed by distribution boys. Out of 50 respondents, *Eenadu* consists of 17 (34 %) distribution boys, *Deccan Chronicle* consists of 12 (24 %) respondents whereas *Vaartha* consists of 4 (8 %) distribution boys. From the analysis it is noted that, *Eenadu* consists of more number of distribution boys and *Vaartha* consists of very less number of distribution boys.

Table–5.15

PUBLICATIONS DISTRIBUTED BY DISTRIBUTION BOYS

Name of the Publication	*Frequency*	*Percentage*
Deccan Chronicle Group	7	14
New Indian Express Group	12	24
Hindu group	5	10
Eenadu group	17	34
Vaartha group	4	8
Others*	5	10
Total	50	100

*Others include *Praja Sakthi*-1, *Andhra Jyothi*-4.

Source: Primary data.

Time Taken to Distribute Newspapers to Subscribers

Table 5.16 shows classification of distribution boys basing on time taken to distribute newspapers to subscribers. Out of 50 respondents, 20 (40 %) respondents can complete entire distribution work with in one hour. Only three (6 %) respondents require 2.50 to 3.00 hours time to distribute newspapers to subscribers. The table further reveals that more number of respondents can distribute entire papers within one hour and very few respondents require more than two hours time to finish the entire distribution of newspapers. That means the average time taken to distribute newspapers for subscribers is 1.24 hours as the mean value is 1.24.

Duration of Working in Field as Distribution Boys

The duration of working is not same for all distribution boys. It is different for different distribution boys. Table 5.17 shows distribution of boys basing on their service of working. The table reveals that 16 (32 %) distribution boys are having less than on year experience and only one distribution boy is working since four to five years. A large majority of distribution boys are doing business during the business for the past twelve months. (one year). The mean value 2.57 indicates the average service period for distribution boys is 2.57 years.

Table–5.16

TIME TAKEN TO DISTRIBUTE NEWSPAPERS FOR SUBSCRIBERS

Time Taken	*Frequency*	*Percentage*
Below one hour	20	40
Between one and one and half hours	12	24
Between one and half and two hours	13	26
Between two and two and half hours	2	4
Between two and half and three hours	3	6
Total	50	100

Source: Primary data.

Table–5.17

DURATION OF WORKING IN FIELD AS DISTRIBUTION BOYS

Time Period	*Frequency*	*Percentage*
Less than 1 year	16	32
1-2 years	13	26
>2-3 years	8	16
>3-4 years	1	2
>4-5 years	1	2
>5-6 years	0	0
> 6 years	11	22
Total	50	100

Source: Primary data.

Distribution of Newspaper Points

Out of 50 distribution boys, nine (18 %) boys are collecting papers from Dutt Island for distribution, nine (18 %) paper boys are collecting papers from Udyog Bhavan, eight distribution boys are collecting papers from Kotta road, five (10 %) paper boys are collecting from Ushodaya junction. Two (4 %) distribution boys are collecting from Meghalaya point, and 12 (24 %) distribution boys are collecting papers for distribution from other areas which are changing from time to time according to convenience. The analysis reveals that eventhough paper points are unevenly distributed efficient distribution is possible.

Distribution Boys Classification Basing on Participation in Collection Work

Out of 50 respondents 36 (72 %) distribution boys are participating in collection work and 14 (28 %) distribution boys are not participating in any collection work. So a majority of distribution boys are participating in collection work.

Out of 36 respondents who are participating in collection work, 33 (91.7 %) respondents are not receiving collection in time whereas three (8.3 %) respondents are receiving collection money in time from subscribers. According to survey, out of 36 respondents, 13 (36.1 per cent) distribution boys usually get the entire money in first ten days of collection work. Eleven (30.6 %) respondents usually get the collection money after two to three times they visit subscribers. Six (16.7 per cent) respondents get subscription money when they made three to four visits. Three (8.3 %) respondents have to make one to two visits to collect money from subscribers. Three (8.3 %) respondents can collect money from first 20 days of collection work started.

Nature of Remuneration

Remuneration for work done is generally of two types. One is fixed remuneration which is fixed irrespective of number of copies distributed and the other one is variable remuneration which is variable according to change in distribution of number of copies. Out of 50 respondents, 36 (72 %) respondents are getting fixed remuneration and only 14 (28 %) are getting variable remuneration. Out of 36 respondents who are getting fixed remuneration, eight (22.2 %) distribution boys are getting less than or equal to Rs.100 month. Seven (19.4 %) respondents are getting greater than Rs.100 to less than or equal to Rs.150 month. Three (8.3 %) respondents are getting greater than Rs.150 to less than or equal to Rs. 200 month. Two (5.6 %) respondents are getting more than Rs. 250 to less than or equal to Rs. 300 month. Seven (19.4 %) respondents are getting more than Rs. 400 to less than or equal to Rs. 500 month. One (2.8 %) respondent is getting more than Rs. 500 to less than or equal to Rs. 600 month. Out of 14 respondents who are getting variable remuneration six (42.9 %) respondents are getting Rs. 5.00 per copy, two (14.3%) respondents are getting Rs. 7.00 copy, two (14.3 %) respondents getting Rs. 7.00 per copy, two (14.3%) respondents are getting Rs. 10 per copy, One (7 %) respondent is getting Rs. 15 per copy. Out of 50 respondents 45 (90%) respondents are not getting any separate remuneration for collection work. Five (10 %) respondents are getting separate remuneration for collection work. Out of five respondents who are getting separate remuneration for work done, One (20 %) respondent is getting Rs. 350 month. One respondent each is getting Rs. 826, Rs. 840, Rs. 900, Rs. 1200 per month. Out of 50 respondents, four (8 %) respondents are getting special incentives in addition to normal earnings when extra copies are sold. 46 (92 %) respondents are not getting any incentives for extra work. Out of four respondents who are earning special incentives, three respondents are getting incentive for every two years. One respondent is getting incentive basing on number of copies sold.

Whether Facing Any Problems While Distributing Newspapers

Out of 50 respondents, 29 (58 %) respondents are facing problems while distributing newspapers and 21 (42 %) respondents are not facing any problems from the newspaper organisations. Significant number of distribution boys are facing problems with newspaper organizations when they were distributing newspapers to the readers. From the subscribers, out of 50 respondents, 18 (36 %) respondents are facing problems and 32 (64 %) respondents are not facing any problems. The analysis reveals that majority of distribution boys are not facing any problems with the subscribers.

Problems of Distribution Boys

The main problem with distribution boys is untimely delivery of newspapers. This is because the parcels sometimes may arrive late from publishers to agent points. If the publisher fails to send the paper parcels on schedule the boys will suffer a lot. The schedule time for paper parcels reaching to all points is 4.00 a.m. This is applicable for all daily newspapers. The boys are habituated to attend the collection point at 4.00 a.m. and arrange all papers and start distribution work. They complete it by 6.00 a.m. every morning. If the publisher does not send the newspaper parcels in time, the distribution boy has to wait till the parcels arrive. This causes a lot of inconvenience to the distribution boys and also to the subscribers.

Because these boys are part-time workers, they would have to attend to their full-time job later after completing newspaper distribution work. The subscriber expects the newspaper early in the morning preferably before 6.00 a.m. If the paper is distributed by distribution boys after 6.00 a.m. the subscriber feels very unhappy and sometimes they decide to discontinue the paper and subscribe to a newspaper delivered early in the morning.

In some posh localities the subscribers lock their entrance gates inside and do not allow anyone to enter into their premises. Sometimes watchmen also obstruct the boys. In this case the boy normally throws the paper into the premises. While throwing the paper in to the premises it may fall into the water, particularly in the rainy season. If the paper is wet it becomes useless and, the reader may complain and discontinue the newspaper for such delivery. Sometimes the pet dogs tear away the newspapers, but the blame is thrown on newspaper boys. Some subscribers, want the paper at their doorsteps. But in apartments, it is very difficult for boys to distribute the paper at their doorsteps. Generally, boys supply the newspapers in the early hours when darkness exist before sunlight. Lack of power supply causes some problems particularly when dogs are barking and also the lanes are narrow. Sometimes, the subscribers repeatedly postpone payment of subscription fee without a valid reason. Because of late printing or for missing pages, subscribers normally blame paper boys even though the mistake is not on their part. Sometimes the subscriptions were cancelled in the middle of the month and the distribution boy may not be aware of it.

REFERENCES

1. Vaile, R.S., E.T. Grether and R. Cox (1952), *Marketing in the American Economy*, New York, Ronald, p. 113.
2. Louis, W. Stern, Adel I.EL-Ansary, Anne T. Coughlan (1996), *Marketing Channels*, Prentice-Hall of India Private Limited, New Delhi, Fifth Edition, pp. 2-3.
3. Drucker, F. Peter (1970), *Marketing for Results*, Allied Publishers (P) Ltd., Bombay, pp. 21-24.
4. Louis, W. Stern, Adel I.El-Ansary, Anne T. Coughlam (1996), *Marketing Channels*, Prentice–Hall of India Private Limited, New Delhi, p. 143.
5. *The International Journal of Logistics Management*, Vol. IV, No. 2 (1993), p. 1.

6. Ronald Henkoff (1994), *Delivering the Goods, Fortune Magazine,* November 28, 1994, pp. 64-66.

7. Primary Data through Interviews with the Circulation Managers of various Publications in Visakhapatnam City.

6

Analysis of Customers' Views, Perception and Satisfaction

The Customer is the most important person in any organization. Customers choose the marketing offer that gives them the most value. Over thirty-five years ago, Peter Drucker observed that a companys' first task is 'to create customers' from their point of view. This is possible only if organizations create and deliver value to the buyers in the market. As such, organizations put their best efforts in understanding the needs of the market and design their offers to suit target markets. Thus, today's customers face a vast array of products and brand choices, prices and suppliers.

Customer Value

We believe that customer estimate which offer will deliver the most value. It is the bundle of benefits customers expect from a given product or service. Total customer cost is the bundle of costs customer expect to incur in evaluating, obtaining and using the product or service.[1] The customers choose the marketing offer that gives them the most value. Customers are value maximizers, within the bounds of search costs and limited knowledge, mobility and income. They form an expectation of value and act on it. Weather or not the offer lives up to the value expectation affects both satisfaction and repurchase ability. Customer compare the prices they must pay for the competitors products. As Adamsmith observed more than two centuries ago, "the real price of anything is the toil and trouble of acquiring it." Total customer cost also include the buyers' anticipated time, energy and psychic costs. The firm will evaluate these costs along with monetary costs to form a complete estimate of its costs.

Customer Perceptions

Customers generally buy the product basing on their perceptions. They buy the product only when it is perceived as less priced and highly qualitative. So simply producing qualitative products is not enough. The job of marketers is to make the people perceive high about the quality of product. "Perception is defined as the process by which an individual selects, organises and interpretes stimuli into a meaningful and coherent picture of the world."[2] So unless the customer perceive the product as qualitative, he will never buy the product, even though it is actually qualitative product. So customer perception plays an important role in consumer buying process.

Customer Satisfaction

"Customer satisfaction is persons' feelings of pleasure or disappointment resulting from comparing a product's perceived performance (or out come) in relation to his or her expectations."[3] Consumers form judgements about the value of marketing offer, and make their buying decisions based upon these judgements. Whether the buyers are satisfied after purchase depends on the offer's performance in relation to the buyers' expectations. Satisfaction is a persons' feelings of pleasure of disappointment resulting from comparing a products' perceived performance in relation to his or her expectations. If the performance falls short of expectations, the customer is dissatisfied. If the performance matches the expectations, the customer is highly satisfied or delighted. The customer expectations are from past buying experience, friends and associates advice, and marketers and competitors information and promise. If marketers raise expectations too high, the buyers are likely to be disappointed. However, if the company sets expectations too low, it cannot attract enough buyers. The brand must represent a promise about the total experience customers can expect. Whether the promise is kept or not depends on the company's ability to manage its value delivery system. The value delivery system includes all the experience the customer will have on the way to obtaining and using the offering. So, in order to know customer satisfaction simply handling complaints is not enough. The organizations should conducts frequent surveys to know about customer satisfaction. In newspaper organisations, the consumers are readers and unless the readers perceive the newspaper as good, they would not prefer to read that particular newspaper, even though it is qualitative one. In order to make the readers feel good about newspaper, they should perceive it as qualitative and at the same time less priced. This chapter analyses readers' views, perceptions and satisfaction of eight different newspapers on coverage of news items, areas of interest, preference of newspapers and so on in Visakhapatnam City. This chapter consists of three parts. First part deals with profile of newspaper readers in Visakhaptanam City. Second part consists of newspaper reading habits of readers and third part explains other media habits of newspaper readers.

Table-6.1
NEWSPAPER READ BY RESPONDENTS

Name of Newspaper	*Frequency*	*Per cent*
The Hindu	117	20.3
The New Indian Express	24	4.2
Deccan Chronicle	64	11.1
The Times of India	7	1.2
Eenadu	211	36.6
Vaartha	120	20.8
Andhra Bhoomi	28	4.9
Andhra Prabha	5	0.9
Total	576	100

Source: Primary data.

Newspaper Reading Habits

The area selected for the study has readers who are reading different types of newspapers. Table 6.1 shows the newspaper reading habits of respondents. The table reveals that, out of 576 respondents, 211 respondents are reading *Eenadu* (36.6 %), 120 (20.8 %) respondents are reading *Vaartha,* 117 (20.3 %) respondents are reading *The Hindu* newspaper, 64 (11.1 %) people are reading *Deccan Chronicle* newspaper. Seven (1.2 %) readers are reading *The Times of India,* and five (0.9 %) readers are reading *Andhra Prabha.* The analysis reveals a large number of respondents read *Eenadu,* considerable number of respondents read *Vaartha* followed by respondents of *The Hindu* and *Deccan Chronicle* newspapers. This explanation reveals the fact that local newspapers are mostly preferred by readers in Visakhapatnam City.

Readers Respondents Basing on Gender

There may be relationship that exists between readers' newspaper reading habit and gender. Out of 576 reader respondents 446 (77.4 %) represent males and 130 (22.6 %) represent female readers. That means 77.4 per cent of readers are males and 22.6 per cent of readers are females. Analysis reveals that a clear majority of newspaper readers are males. This may be because of the reason that in women literacy rate is less when compared with men. As newspaper reading habit is directly proportional to literacy rate, the newspaper reading habit is comparitively less in females. Not only that women are more concerned about household activities and hardly find time to read newspapers. They are also least worried about what has happening in their surroundings, when compared to their family, which is prime concern in a country like India that has strong family values, particularly womens' role and responsibilities in managing household chores.

Table–6.2

GENDER OF READER RESPONDENTS

Gender	*Frequency*	*Per cent*
Men	446	77.4
Women	130	22.6
Total	576	100.0

Source: Primary data.

Table–6.2.1

GENDER AND NEWSPAPER OF RESPONDENT READERS

Name of the Newspaper	*Male*	*Female*	*Total*	*Per cent*
The Hindu	90	26	117	20.3
The New Indian Express	19	6	24	4.2
Deccan Chronicle	50	14	64	11.1
The Times of India	5	2	7	1.2
Eenadu	163	48	211	36.6
Vaartha	93	27	120	20.8
Andhra Bhoomi	22	6	28	4.9
Andhra Prabha	4	1	5	0.9
Total	446	130	576	100.0

Source: Primary data.

Gender and Newspaper of Respondent Readers

There may be relationship between gender and newspaper that read by readers. Table 6.2.1 shows distribution of reader respondents and its relation to gender. Out of 576 respondents, 47 female readers read *Eenadu* and 27 female readers read *Vaartha*. The readership of regional newspapers by women is comparatively high when compared with other national newspapers because of two reasons. One is the newspapers are published in regional language and even less educated people can understand. As women are less educated in a country like India, they prefer regional language newspapers than national newspapers. Another reason is that regional newspapers are publishing supplements relating to women. For example, *Eenadu* newspaper is publishing women supplement known as Vasundhara and *Vaartha* is publishing Cheli. These supplements consist of new relating to women. It consists of women issues, recipes, fashions and other information pertaining to women etc.

Reader Respondents Basing on Age of Readers: There may be relationship exists between the readers' newspaper reading and their age. Table 6.3 shows distribution of reader respondents basing on age. Of the total sample of 576 readers, 99 (17.2 %) readers belong to 26 to 30 years age group, 37 (6.4 %) readers belong to 46 to 50 years age group, nine (1.6 %) readers belong to 61 to 65 age group, and one (0.2 %) reader belong to above 70 years age group. It is observed that majority of readers are middle aged and the newspaper readership is increasing from 15 to 20 years age group to 26 to 30 years age group and the readership slowly declined as age advanced. The mean value of 33.6 indicates middle aged as the major target market for newspapers. The mean value of female respondents 34.7 and the mean value of male respondents 32.5 explain that the males develop newspaper reading habit in the early age than females.

Table–6.3
READER RESPONDENTS – AGE AND GENDER

Age Group (Years)	*Males*	*Females*	*Frequency*	*Per cent*
16–20	65.0	19.0	84	14.6
21–25	66.6	19.4	86	14.9
26–30	76.6	22.4	99	17.2

(Contd.)

Age Group (Years)	*Males*	*Females*	*Frequency*	*Per cent*
31–35	65.9	19.1	85	14.8
36–40	44.9	13.1	58	10.0
41–45	54.3	15.7	70	12.2
46–50	28.6	8.4	37	6.4
51–55	17.0	5.0	22	3.8
56–60	17.0	5.0	22	3.8
61–65	7.0	2.0	9	1.6
66–70	2.3	0.7	3	0.5
70 and above	0.8	0.2	1	0.2
Total	446	130.0	576	100.0

Source: Primary data.

Income of Readers

The annual income of the sample readers includes the income from two sources, viz., primary and secondary. Primary source of income is by employment, business and agriculture. Some people earn money by doing part-time jobs, employees are also do part-time business or agriculture. This is additional source of income. For the purpose of the study income includes income obtained from both primary and secondary sources. Table 6.4 shows distribution of reader respondents' income. Out of 576 reader respondents, 241 (41.9 %) readers are in Rs. 5,001 to Rs. 10,000 income group. Seven (1.2 %) readers are in above Rs. 20,000 income group. The table reveals that more number of readers are in the income group of Rs. 5,001 to10,000 and very less number of readers in above Rs. 20,000 income group. The reading habit increases as income increases up to Rs. 10,000 income level and later on it slowly declined inspite of increased income. The mean value 7,292.20 indicates the average income of respondents is Rs. 7, 292.20.

Readers' Monthly Income and Newspaper Reading

There may be relationship between type of newspaper read and their monthly income. Table 6.4.1 shows distribution of reader respondents in terms of their monthly income. In upto Rs. 5,000 income group *Eenadu* constitutes 64 (37.00 %) readers and *Andhra Prabha* constitutes two (1.20 %) reader respondents. In Rs. 5,001 to Rs. 10,000 income group. *Eenadu* constitutes 88 (36.50 %) readers and

Table–6.4
READER RESPONDENTS – INCOME

Income (Rs.)	*Frequency*	*Percentage*
Up to 5,000	173	30.0
5,001–10,000	241	41.9
10,001–15,000	112	19.4
15,000–20,000	23	7.5
> 20,000	7	1.2
Total	576	100.0

Source: Primary data.

Table–6.4.1
READERS BASING ON NEWSPAPER READING HABIT AND INCOME

Income (Rs.)	*The Hindu*	*The New Indian Express*	*Deccan Chronicle*	*The Times of India*	*Enadu*	*Vaartha*	*Andhra Bhoomi*	*Andhra Prabha*
Up to 5000	35	7	19	2	64	36	8	2
(173)*	(21.3)	(4.0)	(11.0)	(1.2)	(37)	(19.7)	(4.6)	(1.2)
5001–10000	49	10	27	3	88	50	12	2
(241)*	(20.3)	(4.2)	(11.2)	(1.2)	(36.5)	(20.8)	(5.0)	(0.8)
10001–15000	23	5	12	1	41	23	6	1
(112)*	(20.5)	(4.5)	(10.7)	(0.9)	(36.6)	(20.5)	(5.4)	(0.9)
15001–20000	9	2	5	1	15	9	2	–
(23)*	(20.9)	(4.7)	(11.6)	(2.3)	(34.9)	(20.9)	(4.7)	
Total (576)*	117	24	64	7	211	120	28	5

Source: Primary data.
Note: Figures in parenthesis indicates percentages of totals.
* Figures indicates row totals.

Andhra Prabha constitutes two (0.80 %) readers. In Rs. 10,001 to Rs. 15,000 income group *Eenadu* constitutes 41 (36.60 %) reader and *The Times of India* and *Andhra Prabha* constitutes one (0.90 %) reader each. In Rs. 15,001 to Rs. 20,000 income group *Eenadu* constitutes 15 (34.90 %) readers and *Andhra Prabha* constitutes no readers. In above Rs. 20,000 income group *Eenadu* constitutes three (42.80 %) readers and *The New Indian Express, The Times of India, Andhra Bhoomi* and *Andhra Prabha* constitutes zero per cent of readers. As can be seen from the table a majority of readers who read different types of newspapers are in Rs. 5,001 to Rs. 10,000 income group. Of all eight newspapers, *Eenadu* constitutes maximum number of readers in Rs. 5,001 to Rs. 10,000 income group.

Educational Qualification of Readers

There is always a relationship between newspaper reading habit and educational qualification. Readers who are well-qualified always prefer variety of newspapers both English and regional language. People who are less qualified generally prefer regional language newspaper. So readership is more in better-qualified people than less qualified people. Table 6.5 shows distribution of reader respondents basing on educational qualification. Among 576 reader respondents 126 (21.9 %) readers are at intermediate level, 206 (35.8 %) readers are in Graduate/PG (General) category. As can be seen from the table that majority of readers are in Graduate/PG (General) group and least number of readers in PUC category. The Newspaper reading habit slowly increased up to Graduate/PG (General) level and declined after Graduate/PG (Professional) level. Readership is more in youth particularly below graduation level may be because of the reason that newspapers contain information relating to employment, career planning and development etc.

Table-6.5

EDUCATIONAL QUALIFICATION OF READERS

Qualification	*Male*	*Female*	*Frequency*	*Per cent*
Up to 10th	82.8	24.2	107	18.6
Intermediate	97.5	28.5	126	21.9
PUC	10.8	3.2	14	2.4
Graduate/PG (General)	159.0	47.0	206	35.8
Graduate/PG (Professional)	95.2	27.8	123	21.3
Total	446.0	130.0	576	100.0

Source: Primary data:

PG—Post Graduate.

PG (General)—It include general post-graduate courses like M.A. (Master of Arts), M.Com. (Master of Commerce), M.Sc. (Master of Science) etc.

PG (Professional)—It include Post-Graduate Professional courses like M.B.A. (Master of Business Administration), M.C.A. (Master of Computer Applications), B.E. (Bachelor of Engineering) etc.

PUC—Pre-University Course.

Preference of Newspaper in Relation to Readers' Educational Qualification

Table 6.5.1 shows distribution of reader respondents in relation to their educational qualification. In up to 10th class group 39 (36.4 %) readers read *Eenadu* and *The Times of India* and *Andhra Prabha* constitutes one (0.9) reader each. *The Hindu* readers are 22 (20.6 %) in number. In Intermediate 46 (36.5 %) readers read *Eenadu,* One (0.8 %) reader read Andhra Prabha. *The Hindu* readers are 26 (20.6 %) in number. In PUC five (36.5 %) readers read *Eenadu, Andhra Prabha* and *The Times of India* constitutes zero per cent of readers. In Graduate/PG (General) category 75 (36.4 %) readers read *Eenadu,* 41 (19.9 %) readers constitute *The Hindu* readers, two (1.0) constitutes *Andhra Prabha* readers. *Eenadu* constitutes 43 (36.7 %) readers, *The Hindu, Vaartha* constitutes 25 (20.3 %) readers each. *The Times of India* constitutes one (0.8 %) reader each. An insight into the table reveals that in each group *Eenadu* constitutes more number of readers followed by *Vaartha* and in English newspapers, *The Hindu* constitutes more number of readers. *The Times of India* and *Andhra*

Table–6.5.1
EDUCATIONAL QUALIFICATION AND NEWSPAPER READING HABIT OF READERS

Educational Qualification	*The Hindu*	*The New Indian Express*	*Deccan Chronicle*	*The Times of India*	*Eenadu*	*Vaartha*	*Andhra Bhoomi*	*Andhra Prabha*
Up to 10th class (107)*	22 (20.6)	4 (3.7)	1 (11.2)	1 (0.9)	39 (36.4)	23 (21.5)	5 (4.8)	1 (0.9)
Inter (126)*	26 (20.6)	5 (4)	14 (11.1)	2 (1.6)	46 (36.5)	26 (20.6)	6 (4.8)	1 (0.8)
PUC (14)*	3 (21.4)	1 (7.2)	1 (7.2)	–	5 (35.7)	3 (21.4)	1 (7.1)	–
Graduate/PG (General) (206)*	41 (19.9)	9 (4.3)	23 (11.1)	3 (1.5)	75 (36.4)	43 (20.9)	10 (4.9)	2 (1)
Graduate/PG (Professional) (123)*	25 (20.3)	5 (4.1)	14 (11.4)	1 (0.8)	46 (37.4)	25 (20.3)	6 (4.9)	1 (0.8)

Source: Primary data * figures indicates row totals.

Note: Figures in parenthesis indicates percentages as row totals.

Prabha constitutes less number of readers. Of all the newspapers taken for study, majority of readers are either Graduates are Post-Graduates. *Eenadu* has maximum number of readers in either Graduate or Post-Graduate category.

Respondents' Occupation

An attempt is made in the study to know whether there is any relationship between newspaper readership and their occupation. The Table 6.6 furnishes the data about distribution of reader respondents in terms of their occupation. Out of 576 reader respondents 337 (58.5 %) readers are employees,101 (17.5 %) readers are students, 89 (15.5 %) readers are businessmen and 49 (8.5 %) readers are house wives. On the whole anlysis reveals that a majority of newspaper readers are employees and less number of readers are housewives.

Table–6.6

READER RESPONDENTS – OCCUPATION

Occupation	*Frequency*	*Per cent*
Housewives	49	8.5
Businessmen	89	15.5
Employees	337	58.5
Students	101	17.5
Total	576	100.0

Source: Primary data.

Duration of Reading Newspaper

Table 6.7 shows the distribution of reader respondents basing on duration of reading newspaper. Out of 576 respondents, 229 (39.8 %) readers are reading newspaper since more than five years, 302 (52.4 %) readers are reading newspapers since one to five years, 45 (7.8 %) readers are reading newspaper since one year. The analysis reveals that majority of newspaper readers are reading newspapers between one to five years duration.

Respondents' Preferential Contents of Newspaper

Even though a majority of people have the habit of reading newspaper, only some of the readers go through the entire newspaper. Some are interested in specific columns and some readers read only headlines. This is because of some reasons like lack of time, lack of interest, business and so on. An attempt was made to know about

Table–6.7

READERS BASING ON DURATION OF READING NEWSPAPER

Period	*Frequency*	*Per cent*
< 1 years	45	7.8
> 1 year and < 5 years	302	52.4
> 5 years	229	39.8
Total	576	100.0

Source: Primary data.

the readers' preference towards headlines, whole paper, selected columns and specific columns. Table 6.8 shows distribution of reader respondents basing on their preference towards contents of newspaper. The Table shows that 238 (41.3 %) readers are preferring the whole paper, and specific columns are preferred by 18 (3.1 %) readers. The analysis reveals that majority of reader respondents read the entire newspaper and less number of respondents are going through specific columns.

Table–6.8

READERS' PREFERENTIAL CONTENTS IN NEWSPAPER

Newspaper Content	*Frequency*	*Per cent*
Whole paper	238	41.3
Headlines	219	38.0
Selected columns	101	17.6
Specific columns	18	3.1
Total	576	100.0

Source: Primary data.

Table–6.8.1

READERS' PREFERENTIAL CONTENTS IN NEWSPAPERS – AGE

Age Group (576)	*Whole Paper (219)*		*Headlines (238)*		*Selected Columns (101)*		*Specific Columns (18)*	
	f	%	*f*	%	*f*	%	*f*	%
16–20(84)	35	41.7	32	38.0	14	16.7	3	3.6
21–25(86)	35	40.7	33	38.4	15	17.4	3	3.5
26–30(99)	41	41.4	38	38.4	17	17.2	3	3.0
31–35(75)	35	46.7	32	42.7	5	6.6	3	4.0

(Contd.)

Age Group (576)	*Whole Paper (219)*		*Headlines (238)*		*Selected Columns (101)*		*Specific Columns (18)*	
	f	%	*f*	%	*f*	%	*f*	%
36–40(58)	24	41.4	22	37.9	10	17.2	2	3.5
41–45(70)	29	41.4	27	38.6	12	17.1	2	2.9
46–50(37)	15	40.5	14	37.8	7	18.9	1	2.7
51–55(22)	9	40.9	9	40.9	4	18.2	-	-
56–60(22)	9	40.9	8	40.9	4	18.2	1	-
61–65(9)	4	44.5	3	33.3	2	22.2	-	-
66–70(3)	1	33.3	1	33.3	1	33.3	-	-
>70 (1)	1	100.0	-	-	-	-	-	-

Source: Primary data.

Note: *(i)* Percentages are for row totals.
(ii) Figures in parenthesis indicates row and column totals.

Preference of Reading Newspaper Based on Age

Table 6.8.1.shows distribution of reader respondents basing on their preference of reading newspaper in terms of age. In whole paper preference nine (44.5 %) readers are from 61 to 65 group. One (33.3 %) from 66 to 70 age group. In Headlines preference 32 (42.7 %) readers are in 31 to 35 age group. Zero per cent from above 70 age group. In selected columns preference more number of readers (33.3 per cent) are in 66 to 70 group and zero per cent in above 70 age group. In specific column preference three (4 %) readers are in 31 to 35 age group and very less, that is zero per cent in above 70 age group. It is observed that whole paper preference is more in 61 to 65 age group and maximum in above 70 years category. Headline preference is more in 31 to 35 age group and zero in above 70 group. Selected column preference is more in 66 to 70 age group. Specific column preference is more in 35 to 40 age group and it is declining as age group is increasing. In all age groups more respondents prefer whole paper than headlines and specific columns. From 31 to 35 age group, as age increasing the percentage of respondents who prefer to read whole paper are reducing.

Preferential Contents in Newspaper Based on Income

Table 6.8.2 shows distribution of reader respondents basing on their preferential contents in newspaper. In whole paper preference 100

(41.5 %) readers belong to Rs. 5,000 to Rs. 10,000 income group. Three (42.9 %) reader respondents are in above Rs. 20,000 income group. In headline preference 91 (37.8 %) readers are from Rs. 5,001 to Rs. 10,000 income group. Zero per cent of readers are from more than Rs. 20,000 income group. In selected column preference eight (18.6 %) readers are from up to Rs 15,000 to Rs 20,000 income group. One (14.2 %) reader is from above 20,000 income group. In specific columns preference eight (3.3 %) readers belong to Rs. 5,001 to Rs. 10,000 income group and no reader in more than Rs. 20,000 income group. Analysis reveals that whole paper, headline and specific column are preferred by majority of readers in Rs. 5,001 to Rs.10,000 income group. Selected column preference is more in Rs.15,001 to Rs. 20,000 income group than other income groups.

Table–6.8.2

READERS' PREFERENTIAL CONTENTS IN NEWSPAPERS – INCOME

Income (Rs.)	*Whole Paper*		*Headlines*		*Selected Columns*		*Specific Columns*	
	Frequ-ency	*Per cent*	*Frequ-ency*	*Per cent*	*Frequ-ency*	*Per cent*	*Frequ-ency*	*Per cent*
Up to 5,000 (173)	71	41.0	67	38.7	30	17.4	5	2.9
5,001–10,000 (241)	100	41.5	91	37.8	42	17.4	8	3.3
10,001–15,000 (112)	46	41.0	42	37.5	20	17.9	4	3.6
15,000–20,000 (43)	18	41.9	16	37.2	8	18.6	1	2.3
> 20,000 (7)	3	42.9	3	42.9	1	14.2	-	-
Total	238		219		101		18	

Note: (*i*) Figures in parenthesis indicates row totals.
(*ii*) Percentages are for row totals.

Preferential Contents Based on Educational Qualification

Table 6.8.3 shows distribution of readers basing on their preferential contents in terms of educational qualification. Out of 238 respondents who prefer, whole paper 42.9 per cent in PUC level and 40.6 per cent in are Graduate/PG (Professional) level. Out of 219 respondents who prefer headlines are 41(38.3 %) in number in up to 10th class level. 35.7 per cent in PUC level. In selected column preference 22 (17.9 %) readers in Graduate/PG (Professional) level and only two (14.3 %) in PUC category. In specific column preference 7.1 per cent of readers are in PUC category. It is observed that majority of readers are in Graduate/PG (General) level who are reading the whole paper, headlines, selected columns and also specific columns. Majority of readers prefer whole paper in PUC level and less in Graduate/PG (Professional) level. Headline preference is by majority of respondents in up to 10th class and very less in PUC level. Selected columns preference is by majority of reader respondents in Graduate/PG (Professional) level and less in PUC level. Specific columns preference is by majority of readers in PUC and Intermediate level, Graduate/Post-Graduate professional level and very less in Up to 10th class. Analysis reveals that, readers in Intermediate and PUC level get more attracted towards specific columns than other classes.

Table–6.8.3

PREFERENTIAL CONTENT IN NEWSPAPERS AND EDUCATION OF READERS

Income (Rs.)	*Whole Paper*		*Headlines*		*Selected Columns*		*Specific Columns*	
	Frequency	*Per cent*	*Frequency*	*Per cent*	*Frequency*	*Per cent*	*Frequency*	*Per cent*
Upto 10th (107)	44	41.1	41	38.3	19	17.8	3	2.8
Inter (126)	52	41.3	48	38.0	22	17.5	4	3.2
PUC (14)	6	42.9	5	35.7	2	14.3	1	7.1
Graduate/ PG (General) (206)	86	41.7	78	37.9	36	17.5	6	2.9
Graduate/PG (Professional) (123)	50	40.6	47	38.2	22	17.9	4	3.3
Total (576)	238		219		101		18	

Source: Primary data.

Note: Figures in parenthesis indicate row totals.

Time Spent on Reading Newspaper

The time spent by newspaper readers on reading newspaper is different. Some readers spend very less time and some readers spend more time on reading newspaper. Table 6.9 shows distribution of reader respondents basing on time spent on reading newspaper. Out of 576 reader respondents 305 (53 %) readers are spending between one to two hours per day while reading newspaper and 21 (3.7 %) readers are reading newspaper more than three hours per day. It is observed that majority of readers are spending one to two hours time in reading newspapers. Very few number of readers are spending time equal to or more than three hours to read newspaper. The mean value is 1.34. So the average time spent by reader is 1.34 hours.

Table–6.9
TIME SPENT ON READING NEWSPAPER

Time	*Frequency*	*Per cent*
Headlines	219	38.0
< 1 hour	156	27.0
> 1 hour and < 2 hours	305	53.0
>2 hours and < 3 hours	94	16.3
> 3 hours	21	3.7
Total	576	100.0

Source: Primary data.

Frequency of Reading Newspaper

Most of the readers read newspaper daily. But some readers may not read newspaper daily. They read newspaper at week end. Table 6.10 analyses reader respondents basing on frequency of reading newspaper. Out of 576 respondents, 571 (99.1 %) readers are reading newspaper daily and five (0.9 %) readers are reading newspaper at weekends. It is observed that maximum number of people are reading newspaper daily and very less percentage of people are reading newspaper at weekends.

Table–6.10
FREQUENCY OF READING NEWSPAPER

Frequency of Reading	*Frequency*	*Per cent*
Daily	571	99.1
Weekends	5	0.9
Total	576	100.0

Source: Primary data.

Nature of Buying Newspaper

Newspaper readers buy newspaper generally in two different ways. First method is by subscription and second method is from a newspaper stand that is from pan shops. Table 6.11 shows distribution of reader respondents basing on nature of buying newspaper. Out of 576 respondents, 62 (10.8 %) readers are reading newspaper by buying from newspaper stand and 514 (89.2 %) readers are reading newspaper by subscription. It is observed that maximum number of readers are reading newspaper by subscription and very less number of people are reading newspaper by buying from newspaper stand. Majority readers prefer subscription because readers by subscription get newspaper at their doorsteps.

Table–6.11

NATURE OF BUYING NEWSPAPER

Nature	*Frequency*	*Per cent*
Newspaper stand	62	10.8
Subscriber	514	89.2
Total	576	100.0

Source: Primary data.

Difficulty in Buying Newspaper from Newspaper Stand

When readers are buying newspaper from newspaper stand some times they may feel difficulty in buying the newspaper because of non-availability of newspaper or some other reasons. Table 6.11.1 shows distribution of readers respondents who feel/do not feel difficulty in buying newspaper from newspaper stand. Out of 62 readers who get newspaper from newspaper stand, 58 (93.5 %) readers are finding difficulty in getting newspaper from newspaper stand and four (6.5 %) readers are not feeling any difficulty in getting newspaper from newspaper stand. It is observed that a majority of readers do not feel any difficulty in getting newspaper and a very less number of readers are feel difficulty in getting newspaper from newspaper stand.

Time of Receiving Newspaper by the Subscribers

All newspaper readers who subcribe newspaper cannot receive the newspaper at a time. If the newspaper organization have excellent distribution system then only timely delivery is possible. Table 6.11.2 shows distribution of reader respondents who subscribe newspapers, basing on time of receiving newspaper. Out of 576 reader respondents, 358 (69.6 %) readers are receiving newspaper before 6.00 a.m. and 26 (5.1 %) readers are receiving the newspaper between 6.30 a.m. to 7.00 a.m. The table reveals that majority of readers are

Table 6.11.1

RESPONDENTS WHO FEEL/DO NOT FEEL DIFFICULTY IN BUYING NEWSPAPER FROM NEWSPAPER STAND

	Frequency	*Per cent*
Yes	4	6.5
No	58	93.5
Total	62	100.0

Source: Primary data.

receiving newspaper before 6.00 a.m. and very less number of subscribers are receiving newspaper after 7.00 a.m. Thus, it can be inferred that the distribution system for most of the newspaper organisations in Visakhaptanam City is satisfactory.

Table–6.11.2

TIME OF RECEIVING NEWSPAPER BY THE SUBSCRIBER

	Frequency	*Per cent*
Before 6.00 a.m.	358	69.7
Between 6.00 a.m. and 6.30 a.m.	120	23.3
Between 6 .30 a.m. and 7.00 a.m.	26	5.1
After 7.00 a.m.	10	1.9
Total	514	100.0

Source: Primary data.

Time of Reading Newspaper

Table 6.12 shows distribution of reader respondents basing on time of reading newspaper. Out of 576 reader respondents 482 (83.7 %) are reading newspaper in the morning, 39 (6.8 %) readers read newspaper in afternoon, 41 (7.1 %) readers read newspaper in evenings and 14 (2.4 %) readers read newspaper at late evening or even night. The analysis reveals that maximum readers are reading newspaper early in the morning and least number of readers read newspapers at night.

Interest of Readers Towards Newspaper Attributes

Different readers prefer different types of newspapers for different reasons. Even though two individuals are interested in same newspaper, the reasons for preferring particular newspaper may differ from one reader to other reader. Table 6.13 shows distribution of reader

Table-6.12
TIME OF READING THE NEWSPAPER

Time	*Frequency*	*Per cent*
Morning	482	83.7
Afternoon	39	6.8
Evening	41	7.1
Night	14	2.4
Total	576	100.0

Source: Primary data.

Table-6.13
REASONS FOR PREFERRING A PARTICULAR NEWSPAPER

Attributes	*Frequency*	*Per cent*
Quality of news	382	66.3
Quantity (Number of pages)	12	2.1
Price	21	3.6
Timely distribution	7	1.2
More number of features	154	26.8
Total	576	100.0

Source: Primary data.

respondents basing on their preference of newspaper attributes. Out of 576 reader respondents 382 (66.3 %) readers are preferring quality of news. 12 (2.1 %) readers are buying newspaper because of more number of pages. Less price influenced 21 (3.6 %) readers to read newspaper because it is cheaper than other media. Seven (1.2 %) readers are reading newspaper because of timely distribution and 154 (26.8 %) readers read newspaper because of more number of features. It is observed in the study that maximum number of people are reading newspaper because of the qualitative news published by newspaper organizations. That is publishing latest news and publishing information that is useful for readers is viewed to be qualitative news. Secondly, some of readers are reading newspaper because of more number of features. Least number of readers are reading newspapers because of timely distribution while timely distribution is concern for continuation loyalty but not determining attribute to attract subscribers. However, timely delivery is perceived to be very important by the readers, if not as an attribute of newspaper but accompanying service of a product.

Newspaper Attribute Preference of Readers

Table 6.14 shows distribution of readers respondents basing on their newspaper attribute preference. Out of 356 respondents who prefer language and style of presentation, 137 (38.4 %) readers are *Eenadu* readers and 87 (24.4 %) readers are *The Hindu* readers. For *Andhra Prabha* only two (0.7 %) readers prefer language and style of presentation. Out of 212 readers who prefer qualitative printing, 90 (42.4 %) respondents are *Eenadu* reader, 65 (30.7 %) readers belongs to *The Hindu*, None of them preferring *Andhra Prabha* printing. Out of 248 respondents who prefer News coverage, 75 (30.3 %) readers belongs to *Eenadu* and 61 (24.6 %) are *Vartha* readers. Only two (0.8 %) readers of *Andhra Prabha* prefer news coverage attribute. Out of 269 respondents who prefer Timely distribution, 96 (35.7 %) readers are in *Eenadu* category, 54 (20.1 %) respondents belongs to *The Hindu*, 49 (18.2 %) for *Vaartha* as well as *Deccan Chronicle*. Only one (0.4 %) reader prefer timely distribution of *Andhra Prabha*. Out of 258 respondents who prefer price, 101 (39.1 %) are *The Hindu* readers, 52 (20.2 %) are *Deccan Chronicle* readers, one (0.4 %) reader is from *Andhra Prabha*. Out of 178 readers who prefer quantity (Number of pages), 57 (32 %) are *The Hindu* readers, 48 (27 %) are *Eenadu* readers and only one (0.6 %) is *Andhra Prabha* reader. It is observed that style of presentation in language is preferred mostly by *Eenadu* readers and it is followed by *The Hindu, Andhra Prabha* readers show least preference towards style of presentation in language. News coverage is preferred by more *Eenadu* readers followed by *Vaartha*. Less number of readers in *The Hindu* prefer this because local coverage is less for *The Hindu* compared to *Eenadu* and *Vaartha*. *Andhra Prabha* has least number of readers in news coverage. So it must improve news coverage to strengthen and compete in the market. More *Eenadu* readers prefer this attribute which means *Eenadu* paper is reaching to readers in time. It is followed by *The Hindu* and then *Vaartha* and *Deccan Chronicle*. An insight into the table reveals that *Andhra Prabha* has poor distribution net work. Price attribute is liked by more *The Hindu* readers followed by *Deccan Chronicle*. For *Andhra Prabha* readers, price preference is very less. It is observed that, the price of english newspapers was very much liked by people because the price of english newspapers is reduced because of price wars. *The Times of India* first introduced price reduction and later on all English

Table–6.14
NEWSPAPER ATTRIBUTE PREFERENCE – PUBLICATION

Education	*The Hindu*	*The New Indian Express*	*Deccan Chronicle*	*Eenadu*	*Vaartha*	*Andhra Bhoomi*	*Andhra Prabha*	*Times of India*	*Total*
Style of Presentation in language per cent	87	11	37	137	65	11	2	6	356
	(24.4)	(3.0)	(10.3)	(38.4)	(18.3)	(2.9)	(0.7)	(2.0)	
Qualitative printing per cent	65	6	21	90	26	1	–	-3	212
	(30.7)	(2.8)	(9.9)	(42.4)	(12.3)	(0.5)		(1.4)	
News coverage per cent	47	11	34	75	61	14	2	4	248
	(19.0)	(4.4)	(13.7)	(30.3)	(24.6)	(5.6)	(0.8)	(1.6)	
Timely distribution per cent	54	11	49	96	49	5	1	4	269
	(20.1)	(4.1)	(18.2)	(35.7)	(18.2)	(1.9)	(0.4)	(1.5)	
Price per cent	101	20	52	30	43	5	1	6	258
	(39.1)	(7.75)	(20.2)	(16.7)	(11.6)	(1.9)	(0.4)	(2.3)	
Quantity per cent	57	9	36	48	19	2	1	6	178
	(32.0)	(5.0)	(20.2)	(27.0)	(10.7)	(1.1)	(0.6)	(3.4)	

Source: Primary data.

Note: Figures in parenthesis indicate percentage as row totals.

newspapers like *The Hindu* and *Deccan Chronicle* also reduced price because of severe competition in newspaper industry. Quantity preference is more for *The Hindu* followed by *Eenadu* and least preference by *Andhra Prabha* readers.

Style of Preference in Language Based on Educational Qualification

Table 6.14.1 shows distribution of reader respondents basing on the style of preference in language-educational qualification-wise. In up to 10th class category, out of 66 respondents *Eenadu* readers are 26 (39.4 %) in number followed by 16 (24.3 %) *The Hindu* readers. *Andhra Prabha* constitute zero per cent of readers. In Inter group, out of 79 respondents, *Eenadu* constitutes 30 (38 %) readers followed by *The Hindu* which consists of 19 (24 %) readers. In PUC group, out of eight respondents, *Eenadu* constitutes three (37.5 %) readers. *The Hindu, Vaartha* constitutes two (25 %) each. *The New Indian Express, Andhra Bhoomi, Andhra Prabha* and *The Times of India* constitutes no readers. In Graduate/PG (General) level, out of 127 respondents, *Eenadu* constitute 49 (38.6 %) readers, *The Hindu* constitute 31 (24.4 per cent) readers and *Andhra Prabha* constitutes one (0.8 %) reader. In Graduate/PG (Professional) category, out of 76 respondents *Eenadu* constitutes 29 (38.2 %) readers, followed by 19 (25 %) *The Hindu* readers. *Andhra Prabha* constitutes zero per cent of readers. It is observed that in style of preference in language in terms of educational qualification, *Eenadu* stood first in all levels of education and *Andhra Prabha* constitute least number of readers. So the style of preference in language in *Andhra Prabha* must be improved.

News Coverage Performance Based on Educational Qualification

Table 6.14.1 shows distribution of reader respondents basing on news coverage performance-educational qualification-wise. Out of 46 respondents in up to10th class category, 14 (30.4 %) readers constitute *Eenadu* group followed by *Vaartha* which consists of 11 (23.9 %) readers. *Andhra Prabha* constitutes zero per cent of readers. In Inter group, out of 54 respondents, *Eenadu* consists of 16 (29.6 %) readers, *Vartha* consists of 13 (24 %) readers. In PUC group, Out of five respondents, *Eenadu* consists of two (40 per cent) readers. *The Hindu, Deccan Chronicle, Vaartha* constitute one (20 %) reader each. In Graduate/PG(general) level, out of 89 respondents, 27 (30.3 %) readers are in *Eenadu*, 22 (24.7 %) readers are in *Vaartha, Andhra Prabha* and *The Times of India* consists of one (1.1 %) reader each. In

Table-6.14.1

READERS BASING ON STYLE OF PREFERENCE IN LANGUAGE : EDUCATIONAL QUALIFICATION

Education	*The Hindu*		*The New Indian Express*		*Deccan Chronicle*		*Eenadu*		*Vaartha*		*Andhra Bhoomi*		*Andhra Prabha*		*The Times of India*	
	f	%	*f*	%	*f*	%	*f*	%	*f*	%	*f*	%	*f*	%	*f*	%
Up to 10th (66)	16	24.3	2	3.0	7	10.6	26	39.4	12	18.2	2	3.0	-	-	1	1.5
Inter (79)	19	24	3	3.8	8	10.1	30	38	14	17.7	3	3.8	1	1.3	1	1.3
PUC (8)	2	25	-	-	1	12.5	3	37.5	2	25	-	-	-	-	-	-
Graduate/PG (General) (127)	31	24.4	4	3.15	13	10.2	49	38.6	23	18.1	4	3.15	1	0.8	2	1.6
Graduate/PG (Professional) (76)	19	25	2	2.63	8	10.5	29	38.2	14	18.4	2	2.6	-	-	2	2.63
Total: 356																

Note: Figures in parenthesis indicate row totals.
Source: Primary data.

Graduate/PG (Professional) level, *Eenadu* consists of 16 (29.6 %) readers, *Vaartha* consists of 14 (25.9 %) readers and *Andhra Prabha* and *The Times of India* constitute one (1.9 %) reader each. It is observed that, in all categories *Eenadu* readers are maximum. It is followed by *Vaartha*. So *Eenadu* is liked by all levels of readers irrespective of their educational qualification. *Eenadu* and *Vaartha* are newspapers which are publishing in regional language. So regional news coverage is high in these newspapers. Even though *The Hindu* style of presentation in language is good, it is not even in second position in news coverage because readers now-a-days interested in more regional and local news than national news. So *The Hindu* must publish more local and regional news.

Table–6.14.2.
NEWS COVERAGE PREFERENCE OF READERS BASED ON EDUCATION

Education	*The Hindu*	*The New Indian Express*	*Deccan Chronicle*	*Eenadu*	*Vaartha*	*Andhra Bhoomi*	*Andhra Prabha*	*Times of India*	*Total*
	f	*f*	*f*	*f*	*f*	*f*	*f*	*f*	
Up to 10th	9	2	6	14	11	3		1	46
Percentage	19.6	4.3	13.0	30.4	23.9	6.5	-	2.3	100.0
Inter	10	3	8	16	13	3		1	54
Percentage	18.5	5.6	14.8	29.6	24.0	5.6	-	1.9	100.0
PUC	1	-	1	2	1	-	-	-	5
Percentage	20.0		20.0	40.0	20.0				100.0
Graduate/ PG (General)	17	4	12	27	22	5	1	1	89
Percentage	19.1	4.5	13.5	30.33	24.7	5.6	1.1	1.1	100.0
Graduate/PG (Professional)	10	2	7	16	14	3	1	1	54
Percentage	18.5	3.7	13.0	29.6	25.9	5.5	1.9	1.9	100.0
Total: 248									

Source: Primary data.

Quantity Preference Based on Educational Qualification

Table 6.14.3. Shows distribution of reader respondents basing on quantity preference-educational qualification-wise. Out of 34 respondents, in up to 10th class group, 11 (32.3 %) respondents are *The Hindu* readers and it is followed by *Eenadu* which consists of nine (26.5 %) readers. *The Times of India* consists of one (2.9 %) reader. *Andhra Bhoomi* and *Andhra Prabha* consist of zero per cent of readers. In Inter group, out of 38 readers 12 (31.5 %) readers are in *The Hindu* group followed by *Eenadu* consisting of 11 (28.9 %) readers. *Andhra Prabha* and *Andhra Bhoomi* consist of no readers. In PUC group, out of five readers *The Hindu, Deccan Chronicle, Eenadu, Andhra Bhoomi, The Times of India* consist of one (20 %) reader each. *The New Indian Express, Vaartha, Andhra Prabha* consists of zero per cent of readers. In Graduate/PG (General), Out of 63 readers, *The Hindu* consists of 20 (31.7 %) readers followed by 17 (27 %) readers for *Eenadu. Andhra Bhoomi* consists of one (1.6 %) reader and *Andhra Prabha* consists of zero per cent of readers. In Graduate/PG (Professional), Out of 38 readers, *The Hindu* consists of 13 (34.2 %) readers, *Eenadu* consists of 10 (26.4 %) readers, and *Deccan Chronicle* consists of seven (18.4 %) readers. *Andhra Bhoomi* consists of zero per cent of readers. It is observed that, in all categories *The Hindu* consists of maximum readers and it is followed by *Eenadu. Andhra Prabha* and *Andhra Bhoomi* in almost all categories consist of least number of readers.

Table-6 14.3

QUANTITY PREFERENCE BASED ON EDUCATION

Education	*The Hindu*	*The New Indian Express*	*Deccan Chronicle*	*Eenadu*	*Vaartha*	*Andhra Bhoomi*	*Andhra Prabha*	*Times of India*	*Total*
	f	*f*	*f*	*f*	*f*	*f*	*f*	*f*	
Up to 10th	11	2	7	9	4	-	-	1	34
per cent	32.3	5.9	20.6	26.5	11.8			2.9	
Inter	12	2	8	11	4	-	-	1	38
per cent	31.6	5.3	21.1	28.9	10.5			2.6	
PUC	1	-	1	1	-	1	-	1	5
per cent	20		20	20		20		20	
Graduate/PG (General)	20	3	13	17	7	1	-	2	63
per cent	31.7	4.8	20.6	27	11.1	1.6		3.2	
Graduate/PG (Professional)	13	2	7	10	4	-	1	1	38
per cent	34.2	5.3	18.4	26.4	10.5		2.6	2.6	178
Total: 178									

Source: Primary data.

Lending or Borrowing of Newspaper

Unlike other media newspaper is very easy to carry for readers and readers can exchange their newspapers. Table 6.15 shows distribution of readers respondents basing on lending or borrowing of newspaper. Out of 576 respondents, 483 (83.9 %) respondents neither lend nor borrow the newspaper where as 52 (9 %) of readers lend the newspapers and 41 (7.1 %) readers borrow newspaper. It is observed that majority of readers neither borrow nor lend newspaper. A very few readers lend or borrow newspaper. This is because the price of newspaper is very less when compared to other commodities.

Table-6.15
LENDING / BORROWING OF NEWSPAPER BY READERS

	Frequency	*Per cent*
Lend	52	9.0
Borrow	41	7.1
None of these	483	83.9
Total	576	100.0

Source: Primary data.

Lending of Newspaper to Others Based on Income

Table 6.15.1 shows distribution of reader respondents basing on lending of newspaper to others based on income. Out of 52 respondents who lend newspapers to others, in Rs. 5,001 to Rs. 10,000 income group 22 (42.3 %) readers are lending newspaper to others. In Rs. 20,000 income group only one (2 %) reader lends newspaper to others. It is observed that the lending habit of newspaper is more in Rs. 5,001 to Rs. 10,000 income group and it is very less in more than Rs. 20,000 income group.

Areas of Interest

Generally all newspaper readers are not interested in the same or similar type of news. Some readers interested in local news whereas some readers prefer international news. Table 6.16 shows distribution of reader respondents basing on areas of interest. Out of 576 respondents, regional news is preferred by 387 (67.2 %) and international news is preferred by 122 (21.2 %) readers. It is observed that local news is preferred by majority of readers followed by regional news, national news. The least preference category constitute international news followed by national news. The reason for this may be that, people give more importance to local and regional news because they want to know about happenings in the particular locality or region in which they live.

Table–6.15.1
LENDING OF NEWSPAPER BASED ON INCOME OF RESPONDENT

Income (Rs.)	*Lend*	
	Frequency	*Per cent*
Up to 5,000	15	28.8
5,001–10,000	22	42.3
10,001–15,000	10	19.2
15,000–20,000	4	7.7
> 20,000	1	2.0
Total	52	100.0

Source: Primary data.

Table–6.16
AREAS OF INTEREST IN NEWSPAPER READING

Areas of Interest	*Most Preferred*		*Preferred*		*Least Preferred*	
	f	%	*f*	%	*f*	%
Local News (576)	327	56.8	228	39.6	21	3.6
Regional News (576)	178	30.9	387	67.2	11	1.9
National News (576)	183	31.8	329	57.1	64	11.1
International News (576)	118	20.5	336	58.3	122	21.2

Source: Primary data.
M.P.—Most Preferred; P—Preferred; L.P—Least Preferred.

Note: Figures in parenthesis indicates row totals.

Areas of Interest Based on Age

There may be some relationship between areas of interest and age. Table 6.16.1, shows distribution of reader respondents basing on areas of interest and age. Out of 576 respondents, local news is mostly preferred by 56 (17.1 %) readers in 26 to 30 age group. Regional news is mostly preferred by 30 (16.9) of readers in 26 to 30 age group and it is not preferred by readers in above 70 age group. Out of 576 respondents national news is mostly preferred by 31 (16.9 %) readers in 26 to 30 age group and zero per cent in above 70 age group. Out of 576 respondents international news is most preferred by 20 (18.6 %)

readers in age group of 26 to 30 and zero per cent in above 70 age group. Analysis reveals that as age group is increasing, the number of readers who mostly prefer all types of news goes on decreasing. Majority of the readers who strongly prefer international news are in the age group of 31 to 35 years.

Table–6.16.1

AREAS OF INTEREST BASED ON AGE OF READERS

			15-20		*21-25*		*26-30*		*31-35*		*36-40*		*41-45*	
			f	*%*	*f*	*%*	*f*	*%*	*f*	*%*	*f*	*%*	*f*	*%*
Local	327	M.P	48	14.7	49	15.0	56	17.1	48	14.7	33	10.0	40	12.2
	228	P	33	14.5	34	14.9	39	17.1	34	14.9	23	10.0	27	11.8
	21	L.P	3	14.3	3	14.3	4	19.0	3	14.3	2	9.5	3	14.3
Reg-	178	M.P	26	14.6	26	14.6	30	16.9	27	15.2	18	10.1	22	12.4
ional	387	P	56	14.5	58	15.0	66	17.0	57	14.7	39	10.0	47	12.1
	11	L.P	2	18.2	2	18.2	3	27.3	1	9.0	1	9.0	1	9.0
National	183	M.P	27	14.8	27	14.8	31	16.9	27	14.8	19	10.4	22	12.0
	329	P	48	14.6	49	14.9	57	17.3	49	14.9	31	9.4	40	12.2
	64	L.P	9	14.0	10	15.6	11	17.2	9	14.0	8	12.5	8	12.5
Inter-	118	M.P	17	15.7	18	16.7	20	18.6	17	15.7	12	11.1	14	13.0
national	336	P	49	14.6	50	14.9	58	17.3	50	14.9	34	10.1	41	12.2
	128	L.P	18	16.0	18	16.0	21	18.7	18	16.0	12	10.7	15	13.4

		46-50		*51-55*		*56-60*		*61-65*		*66-70*		*70 above*	
		f	*%*	*f*	*%*	*f*	*%*	*f*	*%*	*f*	*%*	*f*	*%*
Local	M.P	21	6.4	12	3.7	12	3.7	5	1.5	2	0.6	1	0.3
(576)	P	15	6.6	9	3.9	9	3.9	4	1.8	1	0.4	0	0
	L.P	1	4.8	1	4.8	1	4.8	0	0	0	0	0	0
Regional	M.P	11	6.2	7	3.9	7	3.9	3	1.7	1	0.6	0	0
(576)	P	25	6.4	15	3.9	15	3.9	6	1.6	2	0.5	1	0.3
	L.P	1	9.0	0	0	0	0	0	0	0	0	0	0
National	M.P	1	6.6	7	3.8	7	3.8	3	1.6	1	0.5	0	0
(576)	P	21	6.4	13	4.0	13	4.0	5	1.5	2	0.6	1	0.3
	L.P	4	6.2	2	3.1	2	3.1	1	1.6	0	0	0	0
International	M.P	8	7.4	5	4.6	5	4.6	2	1.9	0	0	0	0
(576)	P	22	6.5	12	3.6	12	3.6	5	1.5	2	0.6	1	0.3
	L.P	7	6.2	5	4.5	5	4.5	2	1.8	1	0.9	0	0

Total: 576

*M.P.— Most Preferred; P—Preferred; L.P—Least Preferred.

Source: Primary data.

Note: Figures in parethesis indicate row totals.

Table-6.16.2
AREAS OF INTEREST BASED ON EDUCATIONAL QUALIFICATION

			Up to 10th		*Inter*		*PUC*		*PG/Degree (General)*		*PG/Degree (Professional)*	
			f	*%*	*f*	*%*	*f*	*%*	*f*	*%*	*f*	*%*
Local	327	M.P*	61	18.7	72	22.0	8	2.4	117	35.8	69	21.1
(576)	228	P**	42	18.4	50	21.9	6	2.6	82	36.0	48	21.1
	21	L.P***	4	19.0	4	19.0	-	-	7	33.3	6	28.6
Regional	178	M.P	33	18.5	39	21.9	4	2.2	64	36.0	38	21.3
(576)	387	P	72	18.6	85	22.0	9	2.3	138	35.7	83	21.4
	11	L.P	2	18.2	2	18.2	1	9.0	4	36.4	2	18.2
National	183	M.P	34	18.6	41	22.4	4	2.2	65	35.5	39	21.2
(576)	329	P	61	18.5	72	21.9	8	2.4	118	35.9	70	21.3
	64	L.P	12	18.7	13	20.3	2	3.1	23	35.9	14	21.9
Inter-	118	M.P	22	20.4	26	24.0	3	2.8	42	38.9	25	23.1
national	336	P	62	18.5	74	22.0	8	2.4	120	35.7	72	21.3
(576)	122	L.P	23	20.5	26	23.2	3	2.7	44	39.3	26	23.2
Total: 576												

Source: Primary data.
*M.P – Most Preferred; **P – Preferred; ***L.P – Least Preferred.

Areas of Interest Based on Educational Qualification

There may be some relationship between areas of interest of respondents and their educational qualification. Table 6.16.2 shows distribution of reader respondents basing on areas of interest and educational qualification. Among 327 respondents who are mostly prefer local news, 117 (35.8 %) readers are in PG/Degree (General) category. Out of 21 readers who give less preference to local news, it is least preferred by seven (33.3 %) readers in Degree/PG (General) category. In regional news, out of 387 readers, it is preferred by 138 (35.7 %) readers in Degree/PG (General) category. Out of 329 readers, national news is preferred by 118 (35.9 %) readers in Degree/PG (General) category. Out of 336 readers, international news is preferred by 120 (35.7 %) readers. It is observed that almost all areas are preferred most by majority of readers in Degree/PG (General) category. This may be because of the reason that readers who are in graduate and post-graduate level are very enthusiastic about the happenings surrounding them. So they gain knowledge by reading all different news items.

Perception of Coverage of News Items

Even though newspaper organizations are publishing news which cover different items, it must be perceived by the readers. Then only readers' satisfaction will increase. 6.17 shows distribution of reader respondents basing on their perception of coverage of news items. Out of 576 respondents 452 (78.5 %) readers said local news is adequate. Regional news is adequate for 489 (84.9 %) readers. Out of 576 respondents 485 (84.2 %) readers said national news is adequate. International news is adequate for 449 (78 %) respondents. The analysis reveals that majority of readers get satisfied with present news coverage. However, significant number of readers opined that there is a need for improvement in local news and some reduction in international news.

Table–6.17

READERS' PERCEPTION OF COVERAGE OF NEWS ITEMS

Coverage	*Adequate*		*Need to be Improved*		*Need to be Reduced*	
	f	*%*	*f*	*%*	*f*	*%*
Local (576)	452	78.5	118	20.5	6	1.0
Regional (576)	489	84.9	79	13.7	8	1.4
National (576)	485	84.2	83	14.4	8	1.4
International (576)	449	78	102	17.7	25	4.3

Source: Primary data.
A—Adequate; NI—Need to be Improved; NR—Need to be Reduced.
Note: Figures in parentheis indicate row total.

Readers' Perception of Coverage of Items—Publications-wise

Even though newspaper is publishing different types of news, unless it is perceived by readers, they never get satisfied. So it is important for marketers to study their perceptions about coverage of items. Table 6.17.1 shows distribution of reader respondents basing on perception of coverage of items basing on educational qualification. Local news is adequate for 89 (76 per cent) readers who read *The Hindu* newspaper, where as it is adequate for 57 (89 per cent) readers. Analysis depicts, *Deccan Chronicle* is publishing more local news than *The Hindu*. It is also observed that majority of readers for all newspapers suggested that there need some improvement in local news.

Table–6.17.1

READERS' PERCEPTION OF COVERAGE OF ITEMS – PUBLICATION

	Local News			*Regional News*			*National News*			*International News*		
	A	NI	NR	A	NI	NR	A	NI	NR	A	NI	NR
The Hindu	89	28	0	95	22	0	94	20	3	87	23	7
%	76	24	0	81	19	0	80	17	3	74	20	6
The New Indian Express	16	8	0	18	5	1	22	1	1	15	6	3
%	67	33	0	75	21	4	92	4	4	62.5	25	12.5
Deccan Chronicle	57	6	1	56	7	1	55	9	0	51	12	1
%	89	9	2	87	11	2	86	14	0	80	19	1
Eenadu	165	44	2	181	27	3	173	34	4	169	33	9
%	78	21	1	86	13	1	82	16	2	80	16	4
Vaartha	95	24	1	102	16	2	107	13	0	94	17	9
%	79	20	1	85	13	2	89	11	0	78	14	8
Andhra Bhoomi	21	6	1	25	3	0	24	4	0	24	3	1
%	75	21	4	89	11	0	86	14	0	86	11	3
Andhra Prabha	3	1	1	5	0	0	4	1	0	5	0	0
%	60	20	20	100	0	0	80	20	0	100	0	0
Times of India	6	1	0	6	1	0	5	1	0	4	3	0
%	86	14	0	86	14	0	85	14	0	57	43	0
Total: 576												

A-Adequate; NI – Need to be Improved; NR – Need to be Reduced.
Source: Primary data.

Readers' Perception of Coverage of Items Age-wise

There may be relationship between readers' perception and age. Table 6.17. 2 shows distribution of reader basing on perception of coverage of items age-wise. For local news, out of 576 respondents, local news is adequate for 78 (17.3 %) readers in 26 to 30 age group. For 84 (17.2 %) readers in age of 26 to 30, regional news is adequate. For national news, in 26 to 30 age group, 82 (16.9 %) readers said it is adequate. In the same age group 77 (17.3 %) readers get satisfied with international news. It is observed that majority of readers who get satisfied with different news items belongs to middle age group.

Table–6.17.2
READERS' PERCEPTION OF COVERAGE OF ITEMS — AGE

		16-20		*21-25*		*26-30*		*31-35*		*36-40*		*41-45*	
		f	*%*	*f*	*%*	*f*	*%*	*f*	*%*	*f*	*%*	*f*	*%*
Local	A (452)	66	14.6	67	14.8	78	17.3	67	14.8	46	12.2	55	12.2
	NI (118)	17	14.4	18	15.3	20	16.9	17	14.4	11	9.3	14	11.9
	NR (6)	1	16.7	1	16.7	1	16.7	1	16.7	1	16.7	1	16.7
Regional	A (489)	71	14.5	73	14.9	84	17.2	72	14.7	49	10.0	59	12.0
	NI (79)	12	15.2	12	15.0	14	17.5	12	15.0	8	10.0	10	12.7
	NR (8)	1	14.3	1	14.3	1	14.3	1	14.3	1	14.3	1	14.3
National	A (485)	71	14.6	71	14.6	82	16.9	72	14.8	49	10.1	59	12.2
	NI (83)	12	14.4	14	16.9	15	18.1	12	14.4	8	9.6	10	12.0
	NR (8)	1	12.5	1	12.5	1	12.5	1	12.5	1	12.5	1	12.5
Inter-	A (449)	65	14.5	67	14.9	77	17.1	66	14.7	45	10.0	55	12.2
national	NI (102)	15	14.7	15	14.7	18	17.6	15	14.7	10	9.8	12	11.8
	NR (25)	4	16.0	4	16.0	4	16.0	4	16.0	3	12.0	3	12.0

		46-50		*51-55*		*56-60*		*61-65*		*66-70*		*70 above*	
		f	*%*	*f*	*%*	*f*	*%*	*f*	*%*	*f*	*%*	*f*	*%*
Local	M.P	29	6.4	17	3.8	17	3.8	7	1.5	2	0.4	1	0.2
	P	8	6.8	5	4.2	5	4.2	2	1.7	1	0.8	0	0
	L.P	-	-	-	-	-	-	-	-	-	-	-	-
Regional	M.P	31	6.3	19	3.9	19	3.9	8	1.8	3	0.6	1	0.2
	P	5	6.3	3	3.8	3	3.8	1	1.3	0	0	0	0
	L.P	1	12.5	0	0	0	0	0	0	0	0	0	0
National	M.P	31	6.4	19	3.9	19	3.9	8	1.6	3	0.6	1	0.2
	P	5	6.0	3	3.6	3	3.6	1	1.2	0	0	0	0
	L.P	1	12.5	0	0	0	0	0	0	0	0	0	0
International	M.P	29	6.4	17	3.8	18	4.0	7	1.6	2	0.4	1	0.2
	P	6	5.8	4	3.9	4	3.9	2	2.0	1	1.0	0	0
	L.P	2	8.0	1	4.0	0	0	0	0	0	0	0	0

Source: Primary data.

Readers' Perception of Coverage of News Items—Educational Qualification-wise

There exists a relationship between readers' perception relating to coverage of news items and education. Table 6.17.3, shows distribution of reader respondents basing on readers perception of coverage of news items—education-wise. Out of 452 readers, local news is adequate for 162 (35.8 %) readers in Graduate/PG (General) category. Out of 489 readers, regional news is adequate for 175 (35.8 per cent) readers in Graduate/PG (General) category. Out of 485 readers, national news is adequate for 173 (35.7 %) readers in Graduate/PG (General) category. Out of 449 readers, international news is adequate for 161 (35.9 %) readers in Graduate/PG (General) category. The analysis when viewed from whole, reveals that a majority of readers in Graduate/PG category are satisfied with the coverage of different news items.

Table–6.17.3

READERS' PERCEPTION OF COVERAGE OF NEWSITMES – EDUCATION

		Up to 10th		*Inter*		*PUC*		*Degree PG/ (General)*		*DegreePG/ (Professional)*		*Total (576)*
		f	*%*	*f*	*%*	*f*	*%*	*f*	*%*	*f*	*%*	
Local	A	84	18.6	99	21.9	11	2.4	162	35.8	96	21.3	452
	NI	22	18.6	26	22.0	3	2.5	42	35.6	25	21.1	118
	NR	1	16.7	1	16.7	-	-	2	33.3	2	33.3	6
Regional	A	91	18.6	107	21.9	12	2.5	175	35.8	104	21.2	489
	NI	15	19.0	17	21.5	2	2.5	28	35.4	17	21.5	79
	NR	1	12.5	2	25.0	-	-	3	37.5	2	25.0	8
National	A	90	18.6	106	21.9	12	2.5	173	35.7	104	21.4	485
	NI	15	18.0	18	21.7	2	2.4	30	36.0	18	20.7	83
	NR	2	25.0	2	25.0	-	-	3	37.5	1	12.5	8
Inter-national	A	83	18.5	98	21.8	11	2.4	161	35.9	96	21.4	449
	NI	19	18.6	23	22.5	2	2.0	36	35.3	22	21.6	102
	NR	5	20.0	5	20.0	1	4.0	9	36.0	5	20.0	25
Total: 576												

A – Adequate; NI – Need to be Improved; NR – Need to be Reduced.

Source: Primary data.

Impact of Price Increase on Subscribing Newspaper

Price is one of the important factor which influence readers while subscribing newspaper. Table 6.18 shows distribution of reader respondents basing on the impact of price increase on subscribing newspaper. Out of 576 respondents, 527 (91.5 %) readers said that they continue to subscribe the same newspaper even if there is an increase in price of newspaper. 49 (8.5 %) readers said, if price increased they would stop subscribing newspaper and may shift to other newspaper available at less price. An inference can be drawn that most of readers are not price sensitive. So, a little price increase may not have any adverse impact on sales of newspapers.

Table–6.18

THE EFFECT OF PRICE INCREASE ON SUBSCRIBING NEWSPAPER

Readers Response	*Frequency*	*Per cent*
Continue to purchase	527	91.5
Stopped buying newspaper	49	8.5
Total	576	100.0

Source: Primary data.

Table–6.19

READERS OPINION ABOUT DEGRADATION OF NEWSPAPER ATTRIBUTES AFTER PRICE REDUCTION

Attribute	*Effect*	*Frequency*	*Per cent*
Quality (576)	Yes	256	44.4
	No	254	44.1
	No response	66	11.5
Number of pages (576)	Yes	73	12.7
	No	378	65.6
Attribute	*Effect*	*Frequency*	*Per cent*
	No response	125	21.7
Coverage (576)	Yes	228	39.6
	No	227	39.4
	No response	121	21.0
Total: 576			

Source: Primary data.

Table–6.19.1

PERCEPTION OF NEWSPAPER ARRIBUTES AFTER PRICE REDUCTION BASED ON INCOME

Qualification	*Male*	*Female*	*Frequency*	*Per cent*
Up to5,000	158	15	30	30.6
5,001–10,000	221	20	41.9	40.8
10,001–15,000	102	10	19.4	20.4
15,000–20,000	39	4	7.4	8.2
> 20,000	7	0	1.3	0
Total: 576	527	49	100.0	100.0

Source: Primary data.

Readers Opinion on Degradation of Newspaper Attributes after Price Reduction

Most of the English newspapers reduced the price of newspaper because of tough competition and it necessitates reduction of production costs. So in order to reduce the costs many newspaper organizations reduced the size of newspaper, coverage etc. Table 6.19 shows distribution of reader respondents basing on their opinion on degradation of newspaper attributes after price reduction. Out of 576 respondents, 256 (44.4 %) readers perceived about quality deterioration and only 73 (12.7 %) readers perceived about the decrease in number of pages. According to 228 (39.6 %) readers there is degradation in coverage of news. It is observed that majority of readers are quality conscious. So quality news must be published and at the same time news coverage is to be improved.

Readers Response on Degradation of Newspaper Attributes after Price Reduction Based on Income

There may be some relationship between readers' perception of newspaper attributes and their income. Table 6.19.1 shows distribution of reader respondents basing on response of readers relating to degradation of newspaper attributes after price reduction—income-wise. Out of 527 reader respondents, 221 (41.9 %) readers in Rs. 5,001 to Rs. 10,000 income group opined that there is degradation of newspaper attributes like quality of news, coverage of news etc, after price reduction. Only seven (1.3 %) readers are in more than Rs. 20,000 income group said that there is degradation of newspaper attributes after price reduction. An insight into the table reveals that readers who have developed negative attitude towards newspaper attributes after price reduction are maximum in Rs. 5,001 to Rs. 10,000 income group and very less in above Rs. 20,000 income group. Basing on the analysis it is inferred that degradation of newspaper attributes is less perceived by more than Rs. 20,000 income group and more perceived by Rs. 5,001 to Rs. 10,000 income group.

Liking of Supplements of Newspapers

Every newspaper now-a-days consits of various supplements. (Detailed description of these supplements are mentioned in Chapter III). There might be some reasons for liking of these supplements by newspaper readers. Table 6.20 shows distribution of reader respondents basing on liking of supplements produced by various newspapers along with the main newspaper. Out of 576 respondents 556 (96.5 %) readers said that they like supplements and 20 (3.5 %) readers disliked the supplements. Out of 556 respondents who like supplements, 343 (46.9 %) readers read supplements because of their own interest and only one (0.2 %) reader like supplement for literary reviews. A deep insight reveals that majority of readers read newspaper supplements out of interest and very few readers are reading newspapers for literary reviews.

Newspaper Through Internet

Now-a-days newspapers can be read by browsing internet. Table 6.21, shows distribution of readers who read or not read newspaper through internet. Out of 576 respondents who read newspaper, 48 (8.3 %) readers are reading newspaper through Internet. 528 (91.7 %) readers do not read newspapers through internet. It is observed that majority of the readers are not reading newspaper through internet. This is because of the easy availability of normal newspaper and also much cheaper when compared to reading of newspaper through Internet. Not only that, reading of physical newspaper is more convenient, than browsing Internet to read newspaper.

Table–6.20

LIKING OF SUPPLEMENTS BY THE READERS

Like	*Per cent*	*Dislike*	*Per cent*
556	96.5	20	3.5
Total 576			

Reasons for Liking

Reasons for Liking		*Per cent*
235	Informative	32.1
27	Women issues	3.7
343	Interest	46.9
2	New features	0.3
8	Investigative	1.0
54	Entertainment	7.4
1	Spiritual	0.2
30	Local news	4.1
2	Habit	0.3

(Contd.)

Reasons for Liking		*Per cent*
3	Children news	0.4
18	Comfort	2.5
4	Youth issues	0.5
3	Authenticity	0.4
1	Literary reviews	0.2
Total: 576		

Source: Primary data.

Table–6.21

READING NEWSPAPER THROUGH INTERNET

Response	*Frequency*	*Per cent*
Reading newspaper through internet	48	8.3
Not reading newspaper through internet	528	91.7
Total	576	100.0

Source: Primary data.

Reading of Newspaper Through Internet

There may be relationship between reading of newspaper through internet and age of newspaper reader. Table 6.21.1 shows distribution of reader respondents basing on reading of newspaper through Internet. Out of 48 readers who read newspaper through internet, eight (16.7 %) readers belong to 26 to 30 age group and only one (2 %) reader in 61 to 65 age group. It is observed that, more readers who read Internet are in the age group of 26 to 30 and very less number in 61 and above age group. Basing on above analysis, it is infered that habit of reading newspaper through internet decreases as the age is increasing. The mean value is 33.6 indicate the average age of respondent is 33.6 years.

Table–6.21.1

READING NEWSPAPER THROUGH INTERNET – AGE

Age Group (Years)	*Yes*	*Per cent*
16–20	7	14.6
21–25	7	14.6
26–30	8	16.7
31–35	7	14.6

(Contd.)

Age Group (Years)	*Yes*	*Per cent*
36–40	5	10.4
41–45	6	12.5
46–50	3	6.2
51–55	2	4.2
56–60	2	4.2
61–65	1	2.0
66–70	0	0
70 and above	0	0
Total	48	100.0

Source: Primary data.

Reading Newspaper Through Internet—Income-wise

Table 6.21.2 shows distribution of reader respondents basing on reading of newspaper through internet—income- wise. Out of 48 readers who read newspaper through internet, 20 (41.7 %) readers belongs to Rs. 5,001 to Rs. 10,000 income group and only one (2 %) reader belongs to above Rs. 20,000 income group. Analysis reveals that majority of readers who read newspaper through internet are in the income group of Rs. 5,001 to Rs. 10,000 and very less number in above Rs. 20,000 income group. The study observes that the habit of reading newspaper through internet goes on decreasing as income is increasing.

Table–6.21.2

READING NEWSPAPER THROUGH INTERNET—INCOME

Income (Rs.)	*Yes*	*Per cent*
Up to 5,000	14	29.2
5001–10000	20	41.7
10001–15000	9	18.7
15,000–20,000	4	8.3
> 20,000	1	2.0
Total	48	100.0

Source: Primary data.

Reading of Newspaper Through Internet Based on Education

There may be some relationship between reading newspaper through internet and educational qualification of readers. Table 6.21.3, shows distribution of reader respondents basing on reading of newspaper through internet basing on educational qualification. Out of 48 readers who read newspaper through internet, nine (18.7 %) readers belongs to up to 10th class group and 17 (35.4 %) readers are in Graduate/PG (General) group. It is observed that, majority of readers who read newspaper through internet are more in Graduate/PG (General) category.

Table-6.21.3

RESPONDENTS WHO READ NEWSPAPER THROUGH INTERNET BASED ON EDUCATIONAL QUALIFICATION

Educational Qualification	*Yes*	*Per cent*
Up to 10th	9	18.7
Inter	10	20.8
PUC	1	2.0
Graduate/PG (General)	17	35.4
Graduate/PG (Professional)	11	22.8
Total	48	100.0

Source: Primary data.

Frequency of Browsing Internet for Reading Newspaper

Frequency of browsing for readers who browse internet to read newspaper is not uniform for all readers. Some browse daily and some readers browse only once in a week. Table 6.22 shows distribution of reader respondents who read newspaper through internet. Out of 48 respondents, 23 (47.9 %) readers browse internet to read newspaper once in a week. The table reveals that more readers browse internet to read newspaper once in a week. This may be because of the reason that normal newspaper is more economical and convenient. Readers who browse internet twice in a week are less when compared with the readers who browse internet once in a week or daily.

Readers' Internet Location

All readers who browse internet may not have internet at home. Table 6.23 shows distribution of reader respondents who have Internet at home or office or both. Out of 25 reader respondents who have internet, 17 (68 %) readers have internet at home, five (20 %) readers have internet at office and only three (12 %) readers have internet in home and office. It is observed that maximum number of readers have internet at home and very few readers have internet both in office and home.

Table–6.22

FREQUENCY OF BROWSING NEWSPAPER THROUGH INTERNET

Frequency	*Frequency*	*Per cent*
Once in a week	23	47.9
Twice in a week	12	25.0
Daily	13	27.1
Total	48	100.0

Source: Primary data.

Table–6.23

READERS' INTERNET LOCATION

	f	%
Home	17	68.0
Office	5	20.0
Both in home and office	3	12.0
Total	25	100.0

Source: Primary data.

The readers who browse internet to read newspaper may not have internet facility either at home or in office. Though they do not have internet facility at home or in office, they usually read newspaper by browsing internet from outside that is from internet browsing centres. Table 6.24 shows distribution of reader respondents who read newspaper through internet and have internet in home/at office and outside. Out of 54 reader respondents, 32 (59.7 %) readers browse internet outside and only five (9.2 %) readers browse internet from office. It is observed that readers browse internet outside to read newspaper or more in number than readers who browse internet in home or office or both.

Media Habits of Readers

Generally the readers who read newspaper may have some other media habits also. They may have the habit of reading magazines, watching television etc. Table 6.25 shows distribution of reader respondents basing on media habits. Out of 576 respondents 325 (56.4 %) respondents preferably watch television, 154 (26.7 %) respondents preferably read magazines, 68 (11.8 %) respondents preferably listening to radio and 29 (5.1 %) respondents surf internet.

Table–6.24

READERS' READING NEWSPAPER THROUGH INTERNET WHO HAVE INTERNET AT HOME/ OFFICE / OUTSIDE

	Frequency	*Per cent*
Home	14	25.9
Office	5	9.2
Both in home and office	3	5.6
Outside	32	59.7
Total	54	100.0

Source: Primary data.

Table–6.25

MEDIA HABITS OF READERS

Media	*Frequency*	*Per cent*
Whole Paper	238	41.3
Watching Television.	325	56.4
Listening to Radio	68	11.8
Reading Magazines	154	26.7
Surfing Internet	29	5.1
Total	576	100.0

Source: Primary data.

It is observed that majority of respondents have watching television as other media habit. Very less number of respondents have the habit of surfing internet.

Media Habits of Readers Basing on Age

There exists some relationship between media habits and age group of individuals. Table 6.25.1 shows distribution of respondents basing media habits age-wise. In all age groups, more respondents have television as media habit. Watching television is more in 26 to 30 age group and secondly in 21 to 25 age group. Watching Television is least preferred by 66 and above age group people. The habit of listening to the radio is slowly decreasing as age group is increasing. The listenership is more in 16 to 30 age people. The radio listenership is increased in 2003 when compared with listenership in 2001 and 2002. The increase in listenership in recent time is because of entry of private FM channels and more entertainment programmes offered by these FM private channels. Eventhough listernership increased

Table–6.25.1
RESPONDENTS MEDIA HABITS – AGE

Age (Years)	*Watching T.V.*		*Listening Radio*		*Reading Magazines*		*Surfing Iternet*	
	f	%	*f*	%	*f*	%	*f*	%
16–20 (84)	47	56	10	11.9	22	26.2	5	5.9
21–25 (86)	49	57	10	11.6	23	26.7	4	4.7
26–30 (99)	56	56.6	12	12.1	26	26.3	5	5.0
31–35 (85)	48	56.5	10	11.8	23	27	4	4.7
36–40 (58)	33	56.9	7	12	16	27.6	2	3.5
41–45 (70)	39	55.7	8	11.4	19	27.2	4	5.7
46–50 (37)	21	56.8	4	10.8	10	27	2	5.4
51–55 (22)	12	54.6	3	13.6	6	27.3	1	4.5
56–60 (22)	12	54.6	3	13.6	6	27.3	1	4.5
61–65 (9)	5	55.6	1	11.1	2	22.2	1	11.1
66–70 (3)	2	66.7	0	0	1	33.3	0	0
> 70 (1)	1	100	0	0	0	0	0	0
Total: 576								

Source: Primary data.
Note: *(i)* Percentages are for row totals.
(ii) Figures in parenthesis indicate row totals.

for radio after the entry of private F.M. the listening habit of radio (FM channels) is more for entertainment than news. Market share of All India Radio (AIR) increased from 1.5 per cent to 3.5 per cent. The advantage radio offers to a retailers is low cost, focused local reach and high speed of production. Radio can act as a persuader. Magazine reading habit is more in 26 to 30 age group and very less in 66 and above age group. Surfing internet is more in 16 to 20 and 26 to 30 age group. It is very less in above 66 age group. The analysis reveals the fact that modern media is fast penetrating into the readers habits and posing threat to newspaper organizations. This may be kept in defining target market of each newspaper before formulating marketing strategy.

Media Habits of Readers Based on Income

There may be some relationship between media habits and income of individuals. Table 6.25.1 shows distribution of respondents basing

Table–6.25.2

READERS' MEDIA HABITS – INCOME

Income (Rs)	*Watching T.V.*		*Listening to Radio*		*Reading Magazines*		*Surfing Internet*	
	f	%	*f*	%	*f*	%	*f*	%
Up to 5,000 (173)	98	56.6	20	11.6	46	26.6	9	5.2
5,001–10,000 (241)	136	56.4	28	11.6	65	27	12	5
10,001–15,000 (112)	63	56.2	13	11.6	30	26.8	6	5.4
15,001–20,000 (23)	24	17.4	6	26.1	11	47.8	2	8.7
< 20,000 (7)	4	57.1	1	14.3	2	28.6	-	-

Source: Primary data.

media habits basing on age. In all income groups except Rs. 15,000 to Rs. 20,000 income group the habit of watching Television is more. In Rs. 15,000 to Rs. 20,000 age group majority readers have magazine as their reading habit. The people who listen to radio, watch television, read magazines and surf internet are more in Rs. 5,001 to Rs.10,000 income group. All media habits are declining as age group is increasing.

Table 6.25.3

READERS' MEDIA HABITS – EDUCATION

Income (Rs)	*Watching T.V.*		*Listening to Radio*		*Reading Magazines*		*Surfing Internet*	
	f	%	*f*	%	*f*	%	*f*	%
Up to 10th (107)	60	56	13	12.2	29	27.1	5	4.7
Inter (126)	71	56.3	15	11.9	34	27	6	4.8
PUC (14)	8	57.2	2	14.3	3	21.4	1	7.1
Graduate/PG (General) (206)	116	56.3	24	11.7	55	26.7	11	5.3
Graduate/PG (Professional) (123)	70	56.9	14	11.4	33	26.8	6	4.9

Source: Primary data.

Media Habits of Readers Based on Education

There may be some relationship between media habits and educational qualification of individuals. Table 6.25.1 shows distribution of respondents basing media habits basing on educational qualification. In all educational levels, watching television is preferred media habit. For watching television, listening to radio, reading magazines and for surfing internet, majority of readers are in Graduate/PG (General) category.

Reasons for Preferring Particular Media

There may be some reason for people to develop such media habits. Table 6.26 shows distribution of reader respondents basing on reason for preferring particular media. Out of 576 respondents, 149 (45.8 %) respondents watch television for news and 176 (54.2 %) respondents watch television for entertainment and only ten (34.5 %) readers surf internet for news and 19 (65.5 %) readers browse internet for entertainment. Respondents who listen to radio are 40 (58.8 %) in number. As can be seen from the analysis that a majority of respondents watch television for entertainment, than the respondents who watch television for news. In all types of media, respondents who prefer entertainment are more in number than respondents who prefer news in different types of media.

Table-6.26

NUMBER OF READERS WHO ARE WATCHING TV/LISTEN RADIO/READ MAGAZINE/SURF NET

Media	*News*		*Entertainment*	
	f	%	*f*	%
Watching T.V. (325)	149	45.8	176	54.2
Listening to Radio (68)	28	41.2	40	58.8
Reading magazines (154)	55	35.7	99	64.3
Surfing internet (29)	10	34.5	19	65.5
Total: 576	242	100.0	334	100.0

Source: Primary data.
Note: Figures in parenthesis indicate row totals.

Reader Choice of Media—Age

There may be relationship between the reasons for preferring particular media and the age of readers. Table 6.26.1 shows distribution of reader respondents basing on reason for preferring particular media. Out of 84 respondents in 21 to 25 age group, 26 (30.9 %) readers watch television for entertainment. Out of 99 respondents in 26 to 30 age group, 26 (26.3 %) readers watch television for news and 30 (30.3 %) readers watch television

Table-6.26.1

READERS WHO ARE WATCHING TV/LISTEN RADIO/ READ MAGAZINE/SURF NET – AGE

Age (Years)	Watching TV				Listening to Radio				Read Magazines				Surfing Internet			
	News		Entertainment		News		Entertainment		News		Entertainment		News		Entertainment	
	f	%	f	%	f	%	f	%	f	%	f	%	f	%	f	%
16–20(84)	22	45.8	26	54.2	4	40	6	60	8	36.4	14	63.6	1	25	3	75
21–25(86)	22	45.8	26	54.2	5	45.5	6	54.5	8	34.8	15	65.2	1	25	3	75
26–30(99)	26	46.4	30	53.6	5	41.7	7	58.3	9	34.6	17	65.4	2	40	3	60
31–35(85)	22	45.8	26	54.2	4	40	6	60	8	34.8	15	65.2	1	25	3	75
36–40(58)	14	43.8	18	56.2	3	42.9	4	57.1	6	37.5	10	62.5	1	33.3	2	66.7
41–45(70)	18	46.2	21	53.8	3	37.5	5	62.5	7	36.8	12	63.2	2	50	2	50
46–50(37)	10	47.6	11	52.4	2	40	3	60	4	44.4	5	55.6	1	50	1	50
51–55(22)	6	46.2	7	53.8	1	50	1	50	2	33.3	4	66.7	-	-	1	100
56–60(22)	6	46.2	7	53.8	1	50	1	50	2	33.3	4	66.7	-	-	1	100
61–65(9)	2	40	3	60	-	-	1	100	1	33.3	2	66.7	-	-	-	-
66–70(3)	1	50	1	50	-	-	-		-	-	1	100	-	-	-	-
70 above(1)	-		-		-	-	-		-		-		1	100	-	-

Source: Primary data.

Note: Figures in parenthesis indicate row totals.

for entertainment. In 56 to 60 age group, out of 22 respondents, six (27.3 %) watch television for news and seven (31.8 %) watch television for entertainment. Analysis predicts that readers who watch television for news and entertainment are more in 26 to 30 age group and very less in above 66 age group. For listening to radio, news listeners are more in 21 to 30 age group, and for entertainment listeners are more in 26 to 30 age group. For reading magazines for news as well as entertainment, readers are more in 26 to 30 age group. In surfing internet majority of respondents surf internet for news, are in 41 to 45 age group. For entertainment more readers are in 16 to 35 age group. The readers who watch television/read magazine/listening to radio/surf internet are middle aged.

Time Spent on Media by the Readers

Readers who have other media habits may not spent time uniformly to all media. One reader may spend less time to read magazine and another may spend more time to read it. Table 6.27 shows distribution of readers respondents basing on Time spent on media. Out of 325 respondents who watch television, 86 (57.7 %) respondents are spending less than one hour to watch television news and only one (0.7 %) reader is spending greater than or equal to three hours time to watch television news. As many as 83 (47.1 %) people spending two to three hours time. Out of 68 respondents who are listening to radio for entertainment, 26 (65 %) respondents spend less than one hour time to listen radio. Among readers who read magazines for entertainment, 70 (70.7 %) readers are spending less than one hour time to read magazines. Out of 29 respondents who browse internet for entertainment 13 (68.4 %) people spend less than hour to browse. The analysis reveals that a majority of respondents spend less than one hour time for watching television for news and spend two to three hours for entertainment. In reading magazines for news maximum number of people are spending less than one hour time. Majority of the readers browse internet for entertainment only.

Reading of Magazines/ Journals/ Periodicals

Readers who read newspaper may have other reading habits also. Table 6.28 shows distribution of reader respondents who read or not read magazines/journals/periodicals. Out of 576 reader respondents, 372 (64.6 %) readers read other magazines, periodicals or journals so on and 204 (35.4 %) readers does not have any other

Table–6.27
TIME SPENT BY READERS ON MEDIA

Media	*A*		*B*		*C*		*D*		*A*		*B*		*C*		*D*	
	f	%	*f*	%	*f*	%	*f*	%	*f*	%	*f*	%	*f*	%	*f*	%
Watching T.V (325)	86	57.7	55	36.9	7	4.7	1	0.7	11	6.2	50	28.4	83	47.0	32	18.2
Listening Radio (68)	17	60.7	4	14.3	7	25.0	-	-	26	65.0	12	30.0	2	5.0	-	-
Reading Mgazines (154)	47	85.5	8	14.5	-	-	-	-	70	70.7	26	26.3	3	3.0	-	-
Surfing Iternet (29)	9	90.0	1	10.0	-	-	-	-	13	68.4	-	-	6	31.6	-	-

Source: Primary data.
Note: Figures in parenthesis indicate row totals.

reading habit. It is observed that, majority of readers have other types of reading habits in addition to newspaper reading habit.

Table–6.28
READERS' OTHER READING HABITS

	f	%
Readers	372	64.6
Non-readers	204	35.4
Total	576	100

Source: Primary data.

Table–6.29
READERS WHO ARE READING MAGAZINE/ JOURNAL/ PERIODICAL/ OTHERS

	f	%
Magazines	357	96
Journals	7	1.9
Periodicals	2	0.5
Others	6	1.6
Total	372	100

Source: Primary data.

Readers Who Read Magazine/Journal/Periodical/Others

The readers who read newspaper may have other reading habits like reading of journals, magazines etc. Table 6.29 shows distribution of readers respondents who read magazine/journal/periodical/ others. Out of 372 respondents, 357 (96 %) readers read magazines and only two (0.5 %) readers read periodicals. It is observed that, maximum number of readers read magazines. So magazine reading habit is more, when compared with other journals and periodical reading habit.

Reading Habits Other than Newspaper Reading Based on Education

There may be relationship between reading habits and education. Table 6.29.1 shows distribution of reader respondents basing on reading habits, other than newspaper reading. In Graduate/PG (Professional) level 76 (97.4 %) readers are reading magazines. It is observed that, in reading habits, other than newspaper reading, magazines are read by majority of readers than journals and periodicals. In Graduate/PG (Professional) level more percentage of readers are reading magazines. Journal and periodical habit is more in inter group.

Table-6.29.1
READERS' OTHER READING HABITS – EDUCATION

Education	*Magazines*		*Journals*		*Periodicals*		*Others*	
	f	%	*f*	%	*f*	%	*f*	%
Up to 10th (68)	66	97	1	1.5	-	-	1	1.5
Inter (83)	78	94	2	2.4	1	1.2	2	2.4
PUC (9)	9	100	-	-	-	-	-	-
Graduate/PG (General) (134)	128	95.5	3	2.3	1	0.7	2	1.5
Graduate/PG Professional) (78)	76	97.4	1	1.3	-	-	1	1.3
Total	357		7		2		6	

Source: Primary data.
Note: Figures in parenthesis are row totals.

Magazine Reading Habit

In readers who read magazines some readers prefer Telugu magazines and some readers prefer English magazines. Table 6.30 shows distribution of reader respondents basing on magazine reading habit. Out of 337 respondents, who read magazines, 169 (50.1 %) readers read Telugu magazines and 168 (49.9 %) readers read English magazines. It is observed that Telugu magazines are read by more number of readers than English magazines. This is because, the magazines which are printed and published in Telugu language are regional local magazines and are more in number and, this increase in readership is because of greater readership of famous magazine called *Swathi*. The survey reveals that out of 357 readers who read magazines (both Telugu and English), 132 (37 %) readers are *Swathi* readers.

Magazines Reading – Income

There may be some relationship between reading of magazines and income of readers. Table 6.30.1 shows distribution of reader respondents who read magazines basing on income. Out of 102 respondents in Rs. 5,000 to Rs. 10,000 income group, 51 (50 %) readers

Table–6.30
READERS' MAGAZINE READING HABIT

Magazine	*Frequency*	*%*
Telugu magazines	169	50.1
English magazines	168	49.9
Total	337	100.0

Source: Primary data.

Table–6.30.1
MAGAZINE READING HABIT – INCOME

Income (Rs.)	*Telugu Magazines*		*English Magazines*	
	f	*%*	*f*	*%*
Up to 5,000 (102)	51	50	51	50
5,001–10,000 (140)	70	50	70	50
10,001–15,000 (66)	34	51.5	32	48.5
15,001–20,000 (26)	13	50	13	50
> 20, 000(3)	1	33.3	2	66.7

Source: Primary data.
Note: Figures in parenthesis indicate row totals.

read Telugu magazines and 51 (50 %) readers read English Magazines. In above Rs. 20,000 income group, out of three respondents, only one (33.3 %) reader is reading Telugu magazine and two (66.6 %) readers are reading English magazines. It is observed, that as income increasing, the number of readers who read magazines are decreasing. Not only that it is observed that English magazines are mostly read by high income group people and Telugu magazines by low income group people.

Magazine Reading Habit – Education

There may be some relationship between magazines preference and educational qualification of readers. Table 6.30.2 shows distribution of readers respondents basing on their magazine reading habit. In Up to 10th class category, out of 61 respondents, 31 readers are reading Telugu magazines. In Graduate/PG (General) category, out of 122 respondents, 61 (50 %) readers are reading Telugu magazines and same 61 (50 %) readers are reading English magazines. It is observed that, in up to 10th class category more readers are reading Telugu magazines than English magazines because it is easy for them to read magazine when it is in printed in Telugu than in English since Telugu is the mother tongue for majority of readers in Visakhapatnam. In all educational levels except 10th class, both English and Telugu magazines are equally preferred by readers at all levels.

Table–6.30.2

MAGAZINE READING HABIT – EDUCATION

Education	*Telugu Magazines*	*%*	*English Magazines*	*%*	*Total*
Up to 10th	31	50.8	30	49.2	61
Inter	37	50.0	37	50.0	74
PUC	4	50.0	4	50.0	8
Graduate (General)	61	50.0	61	61.0	122
Graduate (Professional)	36	50.0	36	36.0	72
Total	169		168		337

Source: Primary data.

Note: Percentages are for row totals.

Reading of Business Magazines

The readers who read newspaper may read business magazines also. Table 6.31 shows distribution of reader respondents who read or not read business magazines. Out of 576 respondents, 523 (91 %) readers dos not read any type of business magazines and only 53 (9 %) readers read business magazines in addition to reading of newspaper. The analysis reveals that majority of readers who read newspaper, not read any business magazines and among readers who read business magazines, more readers found *Business World.*

Table–6.31

READERS WHO READ BUSINESS MAGAZINES AND THEIR CHOICE

Choice	*No*	*%*	*Name*	*No.*	*%*
No. of people read business magazines (Yes)	53	9.0	*(a)* Business India	16	30.0
			(b) Business World	19	35.0
			(c) Business Today	16	29.0
			(d) Others	3	6.0
No. of people do not read business magazines (No)	523	91.0		–	100.0

Source: Primary data.

Reading of Business Magazines—Occupation of Readers

There may be relation between readers' reading of business magazines and their occupation. Table 6.31.1 shows distribution of reader respondents basing on reading of business magazines in terms of occupation. Out of total 53 respondents who read business magazines, five (35.7 %) businessmen read either *Business India* or *Business World* and only one (7.1 %) businessman read other types of business magazines like *Industrial Economist, A&M,* etc. The study observes that in all categories of people, *Business World* is preferred by majority of readers.

Table 6.31.1
READERS WHO READ DIFFERENT BUSINESS MAGAZINES BASED ON OCCUPATION

Occupation	*Business India*		*Business World*		*Business Today*		*Others*	
	f	*%*	*f*	*%*	*f*	*%*	*f*	*%*
Businessmen (14)	5	35.7	5	35.7	3	21.4	1	7.1
Employees (31)	8	25.8	12	38.7	11	32.2	1	3.2
Students (7)	2	28.6	2	28.6	2	28.6	1	14.2
Housewives(1)	1	100	-	-	-	-	-	-

Source: Primary data.
Note: Figures in parenthesis indicate row totals.

REFERENCES

1. Philip, Kotler (1998), "Marketing Management, Analysis, Planning, Implementation and Control", Prentice Hall of India Private Limited, New Delhi, 9th edition, p. 38.
2. Leon, G. Schiffman and Leslie Lazar Kanuk (1997), "Consumer Behaviour", Prentice Hall India, New Delhi, p. 146.
3. Philip, Kotler (1998), "Marketing Management Analysis, Planning Implementation and Control", Prentice Hall of India Private Limited, New Delhi, 9th edition, p. 40.

7

Summary and Suggestions

Summary

The Press in modern times became a powerful social institution known as the 'Fourth Estate'. It facilitates the exchange of thoughts and help to solve many problems. It is an effective media available and it will be helpful to people in reaching the most influential and educated section of society. The press is an effective medium in the hands of nationalists as well as social reform groups. The newspapers aimed at the enlarging masses of literate persons with low journalistic expectations. This is reflected in increased space given to 'features' and 'sensational pip' on one hand and growing fascination with 'sophisticated technology' on the other. The newspaper industry enjoyed a banner year in 1997 with 19.5 per cent for operating income. Revenues were also increased. This was because of better staffing and more promotional efforts. For 1999-2004 period overall growth is expected to be slightly higher than 5.6 per cent rate posted in the 1994-1999 period. In order to increase growth in circulation, the newspaper businessmen have to follow 'adaptive' culture than 'defensive' culture.

The Times of India's readership increased to 33 per cent compared with previous year according to NRS survey results. Among *The Times of India* readers, more than 75 per cent of readers belongs to the highest socio-economic class 'A' and more than half the readers belongs to households with a monthly income over Rs.10,000. In India the Vernacular press started its origin in 1780 by James Augustus Hicky. The vernacular newspapers stirred deep concern among British authorities. The history of newspapers and journals in Telugu and as in other languages is a saga of sacrifices and devotion to nationalistic ideals.

The decadal study except in 1993 confirms that the India press has advanced at a fast pace, considerably faster than population which, of course is growing. The reasons for the growth of newspapers are literacy growth, reduction of cover price, special supplements and other promotional activities like hawker promotion, campaigning and so on.

The ownership pattern of newspapers in India shows individuals, societies and associations, firms, partnerships so on. After 1980, many structural changes have occurred in Indian journalism. Indian society is witnessing momentous changes in social and economic spheres. The newspapers too is changing along with the society. They are acquiring new technologies and modernizing to discharge their functions efficiently and effectively. Several newspapers started expanding to other areas. The advent of news technology facilitated this expansion. The Indian Government on 25th June, 2002 decided to allow 26 per cent FDI in news and current affairs. Some media groups opposed but advantages are more than disadvantages when FDI is allowed in newspaper industry. So government proposed some guidelines to allow FDI in newspaper industry.

The advent of newspapers in Andhra Pradesh was when the Telugu journal Satya Doota was published in 1836. Later on so many newspapers like *Andhra Patrica, Andhra Janata, Andhra Bhoomi, Andhra Prabha, Andhra Jyothi, Eenadu, Vaartha, Leader* so on were launched.

The circulation and readership of Indian newspapers are increasing every year. Even though circulation from 1999-2000 increased up to 0.50 per cent, the readership from 1999-2000 increased to 10.00 per cent. The readership of newspapers is increasing day-by-day, but only some big newspapers can survive in present-day competitive situation. The newspaper industry is facing stiff competition from other media as well as within the industry. Now-a-days price wars are quite common in newspaper industry which leads to unfair competition. The rise of newsprint cost, obsolete technology and lack of research data also ıed newspaper industry into recession.

Need for this study is the absence of proper research data especially in Indian newspapers even though tough competition prevailed. The main of this study is to examine the structure, conduct and performance of marketing in newspaper organizations. It examines the role of intermediaries and readers' preferences towards selected newspapers in Visakhapatnam City. The area of study is entire Visakhapatnam City. The sources of study include both primary and secondary data. Primary data was collected through questionnaires and secondary data is from the records of newspaper organizations, published journals. Universe of study for readers comprises entire readers in Visakhapatnam City. For agents, the universe for the study is total number of agents in Visakhapatnam City. For middlemen, the universe of study is total number of panshop owners in Visakhapatnam City. For distribution boys, the universe is total number of distribution boys present in Visakhapatnam City. Readers sample consists of 0.5 per cent of total readers. Agents sample consists of 7.5 per cent of total population. Retailers sample consists of 12.5 per cent of total population. Distribution boys sample consists of 4.2 per cent of total number of distribution boys. The organisational heads interviewed for this study are *Eenadu, The Hindu, Deccan Chronicle, Vaartha* of Visakhapatnam City. Instrument used in data collection was self-administered questionnaire. Five different types of questionnaires were administered separately to Readers, Organisational heads, Agents, Retailers and Distribution boys. Readers are classified on the basis of Gender, Age, Income, Educational qualification and Occupation. The study was limited to Visakhapatnam City because of time and cost factors.

Visakhapatnam is the second largest city in Andhra Pradesh. It is on the east coast of Andhra Pradesh with major natural harbour and sea shore. The city is unique in its beauty and landscape. The city is as old as mankind. Visakhapatnam is a fast developing industrial city with a population of 13.2 lakhs approximately, with growing literacy. The number of newspaper readers also increased enormously due to the efforts of newspapers in attracting readers by improving both quality as well as finished product. In Visakhapatnam *Eenadu* is the largest circulated daily.

The interviews coducted on heads of selected newspaper organizations reveals that the price wars are are opposed by most of the newspaper organizations in Visakhapatnam city. *The Hindu* management said, even though it is not unfair competition, by reducing newspaper prices, it slowly develops newspaper reading habit among readers. So it is beneficial to newspaper organisations because now-a-days there is declining trend in reading of newspapers. Allowing 26 per cent FDI in newspaper is not liked by more number of newspaper organisations because newspaper media is not just like other commodity. Here foreigners not only involve in corporate decision-making process, they can also influence people which is not good according to majority of newspaper organizations. The selected newspaper organizations believe that if newspaper go for localisation and improve regional news, that newspaper have better future in coming days. Electronic media no way a competitor to newspaper media is the opinion of majority of organizations in newspaper markets. After telecasting news frequently and after emergence of FM the newspaper readership has not declined but increased. A majority of organisations are using mix of imported and indigenous newsprint for their newspapers.

An understanding of the modern marketing concept reveals that consumer is the focal point and everything revolves around him. By satisfying the consumer every seller can survive and pocket some profit. Hence, the marketing efforts are to be successfully planned, implemented and directed towards satisfying the consumers. The organisations should chalk out proper strategies relating to the marketing mix consisting of four 'P's that is product, price, place and promotion as ingrediants.

As circulation of newspapers in India had witnessed zero growth or negative growth during the period 1993-2003. During the period intense competition among newspapers has been centred on the factors of circulation and cover price. Better staffing, promotional methods like gifts, prize schemes and related activities, use of colour, zoned editions are the methods adopted by the organisations to increase their newspaper circulation. The papers are designed to appeal to a wide range of interests and to address as many population groups as possible, which means more features and sections and thus more pages and ultimately cost of production increases apart from increased market promotion costs.

Survey of Newspaper Agents

Maximum number of agents are males and only 14 per cent of agents are females. These agencies in the name of females, the males are doing the business. The females in any case are not participating in decision-making process relating to agencyship. So women are conspicuously absent in newspaper agency system. Majority of agents belongs to middle age group. Many agents are doing newspaper business as part-time business. Half of the agents are distributing copies up to 500. Duration of carrying newspaper is 1-10 years for 60 per cent of agents. Many of them invested less than or equal to Rs. 25,000. Maximum number of agents receive paper bundles between 3.31 a.m. and 4.00 a.m. Majority of agents earned Rs. 5,000 as return on their investment. Majority of agents are not given any remuneration by the newspaper organizations by collecting money from subscribers. Most of the agents are paying Rs. 300-400 as fixed salary for distribution boys. Majority of retailers have the facility of returning unsold newspapers. A large number of agents said, newspaper business is profit making. According to the newspaper agents are the special supplements catching attention in respect of selected newspapers are *Vaartha:* Career, Cinema and Nadi, *Eenadu:*Vasundhara, *Andhra Bhoomi;* Vennela, *The Hindu:* Young World, *The New Indian Express:* Sunday Magazine, Vibes, Health., and *Deccan Chronicle:*Life style, Career Chronicle. Half of the agents are facing problems either with subscribers or with newspaper organizations and distribution boys. *The Hindu, Eenadu* Agencyship is more beneficial for a majority of newspaper agents than other newspapers. Many of them have positive opinion on the future of newspaper business.

The Survey of Retailers

Majority of retailers belongs to middle age group. Majority of retailers are selling on an average selling 0-10 copies of newspaper per day. Newspapers include *The Hindu, The New Indian Express, Deccan Chronicle, Eenadu, Vaartha, Andhra Bhoomi* and *Andhra Prabha.* For maximum number of retailers, *Eenadu* is the fast moving newspaper. Majority of retailers are selling 0-10 copies of magazines per day. Magazines include *Swathi, Andhra Bhoomi, Andhra Prabha, India Today, Week, Outlook.* Many of them are getting commission of 10 per cent. Less number of retailers are getting six per cent of commission. Majority of retailers have no unsold facility. Unsold facility means, if newspaper is not sold, some concession is given to them while paying money to newspaper organisations. No retailer is getting any special type of incentive.

Survey of Distribution Boys

All distribution boys are males only. Majority of distribution boys belongs to 21 and 25 age group. Many of them are having educational qualification up to 10th class. For *Eenadu* newspaper have more number of distribution boys when compared with other newspaper organizations in Visakhapatnam City. Time taken to distribute newspapers for majority of distribution boys was less than or equal to one hour. The duration of working in newspaper field is less than one year for majority of distribution boys. Nearly 75 per cent of distribution boys are participating in collection work. More than half the percentage of distribution boys are facing problems from newspaper organisations, while distributing newspaper where as less than 50 per cent of distribution boys are facing problems from subscribers.

The Demographic Profile of Readers

The Demographic segmentation of readers in Visakhapatnam shows following results. The readers in Visakhapatnam City mostly prefer *Eenadu* newspaper. It is followed by *Vaartha* and *The Hindu* newspaper. Even though Circulation-wise *The Hindu* newspaper occupies second position, readership is slightly less than *Vaartha* because *The Hindu* newspaper is purchased as second newspaper by some individuals. Many of the readers are males. Age-wise classification shows, majority of readers belongs to middle age group. Very less number of readers are reading newspaper in above 70 age group. This shows declining trend of reading habit as age group is increasing. Income-wise classification shows majority of readers are in Rs. 5,001 to Rs. 10,000 income group. Very less number of readers in above Rs. 20,000 income group. Educational-wise qualification of readers shows majority of readers are in Graduate/ PG (General) category. Occupation-wise classification shows majority of readers are in employee category. Very less number of housewives are reading newspaper.

Newspaper Reading Habits

Majority of readers in Visakhapatnam City are reading newspaper since one to five years. Many of them are reading entire newspaper rather than selected columns and headlines. Only few number of readers are reading specific columns. Majority of readers are spending one to two hours time in reading newspaper. Only few number of readers are spending more than three hours to read newspaper. Maximum number of readers are reading newspaper daily. Negligible number of readers are reading newspaper at week ends. Maximum readers buy newspaper by subscription.

Only less number of readers are reading newspapers by buying newspaper from newspaper stand. Only less number of readers are facing problems while getting newspaper from newspaper stand. In subscribers, majority of readers receive newspaper before six in the morning. Very less number of subscribers are receiving newspaper after seven in the morning. Many of readers read newspaper in the morning time only. Very few number of readers read newspaper at night. Majority of readers are reading newspaper because of quality of news and also quality of newsprint. Maximum number of readers neither borrow nor lend newspapers to others. Only less number of readers lend newspapers to others and they mostly belongs to Rs. 5,001 to Rs. 10,000 income group. More number of readers in Visakhapatnam prefer local news only. Very less number of readers prefer international news. Less than 25 per cent of readers said there must be improvement in local news, regional news, national news and international news. Maximum number of readers does not want to stop buying of newspaper, even if price is increased. In preference of supplements, maximum number of readers like supplements and very less number of readers are disliking supplements. The habit of reading newspaper through internet is very less among readers. Out of the readers who read newspaper through internet, more number of readers are middle aged. Majority of readers who read newspaper through Internet belongs to Rs.5,001-10,000 income group. Majority of readers who read newspaper through internet have Graduation/ PG (General) as their educational qualification. Among readers, who read newspaper through internet, many of them browse internet once in a week. Out of the readers who read newspapers through internet, many readers have internet at home.

Media Habits

Comparison of media habits shows, 56.4 per cent of readers are watching television as media habit and only 5.1 per cent of readers are surfing internet as other media habit. Majority of people who watch television, listening to radio, read magazines and surf internet are in 26 to 30 age group, in Rs. 5,001 to Rs. 10,000 income group and in Graduate/PG (General) category. People who watch television, listening to radio, read magazines and surf internet are have these media habits for entertainment than news.

Other Reading Habits

Out of total readers, 64.6 per cent of readers who read newspapers have other reading habits (Reading magazines, Journals and books) other than newspaper. Among readers who have other reading habits, 96 per cent of readers have magazines as their reading habit. Of the total readers who have magazines as their reading habit, 50.1 per cent of readers read telugu magazines and 49.9 per cent of readers read english magazines, more magazine readers are in Rs. 5,001 to Rs. 10,000 income group. Majority of magazine readers are in Graduate/PG category. Out of total readers, only nine per cent of readers read Business magazines. Readers who read business magazines are more in employee category than in businessmen category.

Suggestions

The newspaper has been one of the oldest media of communication. Due to the technological development, there has been tremendous raise in the number of newspapers being published, to serve the needs of growing population. Competition has increased not only among newspapers, but also because of other media like television, radio and internet. To meet this competition newspaper organizations have adapted many changes and introduced many policies. Still newspaper industry is facing severe problems. Several suggestions were mentioned here to increase the efficiency of newspaper organizations.

The Newspapers should Focus on Social Problems

In the present scenario, real issues which have a real bearing on the people of this country like illiteracy, ill health, cancer of corruption are often ignored. The newspapers with a commercial angle have political fall-outs, scandals and scams as priority issues rather than major concerns and needs of the society. Newspaper media should concentrate on news that threatens peoples' peace, prosperity or well-being and issues like drinking water, untouchability, public health concerns and civic awareness should be given priority. It should not prefer only profits and it should not go for commercialization because newspaper media is not just like any other media which prefer profits and tries to be commercialized. The newspaper is a mirror of society. It is for the mass media to project the voice of those who are not vociferous. Newspaper media should help to improve society.

Newspapers Need to Play a Vital Role in Social Marketing

In India more than one-third of population lives below the poverty line. Waterborne and infectious diseases make public health a major concern. It is the responsibility of newspaper media to increase social awareness. It should publish human interest stories. Conditions of present and former soldiers who felt neglected for years must occupy prime newspaper space. News stories about dalits, tribals who lived on nature and forest produces for generations are now being threatened or hunted out of their natural habitats by activists in the name of environment protection. Newspapers should publish news consisting of exploitation of the weaker sections of the society. It should also concentrate on issues like child labour, minority communities etc., to increase awareness and understanding of their problems.

Newspaper should Strive for Women Empowerment

Newspapers influence women in society in a major way. Newspapers effect women in all walks of life including their self image. It influences women development also. Womens' pages in newspapers are of a relatively recent phenomenon. *Eenadu* has come out with women page entitled 'Vasundhara' and *Vaartha* has come out with 'Cheli.' These special supplements influence women in many ways. It is the responsibility of newspapers to publish news which is useful to women and there should not be any gender discrimination and it should not be stereotypical information. Stories of working women who are Lawyers, Journalists, Doctors, Advertising Executives, Business women etc should be published so that women get motivated and the confidence among women is built. Instead of publishing news which consists of suicide attempts, rape victims and so on, if newspapers publish women related news which enhances the self-respect of women, then women readership will be increased. Articles written by women can be published to get better results.

Make the Newspaper Easy to Navigate

Navigation means turning of pages of newspaper from up side to down and vice versa. While reading news in any one page of the newspaper, sometimes it is required for the reader to refer to news from other pages also. Generally while reading the newspapers the readers feel a sort of inconvenience because unlike magazines and journals, the newspapers are not easy to navigate. If the newspaper is made easy to navigate then it is easy for the reader to read them. Now-a- days, the people are travelling distant places through trains and buses to do jobs. When compared with the past, in the present-day the time spent on travelling has increased enormously, because people now-a-days prefer to travel to do jobs which are at distant places and also want to spend their leisure time on pleasure trips which mostly includes travelling. If newspaper is made easy to navigate, then more people would prefer reading newspaper to magazines and others books while they are travelling in buses because newspaper contains latest information. Thus newspaper readership would increase. By reducing the size of the newspaper and by increasing the number of pages in the newspaper, it can be easily navigated without losing the news content. So organizations should produce a newspaper that is easy to navigate in order to increase the readership.

Enhancement of Newsprint Quality

Some newspapers are using newsprint which is not qualitative. The readers will be impressed and attracted if the newspaper is attractive at a glance. Newspapers can be made attractive only if it is prepared from qualitative newsprint. If quality of newsprint used by newspaper organizations is not good then the newspaper will not be attractive. If the reader's first impression is not good, then however good the content of news in newspaper, it will not catch the attention of viewers. The first impression is the best impression and in order to make the first impression good, the newspapers must use qualitative newsprint.

Cross Media Deals Like Radio Plus Print Media

Cross media deals means advertisement relating to one media can be telecast or published in other media. If an advertisement relating to one newspaper is listened through radio, then radio listeners also may buy the newspapers. Now-a-days radio listenership is increasing as private players like FM have emerged. It is not possible to club print that is newspaper or magazine with television media, because, between these two media, there is a large gap in advertising tariffs, and the high amount of advertising tariffs are not affordable by newspaper media. But there is not much of a difference in tariff rates between radio media and newspaper media. So radio plus newspaper media deal may work. In order to get mutual advantage and to increase awareness among readers and to improve reputation, the newspaper media can go for cross media deals like radio plus newspaper media. It not only increases awareness among newspaper readers, it also increases advertising revenues for newspaper organizations. Not only that within the newspaper media also cross media deals are possible. For example *Eenadu* and *The Hindu* have cross media deal in the form of concessional tariff. For the same advertising tariff the advertiser get advertisement in both newspapers which is known as concessional tariff. If other newspapers also can follow this deal to get mutual advantage to increase awareness among readers.

Increase Local Advertising

Newspapers are publishing different types of news like international, national, state news and local news. But now-a-days besides the international, national and regional readers, viewers and listeners now increasingly want to know what is happening in the neighbourhood. They are generally watching, viewing or listening only to local media. For example in Andhra Pradesh people are watching more local channels like ETV, Gemini, Teja, Maa T.V. etc., than national channels. So if advertisement relating to newspapers is given in local media, that is those which are telecasting programmes in local language, then more listeners and viewers may become readers of newspaper because of increased awareness among them.

Absence of Research Data for Effective Marketing Planning

In order to survive and grow any organization should go in for constant innovation and add features to the existing product. Likewise in newspaper media also, constant upgrading and adding more features is very important. Innovation is possible only when there is a continuous research process. The very important limitation, which newspaper industry is suffering are the lack of proper research data. Newspapers lack research data and only IRS, NRS surveys are conducted and that to having six months gap between two consecutive surveys. (Both for Indian Readership Survey (IRS) and National Readership Surveys (NRS) surveys). Both NRS and IRS conduct surveys only two times in a year which is a long time gap as the readers tastes and preferences are changing everyday. So whatever data they have collected becomes obsolete. Conducting surveys twice in a year is not enough for newspaper industry. They should go in for frequent surveys and research and collect opinions of people. Accordingly, they have to add new features and make the product attractive and thus increase reader perception and satisfaction. One should go in for a continuous process to survive and sustain in the market in order to face the tough competition in the market.

Development of Weekly Books for Future Reference

Unlike electronic media like television and radio media, newspapers can be used as future reference because it has the peculiar feature of physical evidence. So a weekly book covering 10 most important news items of the week may be compiled and published as a supplement for reference purposes.

Add Features Appealing and Interesting

Generally people show more interest in reading the newspapers if the news contains more life style features that are appealing. The readership could be greatly improved by fewer stories about natural disasters, more complex stories on science, more stories on food and fashion and more feature stories on life style. This builds the newspaper brand image.

Produce Newspapers Concise

Newspapers now-a-days are publishing lengthy news stories. But it is not possible for readers to go through all stories because they hardly find time to read newspaper. This is because people now-a-days are participating more in organizational activities. So if newspapers cut long stories short and have plenty of briefs they could convey more information and readers would generally be inclined towards a newspaper which is producing shorter and more stories and articles.

Increase Localisation Aspect

Localisation means publishing more local news. Newspapers have a bright future and readership would be greatly improved when newspapers publish local news. Even though newspapers publish news everyday, some national newspapers are publishing only very little local news and sometimes, they are not in a position to publish entire local news. So newspapers have to publish more local and regional news and allocate more space for local and regional news. While publishing regional and local news, they should check that the news contains latest and updated information and it should not contain any obsolete information.

Publish More Local Business News

Business news means, news relating to trading and manufacturing activities, stock exchange information, information about new products etc. If this business news contains business news from all regions, that is general business news. If this business is relating to particular region then it is called as regional or local business news. All newspapers are publishing only general business news and they hardly publish regional business news. But generally businessmen interested in information about the competitors in surrounding areas. Most of the Indian Business is by the local businessmen only. So the general readers as well as people doing business prefer local or regional business news rather than general business news. Such type of news is published, then it is more useful for readers and it improves readership of newspapers.

Focus on Content Relevant and Appealing to Youth

The readership of newspapers is increasing day by day due to increase in teenagers segment in market. If newspapers contain columns relating to youth which caters to their needs, that is publishing news relating to education, puzzles, employment news, career planning, local job opportunities, some famous quotes etc., then they will be more useful to readers in the teenage group. Today because of the busy work schedules and hectic work, students are feeling tensions and experiencing stress. So some columns may be published on stress management and relaxation. Different techniques to spend leisure time in a qualitative manner can be published in newspapers and that would catch the attention of the readers especially teenagers.

Drawing Meaningful and Reliable Conclusions

It is the duty of the newspapers to cover any important event that takes place anywhere in the world. However, sometimes newspapers after giving the news indulge in predictions, like in the case of elections or a cricket match. Sometimes, enough care is not taken and a haphazard guess is made, this resulting in a prediction that becomes false. Newspapers, therefore, should be very careful of predictions and restrain giving guess work so that they do not lead to confusion among the readers. So it is always better for newspaper organizations to publish news which is true and actual. They should not publish news basing on predictions about future activities, but news should be based on actual happenings.

Improve more Sports News Coverage with Adequate Local Emphasis

Sports news means the news relating to sports. Now-a-days people are more interested in sports because they are more health conscious and sports are very important for all. People are giving more importance to sports and readers wants more sports news. Not only that every reader wants to know what has happened surrounding them than the news at national and international levels. So naturally readers prefer local sports news to national and international sports news. So, apart from national and international sports news, newspapers should contain local or regional sports news to improve readership of newspapers.

Editorial Content

Any newspaper readership depends not just on the latest news it is publishing, the editorial plays an important role in increasing the newspaper readership as the editorial projects the bias of the newspaper. So the editorial must be good and it must be prepared in a qualitative way with expertise.

Promotional Pricing

In all English newspapers, the pricing is known as predatory pricing that is the price of newspaper is less than cost of production. To compensate this, the newspaper organisations are going for increasing the number of advertisements to get more advertising revenue. So newspaper contains more number of advertisements and news content is less. In order to overcome this, the newspaper organizations can fix reasonable price for newspapers and even though less number of advertisements are there, it does not reduce the profits of organization. So, without reducing the profits, it improves reader satisfaction. So they should avoid unhealthy competition like price wars and they can publish qualitative news by fixing reasonable price for newspaper.

Advertising

Any product can impress the minds of individuals only when awareness is created. That is possible through advertising only. Most people get awareness of the product only through advertising. For newspapers also, awareness can be increased and brand loyalty can be improved by proper advertisement. Even though all newspapers are going for excellent sales promotional activities, they are spending very little in the form of advertising. So advertising effort can be improved for every newspaper organization because it is must for every newspaper organizations as it has to face severe competition from other media.

Efficient Distribution System

Newspaper is having one important characteristic feature that is perishability. Any newspaper can survive only when the newspaper reach in time to the readers. Now-a-days, because of more employment, most of the people get ready to leave homes to attend to their jobs before nine in the morning. Not only that women participation in organizational activities is also very high. If employees want to attend duties at nine in the morning they should start before nine. For that they should wake up before six in morning time and they should make preparations and if newspaper reaches before six in the morning, then only readers can get through the newspaper. Now-a-days newspaper reading has become a habit and everyday along with a cup of coffee or tea readers want to read the newspaper and before six the newspaper should reach to the readers. So every newspaper organization must be in a position to distribute the newspapers in time. For that an efficient distribution system should be there. Distribution system can be made effective by efficient distribution boys, adequate number of boys and providing good salaries to them, proper monitoring system etc. Physical distribution and transportation can also be improved, so that it can reach in time to rural areas also. Presently most of the newspaper organizations are able to supply newspaper in time to all regions except a few areas which is unavoidable. But distribution of *The Times of India* and *The Hindu* newspaper is somewhat late when compared with other newspapers distribution. So they should do necessary arrangements to improve the distribution system of newspapers. So that they can reach in time to readers and readers satisfaction can be improved.

Suggestions Specific to Newpapers

I. *Deccan Chronicle*

(i) *Improvement of Career Chronicle: Deccan Chronicle* is publishing one supplement known as Career Chronicle on Tuesday, Thursday and Saturday. It contains some news relating to career planning, educational information etc. So, it is good if it contains more career news, more study materials and it should concentrate on student issues. More employment news and more mind power puzzles can be published. It can be improved if more local employment news is published.

(ii) *Bad Taste and Vulgarity: Deccan Chronicle* is publishing seminude photographs of women. When the women are portrayed in vulgar manner, women readers generally consider them to be in bad taste and vulgar. If such types of photographs are published, they have an impact and women readership would get reduced. So *Deccan Chronicle* newspaper should avoid publication of such photographs in order to retain women readership.

(iii) *Authentic and Clear Information:* There should not be any ambiguity in news while people are reading the newspaper. But now-a-days it is a common phenomenon that newspapers always have technical and composing errors. There should not be any composing and technical errors while publishing newspapers and at the same time there should not be any mistakes while publishing the information.

(iv) *Use of Colours to make Newspaper Attractive:* Any presentation can be made attractive, when greater use of colour is there. So in newspapers, colour photographs contribute to the attraction of the newspaper. By using the proper mix of colours, newspapers look good and readership of newspapers can be increased.

(v) *Classifieds should be Made Attractive:* Classifieds means some columns relating to vacancies, buying and selling of movable and immovable property, so on. In *Deccan Chronicle* newspaper, classifieds are not so attractive. If classifieds are made attractive by using colours and with good print, then it is beneficial to readers because they can easily locate the availability of the goods they want. Not only that, newspaper organizations also get more revenue because, if the classifieds are more attractive, then more and more people will be ready to give advertisements in that newspapers generating more advertising revenue.

(vi) *National and International News Coverage:* In *Deccan Chronicle*, generally there is more of regional news and local news because it is a regional newspaper. But now-a-days, national newspapers like *The Hindu* are also going in for localization, that is publishing of local news. If local news is published by national newspapers, then it is better for *Deccan Chronicle* to publish more international and national news also, because people generally want to prefer newspaper which contains all types of news that is local, regional, national and international news. So if newspapers like *The Hindu* are publishing more local news, then to meet the competition and to survive and grow, regional newspapers like *Deccan Chronicle* should also publish more national and international news.

II. *Andhra Bhoomi*

(i) *Updating of News Content:* News relating to education must be improved by publishing more updated information relating to career planning, puzzles and guidance to students. Employment news must be improved by giving more detailed information relating to job opportunities and publish information relating to local employment also.

(ii) *Improvement in Newsprint Quality:* Generally readers get attracted towards a newspaper when it is attractive with qualitative newsprint and if it has a colourful presentations. No doubt, *Andhra Bhoomi* newspaper consists of colourful photographs and presentations. Even then the newspapers is not so attractive because of one reason, that is the quality of news print is somewhat inferior. Because of the less qualitative newsprint, it lost its first impression and even though colours are used and content is good, it is not able to catch the attention of viewers. So it must be improved.

(iii) *Obsolescence of News:* The word obsolete means not in use. Sometimes if newspapers are not in a position to publish the latest news, they publish news which already published in other newspapers or news that is two to three days old. This news is called obsolete news. Readers have the opinion that *Andhra Bhoomi* is sometimes publishing news which is obsolete and that type of perception among readers may lead to loss of readership. So in order to retain readership, *Andhra Bhoomi* newspaper must publish the latest and updated information and avoid obsolete news.

III. *The New Indian Express*

(i) *Improvement in Content of News:* Now-a-days people are more interested in happenings in surrounding areas, and

publishing information relating to surrounding areas is known as local news. *The New Indian Express* must publish local news to improve readership. News relating to business activities like manufacturing and trading activities is known as business news. Business news must be improved by publishing more business news and also by publishing more local business news. Now-a-days, information technology plays a very important role and publishing news about information technology and computer usage, packages etc will improve the readership. Publishing more job related news definitely improves the readership of the younger generation. So, it should contain news relating to jobs, career planning etc. All these different types of news must be improved by *The New Indian Express* newspaper to improve the readership.

(ii) *Improvement in Quality of Newsprint:* In *The New Indian Express* newspapers the news content is very good and it gives wide coverage about national events, national news etc. Though the articles by George are very interesting, the newspaper readership is very less because, the newsprint quality is not so good. The very look of the newspaper, which is bad because of the quality of the newsprint creates an unfavourable impression. So if the newsprint quality is not good, however qualitative the content is, it never catches the attention of the viewers. So newsprint quality must be improved.

(iii) *Use of Colours:* Any presentation can be made attractive if colours are used in presentation of news items. So *The New Indian Express* newspaper must increase the use of colours, while printing and publishing the news.

IV. ***Andhra Prabha***

(i) *Adding New Features:* Any organization can survive and grow, if new ideas are added to existing product or service. By constant innovation, growth is possible and it will be in a position to face severe competition. Newspaper organizations can survive only if new features are innovated and added to existing ones. So new features must be added to its existing product and that will improve newspaper readership.

(ii) *Improvement in Newsprint Quality:* If newsprint quality is not good, immediately after seeing the newspaper, in the first

instance itself people will loose interest without going deep into the content. So if newsprint quality is not good, however qualitative the content is, it fail to catch the attention of the viewers. Hence newsprint quality must be improved.

V. *The Times of India*

Improvement in the Content of News: The Times of India is one of the popular and leading newspapers of India. Its readership is very high when compared with other newspapers. It is giving up-to-date information with very less price. But one of the important limitation relating to this newspaper is less coverage of local and regional news. In order to improve the newspaper readership, it should publish local business news, local sports, local employment news etc. If it concentrates on publishing local news items, in Andhra Pradesh also, it is possible to increase its readership further.

VI. *Eenadu*

(i) *Educational Programmes: Eenadu* is publishing news relating to education that is information relating to job, career planning, study material, so on. One relative advantage *Eenadu* newspaper is having when compared with other newspaper media is along with newspaper media, *Eenadu* organization has television channel also which is called as E - TV. So further improvement of educational programme is possible. In normal circumstances communication can be either oral or written. Both oral as well as written has its own advantages and disadvantages. Written communication can be useful for future reference. Detailed description of any topic is possible through oral communication. So whatever study material publishes in *Eenadu* newspaper, the same material can be explained through E-television channel just like telecasting of UGC (University Grants Commission) programmes and IGNOU (Indira Gandhi National Open University) programmes at some convenient time for students, normally early in the morning from 5.30 a.m. or from 6.30 a.m. on wards. This will definitely help students in a number of ways. They can keep the study material present in newspaper for further reference and at the same time by watching the television programme they get a clearer idea about subjects

that they are studying. This is possible for *Eenadu* newspaper because it is the only organization which own twin media that is newspaper and television. So it can utilize this facility and can get relative advantage over the other newspapers. The student community gets benefited and that ultimately improves the readership of students for *Eenadu* newspaper.

(ii) *News should not be Biased:* While publishing the news, if newspaper publishes news favourable to anybody, it is called as biased news. *Eenadu* readers while reading the newspaper, generally have the opinion that the news is somewhat biased and it appears that it is supporting particular political parties. When people have such a misconception, then it is the responsibility of the newspaper organization to avoid the misconceptions by publishing authentic information. Otherwise it has some adverse effect in the minds of readers and there is a possibility for decline in the readership of the newspaper.

(iii) *Improvement of City Editions:* City editions contains news only relating to cities. These city editions are full of advertisements and news content is very less. So there must be some improvement in publishing news in relating to city editions and the newspaper should see that it contain more news items than advertisements.

VII. *The Hindu*

(i) *Improving the Young World: The Hindu* newspaper is publishing one supplement known as the Young World which contains useful information for children. There is a possibility to improve the readership if it further improves the young world by publishing some study material, exam guidance information, Career planning etc.

(ii) *Employment Opportunities Information: The Hindu* readers have the opinion that *The Hindu* always publish information relating job opportunities in Chennai only. Though sometimes it is publishing employment information relating to other areas also, yet the misconception remains. So *The Hindu* organization should conduct a campaign to create awareness relating to this and should eliminate that type of misconception in the minds of the individuals.

(iii) *Improvement of Entertainment News: The Hindu* newspaper contain all different types of news like national, international etc. Recently it went for localization also by publishing more local and regional news. Now-a-days the readers want the newspaper to be informative as well as entertaining. So *The Hindu* people should give preference to entertainment news also that is information relating to entertainment activities like hollywood movies, television serials, information relating to local entertainment activities, information about food festivals, holiday resorts, movies in local theatres etc. Publishing and improvement of entertainment news definitely improves the readership of newspaper.

(iv) *Guidance for Parents: The Hindu* newspaper is publishing news relating to children in an attractive and useful manner. It is in the form of *Young World* supplement which contain news relating to children. It consists of small stories, puzzles, educational information which are interesting. As it is already publishing news relating to children, as an improvement activity, it can publish news relating to parents and by using that information, parents can better bring up their children. Interviews with child psychologists can be published so that, the parents can follow the instructions carefully and can counsel the children and they can give guidance to children to choose their career paths.

(v) *Social Awareness Programmes: The Hindu* newspaper should also participate in social awareness programmes like aids awareness, child labour etc. Other newspapers like *The New Indian Express* and *Eenadu* already implemented such type of programmes and it is one of the reason for *Eenadu* to become a successful market leader in Telugu newspaper Industry. If *The Hindu n*ewspaper participate in such type of social awareness programmes, then it is beneficial to the readers as well as the newspaper organizations and readers develop a type of positive attitude towards the newspaper. Not only that unlike all other commodities, newspapers should prefer societal objective, than profit objective. If *The Hindu* newspaper participate in social awareness campaigns, then it will have some positive impact on readership of newspaper.

VII. *Vaartha*

(i) *Avoid Technical and Composing Errors:* Any newspaper can increase the readership, if news is clear and there is no ambiguity while reading the newspaper. But in *Vaartha* newspaper, a number of technical and composing errors were present. This leads to ambiguity. Even though *Vaartha* newspaper is publishing updated and latest information, some confusion and ambiguity arises because of technical and composing errors. So the newspaper should publish news without composing and technical errors.

(ii) *Too Many Features: Vaartha* newspaper is containing too many features particularly in local supplements. This creates disinterest and confusion among the readers to go through the entire newspaper. So it is advisable to reduce certain features and publish other features which are interesting.

(iii) *Improvement in Newsprint Quality:* Vaartha newspaper is using newsprint which is not qualitative. So it must use qualitative newsprint.

Suggestions of Newspaper Agents

1. Any newspaper organization can survive and grow only if it has efficient distribution system, because newspaper is a commodity which has a very short life period of one-day. As such perishability is very high for newspapers. So newspaper bundles should reach in time to newspaper points at different localities in order to make distribution more convenient. This enables the timely delivery of newspapers to customers.
2. While packing the newspapers into bundles, ensure there are no errors and discrepancies in counting number of newspaper for each bundle to avoid problems and misunderstandings. So the packing section should be very careful and check again and again so that there should not be any shortages and surpluses while packing the newspapers to different destinations.
3. The newspaper organizations now-a-days are changing the policies that is policies relating to price, distribution policies like fixing of commission to agents, distribution boys etc. very frequently. Policies should be firm and should not changing frequently. Even though it is advisable to have

some flexibility while framing the policies, they should not change the policies very frequently as they have a negative impact.

4. Now-a-days every newspaper contain too much of advertisements. Undoubtedly generating revenues is very important for the newspaper organizations. At the same time creating and satisfying readers is much more important for newspaper organizations. If more advertisements are published in newspapers, it sometimes leads to advertisement cluttering and people get dissatisfied. So, always a balance should be maintained between the advertisements published and the news content. There should not be too much of advertisements in newspapers. Space allotted for advertisements should not be more than space allotted for news items.
5. Now-a-days, as experts said, that there is future for newspapers if newspaper organizations go for regionalisation and according to that all newspapers are trying to localize and regionalize the news. Likewise the national newspapers when they are giving advertisements, they should give preference to local and regional advertisements rather than to the national advertisements.
6. Many newspapers containing many grammatical and language errors. They should be rectified. Even though it is not possible to avoid it completely, errors should be minimized to the extent possible.
7. There must be proper coordination between the newspaper organizations and the agencies. Organisational people must coordinate with newspaper agents and distribution boys for efficient functioning of newspaper organizations.
8. There should be facility of returning unsold newspapers: Some newspaper organizations are providing unsold facility that is if newspapers are unsold, newspaper organizations are reducing some amount which the agents ought to pay to the newspaper organizations or they can return the unsold newspapers. If such type of concessions are given by the other newspaper organizations also, newspaper agents satisfaction improves and they get motivated.
9. For any individual motivation is very important. Unless there

is motivation, even though the individual is of a highly talented and hard working in nature, he is not interested to do work. Motivating individuals is very important to get good results and for improving the efficiency of distribution system. So by giving some financial and non-financial incentives, the individuals get motivated. Organizational people have to offer different types of incentives to distribution boys and proper recognition must be there to motivate the distribution boys.

10. Newspapers should not identify or associate themselves with any political party and should not show the tendency of giving support. The news published should be unbiased, balanced and reliable.
11. Newspapers must publish special supplements for the aged and to the neglected sections of society, just like supplements what they are producing for women (*Eenadu* – Vasundhara) and Children (*The Hindu* – Young World).
12. Quality of newsprint should be improved and in the printing process some news organizations are using certain inks which have pungent smell and may cause harm to health. So in the printing process, they have to use inks which do not produce pungent smell and which do not cause harm to the health of the readers.
13. News must reach in time to the readers and there should not be any obsolescence. They should publish latest news and at the same time the stories should be short and more new stories should be published to increase the readership.

Suggestions of Distribution Boys

1. The distribution system plays an important role in the newspaper organisational network. Timely distribution of newspapers require the proper functioning of distribution boys. If rains, storms occur, definitely they have adverse impact on distribution process when boys are distributing the newspapers. This problem of distributing in improper weather can be overcome by providing the distribution boys raincoats, cycles, etc., and thus maintain punctuality in distribution.
2. People can be motivated by providing some financial and non-financial incentives. Of these distribution boys who are in low income group mainly get satisfied with financial

incentives. So providing good salary and wage structure and incentives motivates the boys and they will pay greater concentration to do the work and put in their best talents.

3. More promotional campaigns should be undertaken for the promotion of newspapers even though some newspaper organizations are already doing that. The advertising budget should be increased and frequency of advertising exposure should be increased.
4. Readers can easily change the newspaper as many alternative newspapers are available in the market. So those who have been reading newspapers from the last several years, some preference must be given to them in the form of early delivery, price preference etc., that will ensure customer retention and loyalty.
5. Sometimes if subscriptions of newspapers get reduced, commission also get reduced. But if copies are increased, then no concession is given to distribution boys, instead additional boys were appointed to distribute the additional subscription copies, which ultimately creates dissatisfaction among the existing distribution boys. Therefore, there should be a proper system of increasing income to the distribution boys along with the growth of business.

Conclusion

Marketing is a key to success in any organization in todays competitive markets. The newspaper market hitherto is a sellers market that gradually emerged into buyers' market in the post-liberalization era. As such, the newspaper organizations surveyed although reflected signs of growth in terms of circulation and product features, they are exposed to different market challenges, particularly from the electronic media that has changed the reading habits of the customers. This necessiated the concern for a true customer orientation in designing newspapers in the organizations chosen for the study. The organizations must put in their resources and efforts to undertake constant research about readers' preferences. Thus, the newspaper organizations should conduct extensive research programmes to publish newspaper according to the tastes and preferences of readers, improve the product and add innovative and appealing features to attract and retain market. The improvement in marketing activities especially distribution system of newspapers without any deficiencies, would certainly enhance the caliber of newspaper organizations not only for survival in today's highly competitive environment but also increase the future prospects of the business.

ANNEXURES

I. QUESTIONNAIRES

Newspaper Organisation Heads

1. What is your opinion on present scenario of Newspaper Industry? (Regarding allowing of 26 per cent FDI in newspapers, Advertising revenues etc.)
2. What is your opinion on competition prevailing in Newspaper Markets? (price wars etc.)
3. What measures are you taking to meet inter media (T.V., Radio after the emergence of F.M.) competition, Intra media competition (competition from other newspapers)?
4. What is the cost of production/unit?
5. Are you importing newsprint or using domestic newsprint?
6. What is the future of Newspaper Industry?

Agents

1. Name
2. Gender
3. Age
4. Address
5. Publication(s) dealing with:
6. Area(s) of operation:
7. Volume:
8. Since how long you have been in this newspaper business?
9. Is it your 'sole' business or 'part time' business?
   - *(a)* Yes ☐
   - *(b)* No ☐
10. If it is your part time business, what is your main activity?
11. Investment made (in Rupees):
12. At what time you receive your paper bundles?

13. Return on investment is at what rate? Any incentives?
14. How many distribution boys are working with you?
15. Specify the salary structure of boys.
16. What are the reasons for choosing this newspaper business:
17. Is there any sale on return facility?
18. Is the business profit making?
    (*i*) If 'Yes' indicate the amount
19. What is your Ranking of newspapers?
    (*a*) Eenadu
    (*b*) Vaartha
    (*c*) Andhara Bhoomi
    (*d*) The Hindu
    (*e*) Deccan Chronicle
    (*f*) The New Indian Express
20. In your opinion what are the features in the special supplements in each of the newspapers that catches attention of readers?
21. What problems are you facing in doing the business?
22. What is your opinion on reading newspaper through internet?
23. What is your opinion on the future of newspaper business in India?
24. Suggestions, If any – –

Retailers (Pan Shop Owners)

1. Name
2. Gender
3. Age
4. Shop address
5. Name of publications (newspapers) selling and number of newspapers selling.

Name of Newspaper	*Copies Sold*	*Commission Given*
The Hindu		
The New Indian Express		
Deccan Chronicle		
Eenadu		
Vaartha		
Andhra Bhoomi		
Andhra Prabha		

6. Are you satisfied with arrival time of newspaper?
   (*a*) Yes ☐
   (*b*) No ☐
7. Name of magazines sold and quantity sold.

Name of Magazine	*Arrival Time*	*Copies Sold*	*Commission Given*
Swathi			
Andhra Bhoomi weekly			
Andhra Prabha weekly			
India Today			
The Week			
Outlook			
Others			

8. What are the newspapers that are fast moving?
   (1)
   (2)
   (3)
9. Reasons for fast moving
10. Do you have unsold facility?
    (*a*) Yes ☐
    (*b*) No ☐
11. Do you influence the customers to buy a particular newspaper? Why?
12. Do you get any special incentives, if more copies were sold?
13. Are you facing any problems while selling newspapers? If 'yes' please mention the problem area.
14. Suggestions if any— — — —.

Distribution Boys

1. Name
2. Age
3. Address
4. Educational qualification
5. Name of the publication(s) distributing
6. Paper point is situated at
7. Arrival time to paper point
8. No. of papers distributing
9. Area(s) of distributing
10. Time taken for distribution

11. Are you participating in collection work?
    (a) Yes ☐
    (b) No ☐
    If answer is 'Yes' how many days are you required to finish the collection work?
12. Remuneration for work done (in Rs.)
13. Is there any separate remuneration for collection work?
    (a) Yes ☐
    (b) No ☐
    If answer is 'Yes' how much amount are getting as remuneration?
14. Are you given any incentives:
    (a) Yes ☐
    (b) No ☐
    If answer is 'Yes', specify the reason?
15. Since how long have you been working in the field?
16. Whether collection is received in time? (How many number of visits are you making to collect the money?
17. Are you facing any problems while distributing the newspapers?
18. Are you facing any problems with the subscribers?
19. Any other information:
20. Any suggestions to improve distribution system of newspapers?

Readers

1. Personal Details of Readers
    (i) Name
    (ii) Gender:
        (a) Male ☐
        (b) Female ☐
    (iii) Age ☐
    (iv) Address ☐
2. Educational Qualification:
    (a) Up to 10th
    (b) Inter
    (c) PUC
    (d) Graduate/PG (General)
    (e) Graduate/PG (Professional)

3. Monthly house-hold income from all sources (in Rs.):
   (*a*) Up-5,000
   (*b*) 5,000-10,000
   (*c*) 10,000-15,000
   (*d*) 15,000-20,000
   (*e*) Above 20,000

Newspaper Reading habits and preferences

4. Since how long have been you reading Newspaper(s)? — — — years.
5. Which of these Newspapers do you read?
   (*a*) The Hindu ☐
   (*b*) The New Indian Express ☐
   (*c*) Deccan Chronicle ☐
   (*d*) The Times of India ☐
   (*e*) Eenadu ☐
   (*f*) Vartha ☐
   (*g*) Andhra Bhoomi ☐
   (*h*) Andhra Prabha ☐
6. What is your readership preference in respect of each newspaper?
   (*a*) Whole paper
   (*b*) Headlines
   (*c*) Selected columns
   (*d*) Specific columns
7. How much time do you spend on reading newspaper(s)? — — hours — — minutes.
8. Do you read newspaper in week ends (   ) or (   ) daily.
9. Do you buy the Newspaper from the Newspaper stand or you a subscriber?
   If you buy newspaper from Newspaper stand, do you find any difficulty to get newspaper from news stand?
10. At what time do you receive your copy of newspaper?
    (*a*) Before 6 am. ☐
    (*b*) Between 6 a.m. and 6.30 a.m. ☐
    (*c*) 6.30 a.m to 7 a.m. ☐
    (*d*) After 7 a.m ☐
11. When do you read the Newspaper?
    (*a*) Morning
    (*b*) Afternoon
    (*c*) Evening
    (*d*) Night

12. What are the reasons for preferring a particular newspaper?
    (a) Quality ☐
    (b) Quantity more number of pages) ☐
    (c) Price ☐
    (d) Timely distribution ☐
    (e) More number of Features ☐
13. Rank your newspaper on 1 to 4 scale (1 for excellent, 2 for good, 3 for moderate, 4 for poor).

Name of Newspaper
(a) Language and style of presentation
(b) Qualitative printing
(c) News coverage
(d) Timely distribution
(e) Price
(f) Quantity

14. Do you lend your newspaper to neighbours?
    (a) Yes ☐
    (b) No ☐
15. Please give your areas of interest in terms of ranking?

	Most Preferred	*Preferred*	*Least Preferred*
(i) Local News			
(ii) Regional News			
(iii) National News			
(iv) International News			

16. Newspaper coverage of following items:

	Adequate	*Need to be Improved*	*Need to be Reduced*
(i) Local News			
(ii) Regional News			
(iii) National News			
(iv) International News			

17. Do you think that price reduce got any effect on you for purchasing the Newspaper?
    (a) Yes ☐

(*b*) No ☐

18. After price reduction, has been there any degradation in newspaper attributes?

(*a*) Quality Yes/No
(*b*) Number of pages Yes/No
(*c*) Coverage Yes/No
(*d*) Others Yes/No

19. If price is hiked will you still continue to be subscriber?

20. Do you like supplements of the paper you read?

(*a*) Yes ☐
(*b*) No ☐
(*i*) If answer is 'Yes' which supplement do you read?
(*ii*) Reasons for liking?

21. Do you read the newspaper on the Internet?

(*a*) Yes ☐
(*b*) No ☐

If answer is 'Yes' how frequently do you browse
Daily ☐
Twice a week ☐
Once in a week ☐

22. Do you have Internet at:

(*a*) Home ☐
(*b*) Office ☐
(*c*) Outside ☐
(*d*) Other Media Habits ☐

23. What are your media habits?

(*a*) Watching Television ☐
(*b*) Listening Radio ☐
(*c*) Read Magazines ☐
(*d*) Surfing net ☐
(*i*) You watch Television/Listen Radio/Read Magazine/ Surf net what for?

	News	*Entertainment*
1. Watching		
2. Listening Radio.		
3. Reading Magazines		
4. Surfing Internet		

(*ii*) How many hours do you spend on the following media?

	News	*Entertainment*
1. Watching		
2. Listening Radio.		
3. Reading Magazines		
4. Surfing Internet		

24. What are other reading habits?
    (*a*) Magazine ☐
    (*b*) Journals ☐
    (*c*) Periodicals ☐
    (*d*) Others ☐
25. Which Magazine do you read?
    (*a*) India Today ☐
    (*b*) Outlook ☐
    (*c*) The Week ☐
    (*d*) Front Line ☐
    (*e*) Swathi ☐
    (*f*) Andhra Bhoomi ☐
    (*g*) Andhra Prabha ☐
    (*h*) Sports Star ☐
    (*i*) Others ☐
26. Do you read any of the business magazines?
    21 Yes ☐
    22 No ☐
    If answer is 'Yes' name of the Business magazine you read?
    (*a*) Business India
    (*b*) Business World
    (*c*) Business Today
    (*d*) A & M
27. Any other suggestions?

II. BRIEF DESCRIPTION OF NEWSPAPER ORGANISATIONS

THE HINDU

Name	:	*The Hindu*
Language	:	English
Established	:	1878, Madras
Status of Newspaper	:	National
Head Office	:	859 and 860, Anna Salai, Chennai-600 002
Local Office	:	50-19-9,T. P. T. Colony Seethammadhara, Visakhapatnam
The Editor	:	N. Ram
The Publisher	:	S. Rangarajan
Number of Pages (Avg.)	:	28
Price	:	Weekdays – Mon, Wed, Sat – Rs. 1.00, Tue, Thurs, Fri – Rs. 2.00, Sunday – Rs. 4.50
Local Circulation	:	29,000 (Approximately)
Other Publishing Centres	:	Chennai, Coimbatore, Bangalore, Hyderabad, Madurai, Delhi, Tiruvananthapuram, Vijayawada

VAARTHA

Name	:	*Vaartha*
Language	:	Telugu
Established	:	1996, Hyderabad
Status of Newspaper	:	Regional
Head Office	:	396, Lower Tank Bund Indira Park Road Hyderabad-500 080
Local Office	:	13-1-1E, Jagadamba Centre Maharanipeta Visakhapatnam-530 002

The Editor	:	Girish Sanghi
The Publisher	:	Girish Sanghi
Number of Pages (Avg.)	:	18
Price	:	Weekdays – Rs. 2. 80 Sunday – Rs. 3. 50
Local Circulation	:	18000
Other Publishing Centres	:	Hyderabad, Vijayawada, Cuddpah, Rajahmundry, Ongole, Nizamabad, Warangal, Tirupati, Ananthapur.

THE NEW INDIAN EXPRESS

Name	:	*The New Indian Express* (Previously called as *Indian Express*)
Language	:	English
Established	:	1949, Bombay
Status of Newspaper	:	National
Head Office		Express Estate, Mount Road Chennai-600 002
Local Office	:	39-21-40. S. No. 25/1 Madhavadhara Visakhapatnam-530 007
The Managing Editor	:	Manoj Kumar Santhalia
The Publisher	:	R. K. Jhunjhunwala
Number of Pages (Avg.)	:	18
Price	:	Weekdays – Mon, Thur, Sat – Rs. 1.00, Tue, Wed, Friday – Rs. 1.50, Sunday – Rs. 5.00
Local Circulation	:	4000
Other Publishing Centres	:	Visakhapatnam, Hyderabad, Bhubaneswar, Chennai, Coimbatore, Madurai, Vijayawada, Bangalore, Belgam, Shimoga, Tiruvananthapuram, Cochin, Kozikhode.

DECCAN CHRONICLE

Name	:	*Deccan Chronicle*
Language	:	English
Established	:	1938, Hyderabad
Status of Newspaper	:	Regional
Head Office	:	36, Sarojini Devi Road, Secunderabad -500 003
Local Office	:	Deccan Chronicle, Pitapuram Colony, Visakhapatnam- 530 003
The Editor	:	A. T. Jayanthi
The Publisher	:	K. Sudhakar
Number of Pages (Avg.)	:	20
Price	:	Weekdays—Rs. 1. 50 Sunday—Rs. 2. 50
Local Circulation	:	16000
Other Publishing Centres	:	Hyderabad, Vijayawada, Rajahmundry and Ananthpur.

ANDHRA BHOOMI

Name	:	*Andhra Bhoomi*
Language	:	Telugu
Established	:	1968, Hyderabad
Status of Newspaper	:	Regional
Head Office	:	36, Sarojini Devi Road Secunderabad - 500 003
Local Office	:	Andhra Bhoomi Pitapuram Colony Visakhapatnam-530 003
The Editor	:	M. V. R. Sastry
The Publisher	:	K. Sudhakar
Number of Pages (Avg.)	:	18

Price	:	Weekdays – Rs. 1.50 Sunday – Rs. 2.50
Local Circulation	:	2400
Other Publishing Centres	:	Hyderabad, Vijayawada, Rajahmundry.

Bibliography

List of Reports

Press Council of India Annual Report (2003). New Delhi: Press Council of India.

Press In India, 1994, being RNI's Annual Report, covering the year 1993.

PTI Story-Origin and growth of Indian Press and News Agency (1987), Press Trust of India Limited, Bombay, Published in 1987.

Readership Institute at North Western University's Media Management Centre of New York, Readership Survey conducted by NWV of *New York* (2002).

Report by the National News Council (1979-1983).61:715, National News Council—in the Public Interest III.

Report of American Marketing Association.

Report of Registrar of Newspapers of India (1994). New Delhi: Government of India Publication.

Report of the First Press Commission, Delhi.

Report of the Second Press Commission, Delhi.

Reports of Audit Bureau of Circulation, 1956-2003.

Reports of National Readership Survey, 1999-2004.

Second Press Commission Report, Vol. I. (1982) Government of India Publication, New Delhi.

List of Books

Aggarwal, N. (1978), "A Third World Perspective of News", *Freedom at Issue,* May-June.

Ahuja, B.N.(1993), *History of Press, Press Laws and Communications,* Surjeet Publications, New Delhi.

Alleyne, Mark.D.(1997), *News Revolution: Political and Economic Decisions About Global Information",* St. Martin's Press, New York.

Ames, Stemen. E. (1989), *Elements of Newspaper Design*, London, Paeger.

Andrea Millwood Hargrave, U.K. *Keeping Pace with Media Convergence. Are Regulations Still Relevant?*

Baistow, T. (1985), *Fourth-Rate Estate: An Anatomy of Fleet Street*, London: Comedia Publishing Group.

Bart Pattyn (2000), *Media Ethics: Operating Social Dialogue*, Leuven, Belgium: Peters.

Basanthi Sinha (1994), *Press and National Movement in India.*

Bathla Souria (1998), *Women, Democracy and the Media: Cultural and Political Representation in Indian Press*, New Delhi, Sage Publications.

Berelson, B. (1952) *Content Analysis in Communications Research*, Glancoe, Free Press.

Beri, G.C. (1993), *Marketing Research*, Tata McGraw-Hill, New Delhi, p. 475.

Bhatnagar,V. (1996), *Role of Press in Women's Development*, Issues, in V. Bhatnagar (ed.) Development Dynamics of Press and Journalism, pp. 128-29, Jaipur: Printwell.

Bhatt, S.C. (1997), *Indian Press Since 1955*, Publication Division, Ministry of Broadcasting, Government of India, p.168.

Bhattacharya, Ajit (1995), Emergency After 20 Years, *Indian Express.*

Bill Sloan and Amherst (2001), *I Watched a Wild Hog Eat my Baby: A Colourful History of Tabloids and their Cultural Impact*, Promethens Books.

Bob Franklin and David Murphy (1991), *Making the Local News: Local Journalism in Context*, London: Routledge.

Bobby Varthan (2000), *Indian Press and National Movement.*

Bonnie Brennen (2001), *For the Record: An Oral History of Rochester New York, News Workers*, New York, New York University Press.

Bronars and Stephen. G. (1998), "Non-Parametric Tests of the Efficiency of Union Employment Contracts." University of Caulifornia at Santa Barbara Department of Economics, *Cambridge University Press*, p. 41.

Bruce Garrison, Miami, U.S. (2002), The Use of Electronic Mail as a News Gathering Resource, *AEJMC Newspaper Division, 2002.*

Bruce I. Newman (1999), *The Mass Marketing of Politics: Democracy in an Age of Manufactures Images.*

Bryce T. Meintyre (1998), *Mass Media in the Asian Pacific*, Multilingual Matters Limited.

Chaturvedi, J.P. (1992), *The Indian Press at Crossroads*, New Delhi: Media Research Foundation.

Denis Mcquail (1997), *Audience Analysis,* Thousand Oaks, Sage Publications.

Desai, A.R. (1993), *Social Background of Indian Nationalism (Second Edition),* Bombay: Popular Prakashan.

Donald, S.Tull, Del I. Hawkins (1996), "Marketing Research", Prentice Hall of India Private Limited.

Doris, A. Graber (1994), Media Power in Politics.

Dorothy, G. Singer and Jerome L. Singer Editors (2001), *Hand Book of Children and the Media,* Thousand Oaks, Sage Publications.

E.S.Venkataramaih (1987), *Freedom of Press: Some Recent Trends.*

Elizabath, M.Perse, Lawrence Eribanm Association (2001), *Media Effects and Society.*

Elliot, C. Rothenberg (1999), *The Taming of the Press,* West Port, London.

Erik Barnown (1997), *Conglomerates and the Media,* New York: The New Press.

Erwin, K.Thomas and Brown H.Carpenter (2001), *Mass Media in 2025: Industries, Organisations, People and Nations,* Green Wood Press.

Everett, E.Dennis(1994), "Reshaping Mass Media: Mass Communication in Information Age."

Friedrich Ebert Stiftung (1999), *Ethics in Journalism – A Reader on his Perception in the Third World.*

George Douglas (1999), *The Golden Age of the Newspapers,* Greenwood Press.

H.D. Lasswell, N. Leites and Associates (Ed.), *Lanaguage of Politics: A Quantitative Semantics,* pp. 55-82, Cambridge:MIT.

Hachten, W.A. (1996) *The World News Prism: Changing Media of International Communication,* Lowa: Lowa State University Press.

Harp, W. Boyd, Ralph, Stanely (1996), *Marketing Research:Text and Cases,* AITBS.

Hendricks and Patrick (1999), *A Lost Cause? Strategic Mangement of Newspaper Firms in the United States and in Netherlands,* p. 251.

Herbert Lee Williams (1982), *Newspaper Organization and Management,* Surjeet Publications, New Delhi.

Indian Institute of Mass Communication (1968), "Role of Daily Newspapers During Elections: Report of a Content Analysis of the Indian Dailies Coverage of Election News and Items" *IIMC,* New Delhi, 1968, p. 12.

Jacklule (2001), *Daily News, Eternal Stories: The Mythological Role of Journalism,* New York and London, The Guliford Press.

James Potter.J. (1999), *On Media Violence,* Thousand Oaks, Sage Publications.

Jan Bekken, (1995), "News Worker: Toward a History of the Rank and File", *University of Minnesota Press* in U.S.

Jay Fogarthy and Fredrick Gren and Levis Ubinas (1998), Rapidly Increasing Newspaper Revenue Through Redesigning Advertising Sales", *Mckinsey and Company,* June 1998.

Jeffrey, L. Palsey (2001), *The Tyranny of Printer: Newspaper Politics in the Early American Republic,* Charlottesville, University Press of Virginia.

Jena, P.K. (1995), *Effective use of Media for Rural Development: A Study of Communication Patterns in Orissa",* Unpublished Ph.D thesis, Mysore University.

Jhingan, M.L.(1994), *The Economics of Development and Planning,* (27th edition), New Delhi: Konark Publishers.

Joanne, P. Sharp (2000), *Condensing the Cold War: Reader's Digest and American Identity,* Minneapolis and London: University of Minnesota Press.

John M. Coward (1999), *The Newspaper Indian: Native American Identity in the Press, 1820-90,* University of Illinois Press.

John Street (2001), *Mass Media, Politics and Democracy,* New York, Palgrane Publishers.

John Vivian (2002), *The Media and Mass Communication, 6th edition, Boston,* Allyn and Bacon.

Julie Hedgepeth Williams (1999), *The Significance of Printed World in Early America: Colonists thoughts in the Role of the Press,* Green Wood Press.

K.S. Padhy (1991), *Battle for Freedom of Press in India,* Delhi, Academic Foundation.

Kamla Bhasin and Bin Agarwal (1984), *Women and Media: Analysis, Alternatives and Action.*

Keane, John, 69:1077, *The Media and Democracy.*

Kenneth Thomson (1997), London, *Media and Cultural Regulation,* Sage Publications.

Khan, M.I. and Kumar K. (1993), *Studies in Modern Mass Media,* Vol.1, New Delhi: Kanishka, pp. 34-35.

Kothari, C.R. (1985), *Research Methodology.*

Krishna Murthy, N. (1966), *Indian Journalism,* Mysore: Mysore University Press.

Kristie Bunton, Thomas Connery, Stacey Kanihan, Mark Riley Neuzil and David Nimmer (1999), *Writing Across the Media.*

Lasswell, H.D. and Leites, N. (1965), *Language of Politics: Studies in Quantitative Semantics.*

Lawrence Grossberg, Ellen Wartella, D.Charles Whitney (1998), *Media Making: Mass Media in a Popular Culture,* Thousand Oaks, London, Sage Publications.

Lockwood, Robert, Denver (1992), *News by Design: A Survival Guide for Newspapers,* Colorado, Quark Press.

Mazharul Haque.S.M. (1988), *What is News in India? A Content Analysis of the Elite Press,* University Press of America, Lanham, M.D. (1988), p. 190.

Mencher, Melvin, Madison: Brown and Bench Mark (1996), *Basic Media Writing.*

More, Shaun (1993), *Audience Research: Interpreting Audiences, the Ethenography of Media Consumption,* London, Sage Publications.

Moses, Sir Charles and Maslog, C. (1978), *Mass Media in Asia,* Singapore: AMIC.

Murthy, D.V.R. (2001, November), *The Path Forgotten: Ringside View, Indian Express.*

Murthy, K.N. (1996), *Indian Journalism,* Mysore: Mysore University Press.

Murthy, D.V.R. (2002), *Mass Communication-Concepts and Issues,* Olive Green Publishers, p. 150.

Nancy, J. Woodhull and Robert W. Snyder(1998), *Media Mergers,* Transaction Publishers.

Parthasarathy, R.(1991), *History of Journalism in India,* New Delhi:Sterling Publishers.

Paschal Preston (2001), *Reshaping Communications: Technology, Information and Social Change,* Thousand Oaks, Sage Publications.

Patrick Hendriks (1999), *Newspapers: A Lost Cause? Strategic Management of Newspaper Firms in the United States and Netherlands,* Kluwer Academic Publishers.

Paul Manning (2001), *News and News Sources: A Critical Introduction,* Sage Publications.

Paula, M. Poindecter and Maxwell E.Mc Combs (2000), *Research in Mass Communication: A Practical Guide.*

Peter, F. Drucker (1987), *The Frontiers of Management,* Heinemann, London.

Philip Kotler (1989), *Marketing Management,* Prentice Hall, New Delhi, 1989.

Philip M. Seib Oxford, England (2001), *Going Line: Getting the News Right in a Real Time, on Line World,* Rowan and Little Field Publishers.

Philip Rayner, Peter wall, Stephen Kruger (2001), *Media Studies: The Essentials of Introduction,* New York, Routledge.

Picard, Robert. G. (1998), *Press Concentration and Monopoly: New Perspectives of Newspaper Ownership and Operation,* p. 231.

Picard, Robert and G., Broady, Jeffrey. H. (1997), *Newspaper Publishing Industry,* Boston, p. 224.

Pippa Norris ed, Boulder (1997), *Politics and the Press: The News Media and Their Influence,* Lynne Publishers.

Pothuri Venkateswara Rao (2002), *History of Telugu Newspapers,* Kesava Memorial Educational Campus, Hyderbad.

Raghavan, G.N.S, *The Press in India: A New History,* Gyan Publishing House, Delhi.

Raghavan, G.N.S., *PTI Story,* PTI Bombay.

Rai, Usha (1992), *Interview in Rama Jha* (Ed.) *Women and Print Media: Portrayal and Performance,* New Delhi: Chanakya Publications Pvt. Limited, pp. 66-68.

Rao, K.V.(1995), *Research Methodology in Commerce and Management,* Sterling Publishers Private Limited, p. 375.

Raymond Kent (1994), *Measuring Media Audiences,* London.

Reinhold Wagnleitner and Elaine Tyler May eds. (2000), *Here,There and Every where:The Foreign Politics of American Popular Culture,* Hanover, University Press of New England.

Richard Campbell (2002), *Media and Culture: An Introduction to Mass Communication,* Middle Tennesse State University, Boston.

Richard Keeble (2000), *The Newspapers Hand Book,* New York, Routledge.

Righter, R. (1979). Whose News? *Politics, Press and the Third World,* New York: Times Books.

Robin Jeffrey (2000), *The Great Indian Newspaper Revolution: Capitalism, Politics and Indian Language Press,* Oxford University Press, New Delhi.

Ruth Walden, Restor, World Press Freedom Committee (2000), *Insult Laws: An Insult to Press Freedom.*

Sadhu and Singh (1996), *Research Methodology in Social Sciences,* Himalaya Publishing House, p. 288.

Sarkar, Chanchal (1969), *Challenge and Stagnation:The Indian Mass Media,* New Delhi, Vikas Publications.

Sarkar, R.C.S., *The Press in India,* S. Chand and Company, New Delhi.

Schramm.W. (1964), *Mass Media and National Development*, California: Stanword University Press.

Shakdhar, B.M.(1974), *Development of Press in India, 1580-1835*, New Delhi: Unpublished Ph.D thesis, University of Delhi.

Shannon, A.Martin and Kathleen (1998), *Newspapers of Record in a Digital Age: From Hot Type to Hot Link*, Westport, Prager Publishers.

Sharma (1994), "Marketing Research", Sulthan Chand and Sons, p. 470.

Shobha De (1988, January) *The Glam Press*, Inkworld, New Delhi.

Srinivasan, V.L. (1985), "A Comparitive Study of Editorials of the three National Dailies", Unpublished Master's Dissertation, Osmania University.

Subhash C Mehta, *Marketing Management*, Tata McGraw Hill, New Delhi, 1980.

Tripathi, P.C. (1987), *Research Methodology*.

Vilanilam, J.V. (1975), "Ownership vs. Development News Coverage: An Analysis of Independent and Conglomerate Newspapers of India", Paper Presented at AEJ Convention, Ottawa.

Viswanth, K. and Karan, K. (2000), *Handbook of the Media in Asia*, New Delhi: Sage Publications, pp. 84-117.

Von Feitlitzen (1999), *Children and Media: Image, Education and Participation*, Cecilia and Ulla Carlson eds.

William G.Jordan (2001), *Black Newspapers and America's War for Democracy (1914-1920)*, The University of North Carolina Press.

William, J. Stanton (1984), *Marketing Management*, McGraw Hill, Auckland, 1984.

William, Mc Gowan (2001), *Coluring the News, How Crusading for Diversity has Corrupted American Journalism*, Sanfransisco Encounter Books.

Yahya R.Kamalipour and Edited by Behmart (2002), *Global Communication*.

List of Journals

Abby Dress, "Running out of Time: An Analysis of Shutting Down New York Newsday by Times Mirror", *Journalism and Mass Communication Quarterly*, 76/4 (1999), pp. 745-56.

Adams, R.C. (1991), Social Survey Methods for Mass Media Research, *68:298, Journalism and Mass Communication Quarterly*.

Agee, Warren K. Philip H. Ault and Edwin Emery (1988), "Introduction to Mass Communication", 65:765, *Journalism and Mass Communication Quarterly*.

Ahmed, S.A. (1986), "The Language Press in India: A Case Study of Malayalam Newspapers", *Gazette*, 38(3):71-82.

Alan Blanchard and Stephen Lacy (2002), Michigan State University, "The Impact of Public Ownership, Profits and Competition on Number of Newsroom Employees and Starting Salaries in Mid- sized Daily Newspaper", *AEJMC Newspaper Division 2002.*

Altheide, David.L (1985), "Media Power", 62:687-88, *Journalism and Mass Communication Quarterly.*

Alyssa Eckman and Thomas R. Lindlof (2002), Kentuchy, "Negotiating the Grey Lines: An Ethnographic Case Study of Organisational Conflict, Better Advertorials and News", *AEJMC Newspaper Division, 2002.*

AMIC Compilation (2000), *Media and Human Rights in Asia.*

Autumn Miller and Dente Ross (2002), Washington State University, "They are not Us: Framing of American Indian by the Boston Globe", *AEJMC Publications Division,* 2002.

Batlin, R. (1954), "San Fransico Newspaper Campaign Coverage 1886, 1952", *Journalism Quaterly,* 31(3):297-302.

Bela Trivedi, Kosha Takera, "Social Dimensions of Media Convergence in India", *Media Asia,* AMIC, 28/3, 2001.

Berger, Arthur Asa (1993), Media Analysis Techniques, *Journalism and Mass Communication Quarterly,* 70:227.

Bill Sillock and Susan Keith, Arizona State University, "Translating the Tower of Babel: Issues of Language and Culture in Covered Newsroom: Pilot Study", *AEJMC Newspaper Division,* 2002.

Black, Jay and Frederick (1984), C.Whitney, "Introduction to Mass Communication", *Journalism and Mass Communication Quarterly,* 61:927-28.

Bogart, Leo(1992), "Preserving the Press: How Daily Newspapers Mobilized to Keep Their Readers", *Journalism and Mass Communication Quarterly,* 69:502.

Bollinger, Lee C. (1993), "Images of Free Press", *Journalism and Mass Communication Quarterly,* 70:458.

Bruce Garrison, Miami, U.S. (2002), The Use of Electronic Mail as a News Gathering Resource, *AEJMC Newspaper Division,* 2002.

Buckman, R.J.(1993), "How Eight Weekly Newsmagazines Covered Elections in six Countries", *Journalism Quarterly,* 70(4):780-792.

Burch (2001), "Framing an Environmental Controversy in India's English Language Press: A Study of Text in Context", *The International Journal of Environmental Studies,* Volume 4, 2001.

Bush, C.R.(1996), "A System of Categories for General News Content", *Journalism Quarterly, 37(2):206-210.*

Cable, John. R. (February, 1997), "Market Share Behaviour and Mobility: An Analysis and Time Series Application, *Review of Economics and Statistics of* U.K. pp. 136-141.

Chango Lee, Texas-Austin (2002), "News Coverage of the U.S. Attack on Afghanisthan: A Comparison of the New York Times, Arab News", *AEJMC Publications Division*, 2002.

Claire E.Taylor and her Associates (Writer for Daily Advertiser in Layfayette, Louisiana, 2000), "Local Press Coverage of Environmental Conflict", *Journalism and Mass Communication Quarterly, 77/1*, pp. 175-93.

Cornwell, E.E.J. (1959), "Presidential News: The Expanding Public Image", *Journalism Quarterly*, 36(3): 275-83.

David, K. Demers (Assistant Professor at the Edward R. Murrow School of Communication at Washington State University, 1998), "Structural Pluralism, Corporate Newspaper Structure and News Source Perceptions: Another Test of the Editorial Vigor Hypothesis", *Journallism and Mass Communication Quarterly, 75/3*, pp. 572-593.

Davis, H. and Rarick, G. (1964), "Functions of Editorials and Letters to the Editor", *Journalism Quarterly*, 41(1):108-09.

Dharma, Adhikari, Tracy Everbach and Shahira Fahmy(Missouri), "Watching the Watch Dogs: An Etheno Methodological Study of News Decision Making at a mid Western Newspaper", *AEJMC Publications Division, 2002.*

Dietram A.Schenfele,James Shanaham and Sei-Hill Kim(Professors in Communication Department in Saint Marys college, "Who cares about local politics? Media influences on local political involvement, issue awareness and attitude strength", *Journalism and Mass Communication Quarterly*, 79/2, pp. 7-26.

Doobrev and Stainisslav, D. "The Dynamics of Bulgarian Newspaper Industry in a Period of Transition: Organisational Adptation, Structural Intertia and Political Change", *Industrial and Corporate Change (Journal of Bulgaria)*, September, 1999, pp. 573-60.5

Edward, E. Adams (2002), "Collusion and Price Fixing in the American Newspaper Industry: Market Preservation Trends", *Journalism and Mass Communication Quarterly*, 79/2, 2002, pp. 1890-1910.

Elli P. Lester-Roushanzamir (Associate professor at the University of Georgia, Grady college of Journalism and Mass Communication), Usha Raman (Received Ph.D. from Same College) (1999), "The Global Village in Atlanta: A Textual Analysis of Olympic News Coverage for Children in the Atlanta Journal Constitution." *Journalism and Mass Communication Quarterly*, 76/4, pp. 699-713.

Fee, C. Edward, Hanlock, Charles. J. (April, 2000), "Management Turnover and Product Market Competition: Empirical Evidence from the U.S. Newspaper Industry", *Journal of Business (American Magazine)*, pp. 205-43.

Frank, E.B.North Carolina (Chapel Hill), "Whose Values are News Values? What Journalists and Citizens Want", *AEJMC Newspaper Division*, 2002.

Fredrick Fico and Olivia Balog, Michigan State University, "Partisans and Non-partisans in News Coverage of Local Conflict", *AEJMC Publications Division*, 2002.

Gall and Gregor, S. (December, 1993), "The Employer's Offensive in the Provincial Newspaper Industry", *British Journal of Industrial Relations* in U.K. pp. 615-24.

George, L. Daniels and C.Ann Holifield (2001), "Times of Turmoil Short and Long Term Effects of Organisational Change of Newsroom Employees", *Journalism and Mass Communication Quarterly*, 78/3, 2001.

Glen L. Bleske, Caulifornia State University, "The Romance and Reality of Copy Editing: A Newsroom Case Study", *AEJMC Newspaper Division, 2002.*

Gregg, J.E. (1965), Newspaper Editorial Endorsements and California Elections 1948-1962, *Journalism Quarterly*, 42(4): 532-538.

Guy Forida and Wayne Wanta, Missouri, U.S.(2002), "Gate Keeping on the New York Times op-ed Pages: How Diverse is the Content?", *AEJMC Publications Division*, 2002.

Haque, M. (1986), "Is Development News More Salient Than Human-Interest Stories in India's Elite Press?", *Gazette*, 38(3): 83-99.

Hugh, J. Martin (1998), "Measuring Newspaper Profits: Developing a Standard of Comparison", *Journalism and Mass Communication Quarterly*, 75/3,1998.

Jean Kelly, Jan Knight, Jason Nedly, Lee Peck and Guy Reel, 2002, (Ohio University), "On the Straight and Narrative: The Effect of Writing Style on Readers' Perceptions of Narrative Story Quality", *AEJMC Compilation, 2002.*

Jensen , Klaus Bruhn (1987), "Making Sense of the News", 64:647, *Journalism and Mass Communication Quarterly*.

Joe Strupp (Associate Editor for Editor and Publisher on line), "Newsroom Consider Policies, Port Blair, New York Times Scandal Forces Changes", "*Editor and Publisher Online*".

John, J. Pauly, (Professor of Communication at Saint Louis University), Melissa Eckert (Student of Masters Programme at Saint Louis

University), "The Myth of 'The local' in American Journalism", *Journalism and Mass Communication Quarterly*, 79/2, 2002, pp. 310-27.

Johnston, North Carolina(Chapel Hill) and Dolores Flamiano, James Madison University (2002), "Practicing Diversity: An Exploratory Study of Implementing Diversity in the Newsroom", *AEJMC Newspaper Division*, 2002.

Joseph, C. Harry (2001), "Covering Conflict: Astructural-Pluralist Analysis of How a Small-Town and Big City Newspaper Reported an Environmental Controversy", *Journalism and Mass Communication Quarterly, 78/3.*

Kaniss, Phyllis, (1993), *Making Local News, Journalism and Mass Communication Quarterly,* 70:986.

Karin Wahl-Jorgensen (Lecturer in the School of Journalism, Media and Cultural Studies at Cardiff University), "The Normative-economic Justification for Public Discourse: Letters to the Editor", *Journalism and Mass Communication Quarterly,* 79/1, 2002, pp. 121-134.

Kathleen, A. Hansen, Mark Nevzil and Jean (1998), "Newsromm Topic Teams: Journalist's Asssessments of Effects on News Routines and Newspaper Quality", *Journalism and Mass Communication Quarterly,* 75/4, pp. 803-22.

Katz, Raul Luciano (1989), 66:753, *The Information Society: An International Perspective, Journalism and Mass Communication Quarterly.*

Keane, John, 69:1077(1992), *The media and Democracy, Journalism and Mass Communication Quarterly.*

Kiron Bansal, "International News Coverage in Four Indian Newspapers: A Content Study", *Media Asia,* AMIC, 29/4, 2002, p. 31.

Kis Kodrich (Assisant Professor in Department of Journalism), "Finding New Way: Nicarguan Newspapers in Globalised World", *Journalism and Mass Communication Quarterly.* 79/1,2002. pp. 101-21.

Knudson, Jerry W.Bolivia (1986), 63:645, *Press Revolution 1932-1964, Journalism and Mass Communication Quarterly.*

Kurtz, Howard (1993), 70:988, "Media Circus: The Trouble with America's Newspapers", *Journalism and Mass Communication Quarterly.*

Lent, John A. and ShantiRao (1979), "A content Analysis of National coverage of Asian news and Information", *Gazette 25,* pp. 17-22.

Lent, John, A. (1979), "Use of Development News: A Case Study of India, Malasia, Thailand and Ghana", Singapore: *AMIC.*

Leonard, N. read and Karen (2000), "A Demand Side View of Media Substitutability in National Advertising. A Study of Advertiser

Opinions about Traditional Media Options", *Journalism and Mass Communications Quarterly*, 77/2.

Lijing Arthur Chang (2002), Nanyang Technological University, "Exploring the Turnover Issue: Why Newspaper Reporters Intend to Quit their Jobs", *AEJMC Newspaper Division*, 2002.

Manoff, Robert Karl, Michael Schudson eds (1987), *Reading the News*, 64:648, *Journalism and Mass Communication Quarterly*.

Mark Deuze (Assistant Professor at the Department of Communication at the University of Amsterdam), "National News Culture: A Comparison of Dutch, German, British, Australian and Journalists", *Journalism and Mass Communication Quarterly*, 79/1, 2002, pp. 134-150.

Mark Miller (1998), 68:299, *Mass Communication: A Step by Step Approach, Journalism and Mass Communication Quarterly*.

Mark Miller, Julie (Professors in School of Journalism at University of Tennessee.)(1998), "Framing the Candidates in Presential Primaries", *Journalism and Mass communication Quarterly, 75/2*, pp. 312-25.

Mary Alice Shaver and Stephen Lacy, "The Impact of Intermedia and Newspaper Competition on Advertising Linage in Daily Newspapers", *Journalism and Mass Communication Quarterly*.

Mohapatra, C. (1984), "The Development News Coverage of Two Typical Newspapers", *Vidura*, 21(5):309-11.

Neiva-Elizabeth(1996), "The Chain Building: The Consolidation of the American Newspaper Industry,1953-80", *American Journal Business History Review in 1996*, pp. 1-42.

Noon, Mike, "Strategy and Circumstance: The Success of the NUJ's New Technology Policy" *British Journal of Industrial Relations"*, 29(2), June 1991, U.K., pp. 259-276.

Philip Meyer and Minheong Kim, (North Carolina-Chapel Hill), "How Many Newspeople does a Newspaper Need?" *AEJMC Newspaper Division*, 2002.

Pierce, Brooks, Winter. Harold (Dec. 1996), Pure Versus Mixed Commodity Building", *Review of Industrial Organisation*, U.S., pp. 811-21.

Preetha, L. and Karippai, R.S. (1996), "Analysis of Farm News Coverage in Dailies" *Communicator*, XXXI(1): 25-27.

Randal, A. Beam (2001), "Does it Pay a Market Oriented Newspaper?" *Journalism and Mass Communication Quarterly*, 78/3,2001. pp. 466-84.

Rankin,W.Parkman (1986), 63:885, "The Practice of Newspaper Management", *Journalism and Mass Communication Quarterly*.

Riffe, D. Sust, C.F. and Lacy, S.R. (1993) "The Effectiveness of Random, Consecutive Day and Constructed Week Sampling in Newspaper Content Analysis", *Journalism Quarterly, 70(1):* 133-139.

Rivers, William.L. (1988), 65:451, "News in Print, Writing and Reporting", *Journalism and Mass Communication Quarterly.*

Sangeeta.V.(2000), "CII Media Unconvention: Too Little, too Much", *Industrial Economist,* 15-29 November, 2000, pp. 30-31.

Sawant, P.B. (2001), "Freedom of the Press and Ethics", *Press Council of India Quarterly,* 22(2), April.

Slade and E.Margaret (October 1998), "The Leverage Theory of Trying Revisited: Evidence from Newspaper Advertising", *Southern Economic Journal,* pp. 204-222.

Sohn, Ardyth, Christine Ogan and John Polich, 64:423(1987), "Newspaper Readership", *Journalism and Mass Communication Quarterly.*

Soley, Lawrence C. (1993) 70:207, "The News Shapers, The Source who Explain the News", *Journalism and Mass Communication Quarterly.*

Stam, Keith R.(1986),63:205, "Newspaper use and Communities: Toward a Dynamic Theory", *Journalism and Mass Communication Quarterly.*

Stephen Lacy (2001), "Sample Size for Newspaper Content Analysis in Multiyear Studies", *Journalism and Mass Communication Quarterly, 78/4(2001),* pp. 836-46.

Steve, J. Collins, (2002), "The Community Integration Hypothesis' and other Predictors of Campus Newspaper Readership", *AEJMC Compilation* 2002.

Thomson, R. Stephen, (March,1989), "Circulation Versus Advertiser Appeal in Newspaper Industry", *Journal of Industrial Economics* in U.K. pp. 259-271.

Thorn, William J. with Mary Patpheil (1987) 64:899, "Newspaper Circulation and Marketing the News", *Journalism and Mass Communication Quarterly.*

Van-Kranenburg H.L.Palem, Franz CP Fann, Geerard, A. (October, 1998), "The Life Cycle of Daily Newspapers in Netherlands (1848-1997)", *De-economist Journal,* pp. 475-494.

Vivek Chaudari (March 1998), "Pricing Efficiency of Ciruclation Industry: The Case of Newspapers", *Information Economics and Policy Journal of Australia* in March 1998, pp. 59-76.

Watten Berg, Ben J. (1985) 62:671, "The Good News: Is the Bad is Wrong", *Journalism and Mass Communication Quarterly.*

Weber, Robert Philip (1986), 63:433, "Basic Content Analysis", *Journalism and Mass Communication Quarterly.*

Willis, Jim(1991),68:288, "Surviving the Newspaper Business:Newspaper Management in Turbulent Times", *Journalism and Mass Communication Quarterly*.

Wilson Lowrey (2002), "The Non-linear Web Story: An Assessment of Readers Perceptions, Knowledge Acquisition, Readers Feedback", *AEJMC Compilation* 2002.

Wolfson,Lewis, (1986), 63:425, "The Untapped Power of the Press", *Journalism and Mass Communication Quarterly*.

Yadav, J.S. (1991), "Press System in India ", *Media Asia*, 18(3):132-36,142.

Yadava, J.S. (1985) "The Changing Social Role of the Indian Press", *Media Asia*, 12(3):111-19.

Yonghoisong, Missouri Columbia (2002), "Sourcing Patterns of National and Local Newspapers: A Community Structure Perspective", *AEJMC Publications Division*, 2002.

List of Newspapers

Amitisen (2002), "Tour Operators Blame Media for Scare Talk", *Financial Express*, Saturday, June 8, 2002, p. 14.

Anita Joshura (2002), "Cabinet Clears 26 per cent FDI in Print Media", *The Hindu*, Wednesday, June 26,2002, p. 11.

Arthabodh Gangadhar Durba (2002), "Who is Afraid of FDI: No Fears for Opening Print Media", *Financial Express*, Monday, July 1, 2002, p. 6.

Arul Aram, I. (2002), "Children and Media", *The Hindu*, Tuesday, July 2,2002, p.17.

Bhagwati, P. N. (1989), "Ombudsman's Report: Ten Months Later", *TheTimes of India*, December 20, 1989.

Chowdhary, T.H. (1995 , May 17) "Revolution Wrought by Radio", *Deccan Chronicle*.

Devi Prasad, B.,Visveswara Rao K. and Sampath Kumar, R.D.(1992), "Civic Concerns in an Emerging City and its Adjoining Regions", A Content-Analytical Study of Critical Letters to the 'Action please' Column, *"Indian Express"*, NAGARLOK, XXIV(2): 32-42.

EFE Bureau, New Delhi, "Green Signal for FDI in Print Media Draws Mixed Reactions", *Financial Express*, Wednesday, June 26, 2002.

Express Bureau *(2002)*, "Guide Lines for FDI in News Category of Print Media", *Financial Express*, Novemebr 21, 2002.

Hindu Bureau (2002), "Panel Against FDI Foreign Investment in Newspapers",*Business line*, Saturday, March 23, 2002, p. 13.

Hindu News Bureau(2000), "Newspaper Industry must Imbibe new Technology", *The Hindu*, September 16, 2000.

Hindu Special Correspondent (2002), "Hindi Newspapers have Greater Reach", *The Hindu*, Friday, *Sepetember 20*, 2002, p. 9.

Hindu Special Correspondent (2002), "Journalist Union Oppose FDI", *The Hindu*, Sunday, July 7, 2002, p. 11.

Hindu Special Correspondent (2002), "Report Against FDI in Print Media tabled", *The Hindu*, Saturday, March 23, 2002, p. 13.

Hindu Staff Reporter, "Print Media Growing with Renewed Vigour", *The Hindu*, Thursday, February 27, 2003.

INS(2001), "FDI will wipe out Newspapers: INS Chief", *The Hindu*, Monday, July 15, 2002, p.13.

Kalpana Sharma (2002), "Gujarat and Freedom of Press", *The Hindu*, Tuesday, April 9, 2002, p. 3.

Kalpana Sharma (2002), "Media Mathmatics", *The Hindu* Sunday Magazine, April 21, 2002, p. 3.

Lal, Sham (1994 , May 22) "Marking Change", *Indian Express*, New Delhi.

Murali.N.(2000), "Newspapers must Imbibe New Technology", *The Hindu*, September 16, 2000.

Nandy, P. (1994a, March 12), "Goodbye Editors, Hello Marketers", *Deccan Chronicle*.

Nandy, Pritish (1994b, April 16), "Will Print Journalism Survive?", *Deccan Chronicle*.

Nayar, Kuldip (1994, July 11), "Niminy-piminy Press: The Fourth Estate has Deviated from Principles", *Indian Express*.

Nayar, Kuldip (2003 , April 8), "Journalism on the Cheap", *The News Indian Express*.

Ninan, Sevanti (2003 , March 2), "Changing Journalism", *The Hindu*

Nivedita Mookerji (2002), "Print Media Opened to foreign Funds", *Financial Express*, Sunday, June 30, 2002, p. 2.

Palkiwala, N (1995, June 25), "Memoirs of Emergency, Can it Happen?", *The* New *Indian Express*.

Peter. S. Prichard (2000), "The Only Mass buy Today is in the Super Bowl", *The New Indian Express*, 18th February, 2000.

Prabhat Patnaik (2002), "Market, Morals and Media", *The Hindu*, Friday, July 5, 2002.

Press Council of India (2002), "Media must Guide to Nation", Friday 26th April, 2002, p. 11.

PTI (2002), "Women How Free, How Equal", *The Hindu Businessline*, Wednesday, August 6, 2002, p. 17.

PTI, "I&B Ministry to move Cabinet with Proposal on FDI in Print, *Financial Express,* April 26, 2002, p. 14.

Reuters, New York (2001), "US Ruling on Freelancers to Hit Newspapers", *The Hindu Businessline,* Wednesday, June 27, 2001.

Reuters, New York (2001), "Ad Slump Hits Earnings at Paper Agencies", *The Hindu Businessline,* p. 6.

Salzberg, Austria (March, 2002), "Journalism as Public Trust", *The Hindu Sunday Magazine,* April 28, 2002, p. 5.

Sevanthi Ninan (2001), "Resorting to Hype", *The Hindu,* Sunday Magazine, December 23, 2001, p. 3.

Sevanthi Ninan (2001), "Unheard Voices of Reason", *The Hindu Sunday Magazine,* November 18, 2001, p. 3.

Sevanthi Ninan (2002), "A Free Press", *The Hindu,* Sunday Magazine, July 7, 2002, p. 3.

Sevanthi Ninan (2002), "Do-gooders on the Met", *The Hindu,* Sunday Magazine, July 21, 2002, p. 3.

Sevanthi Ninan (2002), "High Pitch", *The Hindu,* Sunday Magazine, June 30, 2002, p. 3.

Sevanthi Ninan (2002), "Western Overdrive", *The Hindu,* Sunday Magazine, June 9, 2002, p. 10.

Sevanthi Ninan (2002), "Media and Civil Society", *The Hindu,* Sunday Magazine, March 31, 2002, p. 3.

Sevanthi Ninan (2002), "Media Ethics", *The Hindu,* Sunday Magazine, April 28, 2002, p. 3.

Sevanthi Ninan(2002), "Media on a Rampage", *The Hindu,* Sunday Magazine, March 10, 2002, p. 3.

Shourie, A. (1990 , March 25), "Things to do about the Press", *Indian Express.*

Shourie, A. (1995, June 22), "Facts are Sacred, did you Say?", *Deccan Chronicle.*

Shyam, G. Menon, Lathavenkataraman (2002), "World Tunes to News Channels as Real Life Gets Deadly", *The Hindu Businessline,* Friday, April 19, 2002, p. 1.

Singh, T. (1994 , October 22), "Hacking away Competition", *Indian Express*

Subhash Agarval (2002), "Foreign Media in India: Sensible, but we are Hyping up its Impact", *Financial Express,* Thursday, July 4, 2002, p. 6.

Sumit Mitra (2001),'Swadesi Times', *India Today,* December 2001, p. 59.

Times News Work (2003), "Radio Biggest Gainer in Delhi", *Times of India,* December 23, 2003, p. 13.

UNI (2002), "Committee says, no to FDI in Print Media", *The New Indian Express*, Saturday, March 23, 2002, p. 9.

Vijay, P.N. (2002),"Print Opens up Finally, no Longer Middle Classes Suffer Undemocratic Policies and Monopolies", *Financial Express*, Thursday, July 4, 2002, p. 6.

List of Magazines

A and M (Advertising and Marketing).

Business India.

Business World.

Economic and Political Weekly.

India Today.

Industrial Economist.

The Week.

Vidura.

Index